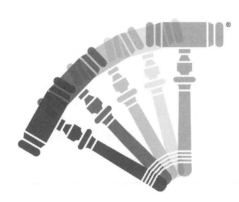

Casenote™ Legal Briefs

BUSINESS ORGANIZATIONS

Keyed to Courses Using

Klein, Ramseyer, and Bainbridge's
Business Associations

Seventh Edition

Wolters Kluwer

Law & Business

AUSTIN   BOSTON   CHICAGO   NEW YORK   THE NETHERLANDS

This publication is designed to provide accurate and authoritative information
in regard to the subject matter covered. It is sold with the understanding that the
publisher is not engaged in rendering legal, accounting, or other professional
services. If legal advice or other expert assistance is required, the services of a
competent professional person should be sought.

— From a Declaration of Principles adopted jointly
by a Committee of the American Bar Association
and a Committee of Publishers and Associates

To contact Customer Care, e-mail customer.care@aspenpublishers.com,
call 1-800-234-1660, fax 1-800-901-9075, or mail correspondence to:

Aspen Publishers
Attn: Order Department
P.O. Box 990
Frederick, MD 21705

Printed in the United States of America.

1 2 3 4 5 6 7 8 9 0

ISBN 978-0-7355-8589-8

About Wolters Kluwer Law & Business

Wolters Kluwer Law & Business is a leading provider of research information and workflow solutions in key specialty areas. The strengths of the individual brands of Aspen Publishers, CCH, Kluwer Law International and Loislaw are aligned within Wolters Kluwer Law & Business to provide comprehensive, in-depth solutions and expert-authored content for the legal, professional and education markets.

CCH was founded in 1913 and has served more than four generations of business professionals and their clients. The CCH products in the Wolters Kluwer Law & Business group are highly regarded electronic and print resources for legal, securities, antitrust and trade regulation, government contracting, banking, pension, payroll, employment and labor, and health-care reimbursement and compliance professionals.

Aspen Publishers is a leading information provider for attorneys, business professionals and law students. Written by preeminent authorities, Aspen products offer analytical and practical information in a range of specialty practice areas from securities law and intellectual property to mergers and acquisitions and pension/benefits. Aspen's trusted legal education resources provide professors and students with high-quality, up-to-date and effective resources for successful instruction and study in all areas of the law.

Kluwer Law International supplies the global business community with comprehensive English-language international legal information. Legal practitioners, corporate counsel and business executives around the world rely on the Kluwer Law International journals, loose-leafs, books and electronic products for authoritative information in many areas of international legal practice.

Loislaw is a premier provider of digitized legal content to small law firm practitioners of various specializations. Loislaw provides attorneys with the ability to quickly and efficiently find the necessary legal information they need, when and where they need it, by facilitating access to primary law as well as state-specific law, records, forms and treatises.

Wolters Kluwer Law & Business, a unit of Wolters Kluwer, is headquartered in New York and Riverwoods, Illinois. Wolters Kluwer is a leading multinational publisher and information services company.

Format for the Casenote Legal Brief

Nature of Case: This section identifies the form of action (e.g., breach of contract, negligence, battery), the type of proceeding (e.g., demurrer, appeal from trial court's jury instructions) or the relief sought (e.g., damages, injunction, criminal sanctions).

Fact Summary: This is included to refresh your memory and can be used as a quick reminder of the facts.

Rule of Law: Summarizes the general principle of law that the case illustrates. It may be used for instant recall of the court's holding and for classroom discussion or home review.

Facts: This section contains all relevant facts of the case, including the contentions of the parties and the lower court holdings. It is written in a logical order to give the student a clear understanding of the case. The plaintiff and defendant are identified by their proper names throughout and are always labeled with a (P) or (D).

Party ID: Quick identification of the relationship between the parties.

Concurrence/Dissent: All concurrences and dissents are briefed whenever they are included by the casebook editor.

Analysis: This last paragraph gives you a broad understanding of where the case "fits in" with other cases in the section of the book and with the entire course. It is a hornbook-style discussion indicating whether the case is a majority or minority opinion and comparing the principal case with other cases in the casebook. It may also provide analysis from restatements, uniform codes, and law review articles. The analysis will prove to be invaluable to classroom discussion.

Palsgraf v. Long Island R.R. Co.

Injured bystander (P) v. Railroad company (D)

N.Y. Ct. App., 248 N.Y. 339, 162 N.E. 99 (1928).

NATURE OF CASE: Appeal from judgment affirming verdict for plaintiff seeking damages for personal injury.

FACT SUMMARY: Helen Palsgraf (P) was injured on R.R.'s (D) train platform when R.R.'s (D) guard helped a passenger aboard a moving train, causing his package to fall on the tracks. The package contained fireworks which exploded, creating a shock that tipped a scale onto Palsgraf (P).

🏛 RULE OF LAW
The risk reasonably to be perceived defines the duty to be obeyed.

FACTS: Helen Palsgraf (P) purchased a ticket to Rockaway Beach from R.R. (D) and was waiting on the train platform. As she waited, two men ran to catch a train that was pulling out from the platform. The first man jumped aboard, but the second man, who appeared as if he might fall, was helped aboard by the guard on the train who had kept the door open so they could jump aboard. A guard on the platform also helped by pushing him onto the train. The man was carrying a package wrapped in newspaper. In the process, the man dropped his package, which fell on the tracks. The package contained fireworks and exploded. The shock of the explosion was apparently of great enough strength to tip over some scales at the other end of the platform, which fell on Palsgraf (P) and injured her. A jury awarded her damages, and R.R. (D) appealed.

ISSUE: Does the risk reasonably to be perceived define the duty to be obeyed?

HOLDING AND DECISION: (Cardozo, C.J.) Yes. The risk reasonably to be perceived defines the duty to be obeyed. If there is no foreseeable hazard to the injured party as the result of a seemingly innocent act, the act does not become a tort because it happened to be a wrong as to another. If the wrong was not willful, the plaintiff must show that the act as to her had such great and apparent possibilities of danger as to entitle her to protection. Negligence in the abstract is not enough upon which to base liability. Negligence is a relative concept, evolving out of the common law doctrine of trespass on the case. To establish liability, the defendant must owe a legal duty of reasonable care to the injured party. A cause of action in tort will lie where harm,

though unintended, could have been averted or avoided by observance of such a duty. The scope of the duty is limited by the range of danger that a reasonable person could foresee. In this case, there was nothing to suggest from the appearance of the parcel or otherwise that the parcel contained fireworks. The guard could not reasonably have had any warning of a threat to Palsgraf (P), and R.R. (D) therefore cannot be held liable. Judgment is reversed in favor of R.R. (D).

DISSENT: (Andrews, J.) The concept that there is no negligence unless R.R. (D) owes a legal duty to take care as to Palsgraf (P) herself is too narrow. Everyone owes to the world at large the duty of refraining from those acts that may unreasonably threaten the safety of others. If the guard's action was negligent as to those nearby, it was also negligent as to those outside what might be termed the "danger zone." For Palsgraf (P) to recover, R.R.'s (D) negligence must have been the proximate cause of her injury, a question of fact for the jury.

▶ ANALYSIS
The majority defined the limit of the defendant's liability in terms of the danger that a reasonable person in defendant's situation would have perceived. The dissent argued that the limitation should not be placed on liability, but rather on damages. Judge Andrews suggested that only injuries that would not have happened but for R.R.'s (D) negligence should be compensable. Both the majority and dissent recognized the policy-driven need to limit liability for negligent acts, seeking, in the words of Judge Andrews, to define a framework "that will be practical and in keeping with the general understanding of mankind." The Restatement (Second) of Torts has accepted Judge Cardozo's view.

Quicknotes

FORESEEABILITY A reasonable expectation that change is the probable result of certain acts or omissions.

NEGLIGENCE Conduct falling below the standard of care that a reasonable person would demonstrate under similar conditions.

PROXIMATE CAUSE The natural sequence of events without which an injury would not have been sustained.

Issue: The issue is a concise question that brings out the essence of the opinion as it relates to the section of the casebook in which the case appears. Both substantive and procedural issues are included if relevant to the decision.

Holding and Decision: This section offers a clear and in-depth discussion of the rule of the case and the court's rationale. It is written in easy-to-understand language and answers the issue presented by applying the law to the facts of the case. When relevant, it includes a thorough discussion of the exceptions to the case as listed by the court, any major cites to the other cases on point, and the names of the judges who wrote the decisions.

Quicknotes: Conveniently defines legal terms found in the case and summarizes the nature of any statutes, codes, or rules referred to in the text.

Aspen Publishers is proud to offer *Casenote Legal Briefs*—continuing thirty years of publishing America's best-selling legal briefs.

Casenote Legal Briefs are designed to help you save time when briefing assigned cases. Organized under convenient headings, they show you how to abstract the basic facts and holdings from the text of the actual opinions handed down by the courts. Used as part of a rigorous study regimen, they can help you spend more time analyzing and critiquing points of law than on copying bits and pieces of judicial opinions into your notebook or outline.

Casenote Legal Briefs should never be used as a substitute for assigned casebook readings. They work best when read as a follow-up to reviewing the underlying opinions themselves. Students who try to avoid reading and digesting the judicial opinions in their casebooks or online sources will end up shortchanging themselves in the long run. The ability to absorb, critique, and restate the dynamic and complex elements of case law decisions is crucial to your success in law school and beyond. It cannot be developed vicariously.

Casenote Legal Briefs represents but one of the many offerings in Aspen's Study Aid Timeline, which includes:

- *Casenote Legal Briefs*
- *Emanuel Law Outlines*
- *Examples & Explanations* Series
- *Introduction to Law* Series
- Emanuel *Law in a Flash* Flashcards
- Emanuel *CrunchTime* Series

Each of these series is designed to provide you with easy-to-understand explanations of complex points of law. Each volume offers guidance on the principles of legal analysis and, consulted regularly, will hone your ability to spot relevant issues. We have titles that will help you prepare for class, prepare for your exams, and enhance your general comprehension of the law along the way.

To find out more about Aspen Study Aid publications, visit us online at *http://lawschool.aspenpublishers.com* or email us at *legaledu@wolterskluwer.com*. We'll be happy to assist you.

Get this Casenote Legal Brief as an AspenLaw Studydesk eBook today!

By returning this form to Aspen Publishers, you will receive a complimentary eBook download of this Casenote Legal Brief in the AspenLaw Studydesk digital format.* Learn more about AspenLaw Studydesk today at *www.AspenLaw.com*.

Name	Phone ( )
Address	Apt. No.
City	State	ZIP Code
Law School	Year (check one) ☐ 1st ☐ 2nd ☐ 3rd

Cut out the UPC found on the lower left corner of the back cover of this book. Staple the UPC inside this box. Only the original UPC from the book cover will be accepted. (No photocopies or store stickers are allowed.)

Attach UPC inside this box.

Email (Print legibly or you may not get access!)

Title of this book (course subject)

ISBN of this book (10- or 13-digit number on the UPC)

Used with which casebook (provide author's name)

Mail the completed form to:

Aspen Publishers, Inc.
Legal Education Division
130 Turner Street, Bldg 3, 4th Floor
Waltham, MA 02453-8901

* Upon receipt of this completed form, you will be emailed a code for the digital download of this book in AspenLaw Studydesk format. The AspenLaw Studydesk application is available as a 60-day free trial at *www.AspenLaw.com*.

For a full list of print titles by Aspen Publishers, visit *lawschool.aspenpublishers.com*.
For a full list of digital eBook titles by Aspen Publishers, visit *www.AspenLaw.com*.

Make a photocopy of this form and your UPC for your records.

For detailed information on the use of the information you provide on this form, please see the PRIVACY POLICY at www.aspenpublishers.com.

How to Brief a Case

A. Decide on a Format and Stick to It

Structure is essential to a good brief. It enables you to arrange systematically the related parts that are scattered throughout most cases, thus making manageable and understandable what might otherwise seem to be an endless and unfathomable sea of information. There are, of course, an unlimited number of formats that can be utilized. However, it is best to find one that suits your needs and stick to it. Consistency breeds both efficiency and the security that when called upon you will know where to look in your brief for the information you are asked to give.

Any format, as long as it presents the essential elements of a case in an organized fashion, can be used. Experience, however, has led *Casenotes* to develop and utilize the following format because of its logical flow and universal applicability.

NATURE OF CASE: This is a brief statement of the legal character and procedural status of the case (e.g., "Appeal of a burglary conviction").

There are many different alternatives open to a litigant dissatisfied with a court ruling. The key to determining which one has been used is to discover *who is asking this court for what.*

This first entry in the brief should be kept as *short as possible.* Use the court's terminology if you understand it. But since jurisdictions vary as to the titles of pleadings, the best entry is the one that addresses who wants what in this proceeding, not the one that sounds most like the court's language.

RULE OF LAW: A statement of the general principle of law that the case illustrates (e.g., "An acceptance that varies any term of the offer is considered a rejection and counteroffer").

Determining the rule of law of a case is a procedure similar to determining the issue of the case. Avoid being fooled by red herrings; there may be a few rules of law mentioned in the case excerpt, but usually only one is *the* rule with which the casebook editor is concerned. The techniques used to locate the issue, described below, may also be utilized to find the rule of law. Generally, your best guide is simply the chapter heading. It is a clue to the point the casebook editor seeks to make and should be kept in mind when reading every case in the respective section.

FACTS: A synopsis of only the essential facts of the case, i.e., those bearing upon or leading up to the issue.

The facts entry should be a short statement of the events and transactions that led one party to initiate legal proceedings against another in the first place. While some cases conveniently state the salient facts at the beginning of the decision, in other instances they will have to be culled from hiding places throughout the text, even from concurring and dissenting opinions. Some of the "facts" will often be in dispute and should be so noted. Conflicting evidence may be briefly pointed up. "Hard" facts must be included. Both must be *relevant* in order to be listed in the facts entry. It is impossible to tell what is relevant until the entire case is read, as the ultimate determination of the rights and liabilities of the parties may turn on something buried deep in the opinion.

Generally, the facts entry should not be longer than three to five *short* sentences.

It is often helpful to identify the role played by a party in a given context. For example, in a construction contract case the identification of a party as the "contractor" or "builder" alleviates the need to tell that that party was the one who was supposed to have built the house.

It is always helpful, and a good general practice, to identify the "plaintiff" and the "defendant." This may seem elementary and uncomplicated, but, especially in view of the creative editing practiced by some casebook editors, it is sometimes a difficult or even impossible task. Bear in mind that the *party presently* seeking something from this court may not be the plaintiff, and that sometimes only the cross-claim of a defendant is treated in the excerpt. Confusing or misaligning the parties can ruin your analysis and understanding of the case.

ISSUE: A statement of the general legal question answered by or illustrated in the case. For clarity, the issue is best put in the form of a question capable of a "yes" or "no" answer. In reality, the issue is simply the Rule of Law put in the form of a question (e.g., "May an offer be accepted by performance?").

The major problem presented in discerning what is *the* issue in the case is that an opinion usually purports to raise and answer several questions. However, except for rare cases, only one such question is really the issue in the case. Collateral issues not necessary to the resolution of the matter in controversy are handled by the court by language known as *"obiter dictum"* or merely *"dictum."* While dicta may be included later in the brief, they have no place under the issue heading.

To find the issue, ask *who wants what* and then go on to ask *why did that party succeed or fail in getting it.* Once this is determined, the "why" should be turned into a question.

The complexity of the issues in the cases will vary, but in all cases a single-sentence question should sum up the issue. *In a few cases,* there will be two, or even more rarely, three issues of equal importance to the resolution of the case. Each should be expressed in a single-sentence question.

Since many issues are resolved by a court in coming to a final disposition of a case, the casebook editor will reproduce the portion of the opinion containing the issue or issues most relevant to the area of law under scrutiny. A noted law professor gave this advice: "Close the book; look at the title on the cover." Chances are, if it is Property, you need not concern yourself with whether, for example, the federal government's treatment of the plaintiff's land really raises a federal question sufficient to support jurisdiction on this ground in federal court.

The same rule applies to chapter headings designating sub-areas within the subjects. They tip you off as to what the text is designed to teach. The cases are arranged in a casebook to show a progression or development of the law, so that the preceding cases may also help.

It is also most important to remember to *read the notes and questions* at the end of a case to determine what the editors wanted you to have gleaned from it.

HOLDING AND DECISION: This section should succinctly explain the rationale of the court in arriving at its decision. In capsulizing the "reasoning" of the court, it should always include an application of the general rule or rules of law to the specific facts of the case. Hidden justifications come to light in this entry; the reasons for the state of the law, the public policies, the biases and prejudices, those considerations that influence the justices' thinking and, ultimately, the outcome of the case. At the end, there should be a short indication of the disposition or procedural resolution of the case (e.g., "Decision of the trial court for Mr. Smith (P) reversed").

The foregoing format is designed to help you "digest" the reams of case material with which you will be faced in your law school career. Once mastered by practice, it will place at your fingertips the information the authors of your casebooks have sought to impart to you in case-by-case illustration and analysis.

B. Be as Economical as Possible in Briefing Cases

Once armed with a format that encourages succinctness, it is as important to be economical with regard to the time spent on the actual reading of the case as it is to be economical in the writing of the brief itself. This does not mean "skimming" a case. Rather, it means reading the case with an "eye" trained to recognize into which "section" of your brief a particular passage or line fits and having a system for quickly and precisely marking the case so that the passages fitting any one particular part of the brief can be easily identified and brought together in a concise and accurate manner when the brief is actually written.

It is of no use to simply repeat everything in the opinion of the court; record only enough information to trigger your recollection of what the court said. Nevertheless, an accurate statement of the "law of the case," i.e., the legal principle applied to the facts, is absolutely essential to class preparation and to learning the law under the case method.

To that end, it is important to develop a "shorthand" that you can use to make margin notations. These notations will tell you at a glance in which section of the brief you will be placing that particular passage or portion of the opinion.

Some students prefer to underline all the salient portions of the opinion (with a pencil or colored underliner marker), making marginal notations as they go along. Others prefer the color-coded method of underlining, utilizing different colors of markers to underline the salient portions of the case, each separate color being used to represent a different section of the brief. For example, blue underlining could be used for passages relating to the rule of law, yellow for those relating to the issue, and green for those relating to the holding and decision, etc. While it has its advocates, the color-coded method can be confusing and time-consuming (all that time spent on changing colored markers). Furthermore, it can interfere with the continuity and concentration many students deem essential to the reading of a case for maximum comprehension. In the end, however, it is a matter of personal preference and style. Just remember, whatever method you use, underlining must be used sparingly or its value is lost.

If you take the marginal notation route, an efficient and easy method is to go along underlining the key portions of the case and placing in the margin alongside them the following "markers" to indicate where a particular passage or line "belongs" in the brief you will write:

N   (NATURE OF CASE)
RL (RULE OF LAW)
I   (ISSUE)
HL (HOLDING AND DECISION, relates to the RULE OF LAW behind the decision)
HR (HOLDING AND DECISION, gives the RATIONALE or reasoning behind the decision)
HA (HOLDING AND DECISION, APPLIES the general principle(s) of law to the facts of the case to arrive at the decision)

Remember that a particular passage may well contain information necessary to more than one part of your brief, in which case you simply note that in the margin. If you are using the color-coded underlining method instead of margin notation, simply make asterisks or checks in the margin next to the passage in question in the colors that indicate the additional sections of the brief where it might be utilized.

The economy of utilizing "shorthand" in marking cases for briefing can be maintained in the actual brief writing process itself by utilizing "law student shorthand" within the brief. There are many commonly used words and phrases for which abbreviations can be substituted in your briefs (and in your class notes also). You can develop abbreviations that are personal to you and which will save you a lot of time. A reference list of briefing abbreviations can be found on page xii of this book.

C. Use Both the Briefing Process and the Brief as a Learning Tool

Now that you have a format and the tools for briefing cases efficiently, the most important thing is to make the time spent in briefing profitable to you and to make the most advantageous use of the briefs you create. Of course, the briefs are invaluable for classroom reference when you are called upon to explain or analyze a particular case. However, they are also useful in reviewing for exams. A quick glance at the fact summary should bring the case to mind, and a rereading of the rule of law should enable you to go over the underlying legal concept in your mind, how it was applied in that particular case, and how it might apply in other factual settings.

As to the value to be derived from engaging in the briefing process itself, there is an immediate benefit that arises from being forced to sift through the essential facts and reasoning from the court's opinion and to succinctly express them in your own words in your brief. The process ensures that you understand the case and the point that it illustrates, and that means you will be ready to absorb further analysis and information brought forth in class. It also ensures you will have something to say when called upon in class. The briefing process helps develop a mental agility for getting to the *gist* of a case and for identifying, expounding on, and applying the legal concepts and issues found there. The briefing process is the mental process on which you must rely in taking law school examinations; it is also the mental process upon which a lawyer relies in serving his clients and in making his living.

Abbreviations for Briefs

acceptance	acp	offer	O
affirmed	aff	offeree	OE
answer	ans	offeror	OR
assumption of risk	a/r	ordinance	ord
attorney	atty	pain and suffering	p/s
beyond a reasonable doubt	b/r/d	parol evidence	p/e
bona fide purchaser	BFP	plaintiff	P
breach of contract	br/k	prima facie	p/f
cause of action	c/a	probable cause	p/c
common law	c/l	proximate cause	px/c
Constitution	Con	real property	r/p
constitutional	con	reasonable doubt	r/d
contract	K	reasonable man	r/m
contributory negligence	c/n	rebuttable presumption	rb/p
cross	x	remanded	rem
cross-complaint	x/c	res ipsa loquitur	RIL
cross-examination	x/ex	respondeat superior	r/s
cruel and unusual punishment	c/u/p	Restatement	RS
defendant	D	reversed	rev
dismissed	dis	Rule Against Perpetuities	RAP
double jeopardy	d/j	search and seizure	s/s
due process	d/p	search warrant	s/w
equal protection	e/p	self-defense	s/d
equity	eq	specific performance	s/p
evidence	ev	statute of limitations	S/L
exclude	exc	statute of frauds	S/F
exclusionary rule	exc/r	statute	S
felony	f/n	summary judgment	s/j
freedom of speech	f/s	tenancy in common	t/c
good faith	g/f	tenancy at will	t/w
habeas corpus	h/c	tenant	t
hearsay	hr	third party	TP
husband	H	third party beneficiary	TPB
in loco parentis	ILP	transferred intent	TI
injunction	inj	unconscionable	uncon
inter vivos	I/v	unconstitutional	unconst
joint tenancy	j/t	undue influence	u/e
judgment	judgt	Uniform Commercial Code	UCC
jurisdiction	jur	unilateral	uni
last clear chance	LCC	vendee	VE
long-arm statute	LAS	vendor	VR
majority view	maj	versus	v
meeting of minds	MOM	void for vagueness	VFV
minority view	min	weight of the evidence	w/e
Miranda warnings	Mir/w	weight of authority	w/a
Miranda rule	Mir/r	wife	W
negligence	neg	with	w/
notice	ntc	within	w/i
nuisance	nus	without prejudice	w/o/p
obligation	ob	without	w/o
obscene	obs	wrongful death	wr/d

Table of Cases

Agency

Quick Reference Rules of Law

CHAPTER 1

Gorton v. Doty

Father of injured student (P) v. Owner of vehicle (D)

69 P.2d 136 (Idaho 1937).

NATURE OF CASE: Appeal from a judgment in favor of guardian ad litem in a vehicle accident case.

FACT SUMMARY: Doty (D) loaned her car to Russell Garst, a high school football coach, to transport members of the team to a game. When Garst had a traffic accident in which Richard Gorton (P) was injured, Richard's father, as guardian ad litem, sued Doty (D), arguing that Garst was Doty's (D) agent while transporting the team in Doty's (D) car, hence Doty (D), as principal in the agency relationship, was liable for the injuries resulting from the accident.

> ## 🏛 RULE OF LAW
> Where one undertakes to transact some business or manage some affair for another by authority and on account of the latter, the relationship of principal and agent arises.

FACTS: Richard Gorton (P), a minor, was a member of his high school's football team which was scheduled to play a game at another school. Russell Garst was his football coach. Doty (D) knew of the game and volunteered her car for use in transporting team members to and from the game. Doty (D) told Garst that he could use her car if he drove it. She was not promised compensation for the use of her car and did not receive any. The school district paid for the gasoline used, although Doty (D) had "not employed" Garst and had not at any time "directed his work or his services, or what he was doing." On route, Garst was involved in a traffic accident, resulting in injuries to Richard Gordon (P), a passenger. Richard's father, as guardian ad litem, brought suit against Doty (D), arguing that Garst was her agent at the time of the accident and that she was accordingly liable as the principal. Judgment was rendered in favor of Richard Gorton (P), and Doty (D) appealed.

ISSUE: Where one undertakes to transact some business or manage some affair for another by authority and on account of the latter, does the relationship of principal and agent arise?

HOLDING AND DECISION: [Judge not stated in casebook excerpt.] Yes. Where one undertakes to transact some business or manage some affair for another by authority and on account of the latter, the relationship of principal and agent arises. Here, Doty (D) volunteered the use of her car to Garst, the school football coach, for the purpose of furnishing transportation of the team to and from its game site. She "designated Garst," and, in so doing, made it a condition precedent that the person she designated should drive her car. That she thereby consented that Garst should act for her and in her behalf, in

driving her car on that occasion, is clear from her act in volunteering the use of her car upon the express condition that he should drive it, and further, that Garst consented to so act for Doty (D) is equally clear by his act in driving the car. Furthermore, the fact of the car's ownership alone (conceded here), regardless of the presence or absence of the owner in the car at the time of the accident, establishes a prima facie case against the owner for the reason that the presumption arises that the driver is the agent of the owner. Affirmed.

DISSENT: (Budge, J.) Agency means more than mere passive permission. It involves request, instruction, or command. Here, Doty (D) simply loaned her car to Garst to enable him to furnish transportation for the team. It was nothing more or less than a kindly gesture on her part to be helpful to Garst.

▶ ANALYSIS

In the *Gorton* case, the court noted that it is not essential to the existence of authority that there be a contract between principal and agent or that the agent promise to act as such, nor is it essential to the relationship of principal and agent that they, or either, receive compensation.

■=■

Quicknotes

AGENCY A fiduciary relationship whereby authority is granted to an agent to act on behalf of the principal in order to effectuate the principal's objective.

AGENT An individual who has the authority to act on behalf of another.

GUARDIAN AD LITEM Person designated by the court to represent an infant or ward in a particular legal proceeding.

PRINCIPAL A person or entity who authorizes another (the agent) to act on its behalf and subject to its authority to the extent that the principal may be held liable for the actions of the agent.

■=■

A. Gay Jenson Farms Co. v. Cargill, Inc.

Farm (P) v. Grain dealer (D)

309 N.W.2d 285 (Minn. 1981).

NATURE OF CASE: Appeal from judgment awarding damages for breach of contract.

FACT SUMMARY: Cargill, Inc. (D), in addition to loaning funds to Warren Grain & Seed Co. (D), also took control of the day-to-day operations of Warren (D).

RULE OF LAW
A creditor who assumes control of his debtor's business may be held liable as principal for the acts of the debtor in connection with the business.

FACTS: Warren Grain & Seed Co. (D) operated a seed elevator and, as a result thereof, purchased grain and seed from local farmers. Cargill, Inc. (D), provided working capital to Warren (D). Warren (D) slowly became less and less financially sound and Cargill (D) became more and more involved in its daily operations. Eventually, Cargill (D) essentially took over the day-to-day operations of Warren (D). Nonetheless, Warren (D) eventually defaulted on two million dollars worth of purchase contracts it had executed with local farmers (P). Eighty-six individual and corporate farmers (P) sued both Warren (D) and Cargill (D). A jury rendered a verdict against both Warren (D) and Cargill (D). Cargill (D) appealed, contending that it had not been a principal of Warren (D).

ISSUE: May a creditor who assumes control of his debtor's business become liable as principal for the acts of the debtor?

HOLDING AND DECISION: [Judge not stated in casebook excerpt.] Yes. A creditor who assumes control of his debtor's business may be held liable as principal for the acts of the debtor in connection with the business. Agency is a fiduciary relationship that results from the manifestation of consent by one person to another that the other shall act on his behalf and subject to his control, and consent of the other to so act. In order to create an agency relationship, the principal must consent to the agency, the agent must act on behalf of the principal, and the principal must exercise control of the agent. All three elements were found in the particular circumstances of this case. Warren (D) acted on Cargill's (D) behalf in procuring grain for Cargill (D), and Cargill (D) interfered in Warren's (D) internal affairs. Affirmed.

▶ ANALYSIS

The court admitted that Cargill (D) and Warren (D) had a unique relationship that transcended the normal debtor-creditor situation. Cargill (D) financed Warren (D) to establish a source of grain for its business, not to make money as

a lender. Cargill (D) was receiving significant amounts of grain and, notwithstanding the risk, the operation was considered profitable.

Quicknotes

AGENT An individual who has the authority to act on behalf of another.

FIDUCIARY RELATIONSHIP Person holding a legal obligation to act for the benefit of another.

PRINCIPAL A person or entity who authorizes another (the agent) to act on its behalf and subject to its authority to the extent that the principal may be held liable for the actions of the agent.

Mill Street Church of Christ v. Hogan

Insured employer (D) v. Injured worker (P)

785 S.W.2d 263 (Ky. App. 1990).

NATURE OF CASE: Petition for review of a workers' compensation board's holding that a worker was a company's employee thus entitled to workers' compensation benefits.

FACT SUMMARY: The Mill Street Church of Christ (D) hired Bill Hogan to paint its church building. Bill hired his brother, Sam (P), to help in completing a difficult part of the job. While painting, Sam (P) broke his leg and filed a claim with the workers' compensation board. The board held that Sam (P) was an employee of the Church (D) (hence entitled to workers' compensation benefits) since Bill had the implied authority to hire Sam (P) because such implied authority was necessary to implement Bill's express authority as an agent of the Church (D) to complete the painting job.

RULE OF LAW
A person possesses implied authority as an agent to hire another worker where such implied authority is necessary to implement the agent's express authority.

FACTS: The Mill Street Church of Christ (D) hired Bill Hogan to paint its church building. In the past, the Church (D) had allowed Bill to hire his brother, Sam (P), to assist if any assistance were needed. After Bill had painted most of the church himself, he realized that he needed assistance to paint the baptistry portion of the church which was very high and difficult to paint. Bill thereupon hired his brother (P) to help in completing the painting job. The Church (D) supplied the tools, materials, and supplies necessary to complete the project. While painting, Sam's (P) ladder broke, causing a fall which broke his leg. After the accident, Sam (P) filed a claim under the Workers' Compensation Act. The New Workers' Compensation Board, reversing a ruling of the Old Workers' Compensation Board, held that Sam (P), at the time of his injury, was an employee of the Church (D), hence entitled to workers' compensation benefits. The Church (D) petitioned for review.

ISSUE: Does a person possess implied authority as an agent to hire another worker where such implied authority is necessary to implement the agent's express authority?

HOLDING AND DECISION: [Judge not stated in casebook excerpt.] Yes. A person possesses implied authority as an agent to hire another worker where such implied authority is necessary to implement the agent's express authority. Here, Bill Hogan had the implied authority of Mill Street Church (D) to hire Sam Hogan (P) as his helper. First, in the past, Mill Street Church (D) had allowed Bill Hogan to hire his brother (P) or other persons whenever he needed assistance on a project. Even though the Board of Elders discussed a different arrangement this time, no mention of this discussion was ever made to Bill or Sam Hogan (P). Furthermore, Bill Hogan needed to hire an assistant to complete the job for which he had been hired. The interior of the church simply could not be painted by one person. Maintaining a safe and attractive place of worship clearly is part of the church's function, and one for which it would designate an agent to ensure that the building is properly painted and maintained. Finally, here, Sam Hogan (P) believed that Bill Hogan had the authority to hire him as had been the practice in the past. The church treasurer had even paid Bill Hogan for the half hour of work that Sam Hogan (P) had completed prior to the accident. Affirmed.

ANALYSIS

It is important to distinguish implied and apparent authority. Implied authority is actual authority circumstantially proven which the principal actually intended the agent to possess and includes such powers as are practically necessary to carry out the duties actually designated. Apparent authority, on the other hand, as noted in the *Mill Street Church* case, is not actual authority, but is the authority the agent is held out by the principal as possessing. It is a matter of appearances on which third parties come to rely.

■=■

Quicknotes

AGENCY A fiduciary relationship whereby authority is granted to an agent to act on behalf of the principal in order to effectuate the principal's objective.

EXPRESS AUTHORITY Authority that is delegated pursuant to expressly stated words.

IMPLIED AUTHORITY Inferred power granted, but not expressly given, to an agent to act on behalf of the principal in order to effectuate the principal's objective.

■=■

Dweck v. Nasser

Minority shareholder (P) v. Majority shareholder (D)

2008 WL 2602169 (Del. Ch. 2008).

NATURE OF CASE: Motion to enforce settlement agreement in action for unlawful termination of employment and breach of fiduciary duties.

FACT SUMMARY: Nasser (D), who had a very longstanding relationship with his primary attorney, Shiboleth, disputed that he had given Shiboleth any kind of authority (express, implied, or apparent) to enter into a settlement agreement in litigation brought by Dweck (P), even though Nasser (D) had told Shiboleth to "get it done" and had so informed Heyman, his attorney of record in the litigation.

RULE OF LAW

An attorney who is not an attorney of record in litigation has authority to settle the litigation where a party to the litigation has had a longstanding relationship with the attorney, has granted authority to the attorney, has permitted the attorney to "speak in his name," and has informed others of the attorney's authority.

FACTS: Dweck (P), a 30% shareholder, officer, and director of Kids International, Inc. (Kids), brought suit against Kids' majority shareholder, Nasser (D), for unlawful termination of employment and breach of fiduciary duties after Nasser (D) terminated her as the corporation's president after he discovered that she had been competing businesses out of Kids' offices. Heyman was Nasser's (D) attorney of record in the matter. After the court upheld Dweck's (P) termination, the parties could not settle the litigation for over a year and a half. To move discussions forward, Dweck (P) retained attorney Wachtel, who reached out to Shiboleth, Nasser's (D) close friend, business associate, and primary attorney for over 20 years. Shiboleth, who was very familiar with the underlying dispute, agreed to work with Wachtel to reach a settlement, and obtained approval from Nasser (D) to do so. Nasser (D) reviewed draft settlement agreements. Initially, he objected to several terms, but then relented as to these terms, informing Heyman that he wanted to reach settlement and that he had directed Shiboleth to "get it done," which Heyman understood to mean settle the litigation. Shiboleth also confirmed to Heyman that Nasser (D) had directed him to settle the dispute. Further negotiations ensued until an agreement satisfactory to both parties was reached. Heyman did not expressly agree to the settlement because he believed that authority was vested with Shiboleth. Shiboleth, who had already secured Nasser's (D) final consent to the agreement, did notify Wachtel that the action was settled and that Nasser (D) would promptly sign the agreement. Wachtel sent the final settlement agreement for Nasser's (D) signature. At that time, Wachtel, Shiboleth, and Heyman believed that a final settlement had been reached between the parties. Nasser (D) also told Heyman that he would sign the agreement. Several days later, however, Nasser (D) objected to several provisions of the agreement—those he had originally objected to but then relented on—and rejected Shiboleth's authority to enter into the settlement. Heyman informed Nasser (D) that he believed Shiboleth had been given the authority to enter into the settlement, but Nasser (D) disagreed. Nasser (D) retained new counsel; Dweck (P) moved to enforce the settlement agreement.

ISSUE: Does an attorney who is not an attorney of record in litigation have authority to settle the litigation where a party to the litigation has had a longstanding relationship with the attorney, has granted authority to the attorney, has permitted the attorney to "speak in his name," and has informed others of the attorney's authority?

HOLDING AND DECISION: [Judge not stated in casebook excerpt.] Yes. An attorney who is not an attorney of record in litigation has authority to settle the litigation where a party to the litigation has had a longstanding relationship with the attorney, has granted authority to the attorney, has permitted the attorney to "speak in his name," and has informed others of the attorney's authority. An attorney of record is presumed to have authority to settle pending litigation. Heyman testified that he believed Shiboleth had such authority, that he (Heyman) did not, and that is why Heyman tried very hard not to demonstrate an acceptance of the settlement. However, because Shiboleth was not the attorney of record, it cannot be presumed that he had authority to agree to the settlement. Instead, it must be ascertained under principles of agency law whether Shiboleth had actual, implied, or apparent authority to enter into the settlement. Actual authority is expressly granted by the principal, either orally or in writing. Implied authority is a derivation of actual authority and often means "actual authority either (1) to do what is necessary, usual, and proper to accomplish or perform an agent's express responsibilities or (2) to act in a manner in which an agent believes the principal wishes the agent to act based on the agent's reasonable interpretation of the principal's manifestation in light of the principal's objectives and other facts known to the agent." Apparent authority "is such power as a principal holds his [a]gent out as possessing or permits him to exercise under such

Continued on next page.

circumstances as to preclude a denial of its existence." As to actual authority, both Shiboleth and Heyman testified that Nasser (D) granted Shiboleth authority to settle the litigation. Nasser (D) had told Shiboleth to "do what you want or what you understand," which, based on 20 years of representing Nasser (D), Shiboleth understood to mean that he was authorized to settle the case. Nasser (D) also testified that he told Shiboleth that he could "talk in my name" in settling the litigation. Because of this evidence, and because Nasser (D) had told Shiboleth and Heyman that he would "blindly" sign a settlement at their direction, Shiboleth had actual authority to enter into the settlement. Because of the actions Nasser (D) took in this regard, it also does not matter that he objected to certain terms or believed that he had reserved the right to sign off on the settlement agreement. Shiboleth also had implied authority to enter into the settlement, based on the course of dealings between Shiboleth and Nasser (D) for over 20 years. Based on Nasser's (D) permitting Shiboleth to speak "in his name" and agreeing to execute any agreement Shiboleth and Heyman would present to him, it was reasonable for Shiboleth to assume that he was authorized to settle the case, especially since Shiboleth had settled numerous other cases for Nasser (D) during the course of their dealings. Finally, Shiboleth also had apparent authority to enter into the settlement since because Nasser (D) had informed other individuals that he did not intend to read the settlement agreement and would sign it when so instructed by Shiboleth and Heyman. Motion to enforce the settlement agreement is granted.

▌ *ANALYSIS*

Agency—as between an attorney (agent) and the attorney's client (principal)—is defined as "the fiduciary relation which results from the manifestation of consent by one person to another that the other shall act on his behalf and subject to his control, and consent by the other so to act." As this decision demonstrates, questions of agency are not subject to absolute rules but, rather, turn on the facts of the individual case.

■■■■

Quicknotes

EXPRESS AUTHORITY Authority that is delegated pursuant to expressly stated words.

FIDUCIARY DUTY A legal obligation to act for the benefit of another, including subordinating one's personal interests to that of the other person.

IMPLIED AUTHORITY Inferred power granted, but not expressly given, to an agent to act on behalf of the principal in order to effectuate the principal's objective.

■■■■

Three-Seventy Leasing Corporation v. Ampex Corporation

Computer dealer (P) v. Computer seller (D)

528 F.2d 993 (5th Cir. 1976).

NATURE OF CASE: Appeal from judgment awarding damages for breach of contract.

FACT SUMMARY: A salesperson at Ampex Corporation (D) agreed to sell certain computers to Three-Seventy Leasing Corporation (370) (P) despite not having been given the authority to do so by Ampex (D).

🏛 RULE OF LAW
A salesperson binds his employer to a sale if he agrees to that sale in a manner that would lead the buyer to believe that a sale had been consummated.

FACTS: Joyce (P) formed 370 (P) to purchase and lease computers. Joyce (P) agreed to lease six mainframe memory units to EDS Corp. He began negotiation with Kays, a salesperson for computer manufacturer Ampex Corp. (D). After negotiations, Kays sent a letter to Joyce (P) confirming the sale of six units. Ampex (D) later reneged on the sale because 370 (P) did not meet its credit requirements. 370 (P) was unable to find other units to lease to EDS, and lost the deal. Joyce (P) and 370 (P) sued for breach, contending that a valid sales contract had been formed. The district court so held, and awarded damages to 370 (P). Ampex (D) appealed, contending that Kays had not been authorized to sell without first checking for creditworthiness.

ISSUE: Does a salesperson bind his employer to a sale if he agrees to that sale in a manner that would lead the vendee to believe that a sale had been consummated?

HOLDING AND DECISION: [Judge not stated in casebook excerpt.] Yes. A salesperson binds his employer to a sale if he agrees to that sale in a manner that would lead the buyer to believe that a sale had been consummated. An agent has apparent authority sufficient to bind the principal when the principal acts in such a manner as would lead a reasonably prudent person to suppose that the agent had the authority he purports to exercise. Further, absent knowledge to the contrary on the part of the buyer, an agent has the apparent authority to do those things which are usually incidental to his capacity. Here, Ampex (D) allowed Kays, a salesperson, to deal with a prospective purchaser. In such a situation the purchaser has a right to believe that when the salesperson says that the transaction is completed, he had the ability to close the deal. Joyce (P) therefore was entitled to his bargain when Kays purported to agree to it, and Ampex (D) was bound. Affirmed.

▶ ANALYSIS

The court here does not appear to distinguish between apparent authority and inherent authority, as it seems to use both concepts at the same time in arriving at the conclusion it did. This sort of nonrigorous analysis is common in cases in this area, particularly when, as here, both concepts would tend to work to the same result.

■■■

Quicknotes

APPARENT AUTHORITY The authority granted to an agent to act on behalf of the principal in order to effectuate the principal's objective, which may not be expressly granted, but which is inferred from the conduct of the principal and the agent.

■■■

Watteau v. Fenwick

Supplier (P) v. Pub owner (D)

Queen's Bench, 1 Q.B. 346 (1892).

NATURE OF CASE: Appeal from judgment awarding damages in action for breach of contract.

FACT SUMMARY: Fenwick (D) had authorized Humble as purchasing agent, but only for specific items, an authority Humble then exceeded.

> ## 🏛 RULE OF LAW
> When one holds out another as an agent, that agent can bind the principal on matters normally incident to such agency, even if he was not authorized for a particular type of transaction.

FACTS: Fenwick (D) purchased a pub from Humble. He retained Humble as manager. Part of Humble's duties as manager was purchasing supplies; however, Fenwick (D) only authorized Humble to purchase ale and mineral water. Humble purchased other pub-related items from Watteau (P) over a long period of time, on credit. Watteau (P) later sued to recover the value of the items sold. The trial court granted judgment in favor of Watteau (P). Fenwick (D) appealed, contending that Humble had not been authorized to purchase on his behalf.

ISSUE: When one holds out another as an agent, can that agent bind the principal on matters incident to such agency even if he was not authorized for a particular type of transaction?

HOLDING AND DECISION: (Wills, J.) Yes. When one holds out another as an agent, that agent can bind the principal on matters incident to such agency, even if he was not authorized for a particular type of transaction. The principal is liable for all the acts of the agent that are within the authority usually confided to an agent of that character, notwithstanding any limitations placed on the agency and not disclosed to third parties. Here, in the context of a public house, one dealing with the manager thereof clearly would expect that such manager would have authority to purchase pub-related items, and therefore Fenwick (D) is liable for the debt incurred by Humble. Appeal dismissed.

▶ ANALYSIS

This case represents an early example of apparent authority. In this context, Humble, having authority to purchase some tavern-related items, had apparent authority to purchase other tavern-related goods, and could bind his principal in doing so. This rule also applies to partnerships; a partner may be held liable for claims made against other partners, even if he does not disclose his identity as a partner and even if the partnership agreement prohibits the transaction underlying the claim.

■══■

Quicknotes

AGENT An individual who has the authority to act on behalf of another.

APPARENT AUTHORITY The authority granted to an agent to act on behalf of the principal in order to effectuate the principal's objective, which may not be expressly granted, but which is inferred from the conduct of the principal and the agent.

PRINCIPAL A person or entity who authorizes another (the agent) to act on its behalf and subject to its authority to the extent that the principal may be held liable for the actions of the agent.

■══■

Botticello v. Stefanovicz

Purchaser of property (P) v. Sellers of property (D)

177 Conn. 22, 411 A.2d 16 (Conn. 1979).

NATURE OF CASE: Appeal by property sellers from an order for specific performance in favor of the property purchaser.

FACT SUMMARY: Mary and Walter Stefanovicz (D) were tenants in common of a farm. Anthony Botticello (P) wanted to purchase the farm. Botticello (P) and Walter (D) agreed upon a price of $85,000 for a lease with an option to purchase and signed papers to that effect. When Mary (D) and Walter (D) subsequently refused to honor the option agreement, Botticello (P) sued them for specific performance.

 RULE OF LAW
Marital status cannot in and of itself prove an agency relationship.

FACTS: Mary and Walter Stefanovicz (D) were tenants in common of a farm. Anthony Botticello (P) visited the farm and offered $75,000 to purchase it. At that time, Mary (D) stated that there was "no way" she could sell it for that amount. Ultimately, Botticello (P) and Walter (D) agreed upon a price of $85,000 for a lease with an option to purchase. The informal agreement was finalized with the assistance of counsel for both Walter (D) and Botticello (P). Neither Botticello (P) nor his attorney, nor Walter's (D) attorney, was then aware of the fact that Walter (D) did not own the property outright. After execution of the lease and option-to-purchase agreement, Botticello (P) took possession of the property and made substantial improvements on it. When Mary and Walter Stefanovicz (D) refused to honor the option agreement, Botticello (P) sued them for specific performance. The trial court ordered specific performance, holding that although Mary (D) was not party to the lease and option-to-purchase agreement, its terms were nonetheless binding on her because Walter (D) had acted as her authorized agent in the negotiations, discussions, and execution of the written agreement. Mary and Walter Stefanovicz (D) appealed.

ISSUE: Can marital status in and of itself prove an agency relationship?

HOLDING AND DECISION: [Judge not stated in casebook excerpt.] No. Marital status cannot in and of itself prove an agency relationship. The existence of an agency relationship is a question of fact. The burden of proving agency is on the plaintiff, and it must be proven by a fair preponderance of the evidence. Here, mere marital status does not prove such a relationship nor does the fact that Mary and Walter Stefanovicz (D) owned the land jointly make one the agent for the other. Although Mary (D) remarked that she would not sell the farm for less than

$85,000, a statement that one will not sell for less than a certain amount is by no means the equivalent of an agreement to sell for that amount. Moreover, the fact that one spouse tends more to business matters than the other does not, absent other evidence of agreement or authorization, constitute the delegation of power as to an agent. Furthermore, although Mary (D) may have acquiesced in Walter's (D) handling of many business matters, Walter (D) never signed any documents as agent for Mary (D) prior to the time of the alleged farm sale. Mary (D) had consistently signed any deed, mortgage, or mortgage note in connection with their jointly held property. Finally, the facts do not indicate intent of Mary (D) to have ratified the agreement of Walter (D) to sell the property to Botticello (P) nor do the facts establish her knowledge of all the material circumstances surrounding the deal. Specific performance reversed and remanded.

▶ *ANALYSIS*

As noted in the *Botticello* case, ratification requires acceptance of the results of the act with intent to ratify and with full knowledge of all the material circumstances. Hence, if the original transaction was not purported to be done on account of the principal, the fact that the principal receives its proceeds, does not make him or her, a party to it.

■==■

Quicknotes

SPECIFIC PERFORMANCE An equitable remedy whereby the court requires the parties to perform their obligations pursuant to a contract.

TENANCY IN COMMON An interest in property held by two or more people, each with equal right to its use and possession; interests may be partitioned, sold, conveyed, or devised.

■==■

Hoddeson v. Koos Bros.

Purchaser (P) v. Furniture store (D)

47 N.J. Super. 224, 135 A.2d 702 (App. Div.1957).

NATURE OF CASE: Appeal from a judgment in favor of a purchaser in an assumpsit suit against a furniture store.

FACT SUMMARY: When Mrs. Hoddeson (P), intending to purchase furniture, gave cash to a man on the sales floor of Koos Brothers furniture store (D) who held himself out to be a salesperson, but later discovered he was not employed by the store but was a con artist who kept the money, she brought an assumpsit suit against the store, alleging privity of contract on the basis of agency.

> ## 🏛 RULE OF LAW
> To establish agency by estoppel, the appearance of authority must be shown to have been created by the manifestations of the alleged principal and not solely by the supposed agent.

FACTS: Mrs. Hoddeson (P) went to Koos Brothers furniture store (D) and purchased furniture from a man on the sales floor whom she assumed was a salesperson of the store. He guided Hoddeson (P) to the furniture she desired to purchase, withdrew from his pocket a pad on which he presumably recorded her order and calculated the total purchase price to be $168.50. Hoddeson (P) handed to him the $168.50 in cash. He told her the articles would be delivered, but gave her no receipt. Subsequently when the articles were not delivered, Hoddeson (P) contacted the store and discovered there was never any such sale and the "seller" of the goods was not a store employee but rather a con artist. She was later unable to recognize the salesman among any of the store's regularly employed sales force. Hoddeson (P) brought an assumpsit suit against Koos Brothers (D), alleging a privity of contract with Koos Brothers (D) through the relationship of agency between the latter and the man who had "sold" her the goods. The trial court found in favor of Hoddeson (P). Koos Brothers (D) appealed.

ISSUE: To establish agency by estoppel, must the appearance of authority be shown to have been created by the manifestations of the alleged principal and not solely by the supposed agent?

HOLDING AND DECISION: [Judge not stated in casebook excerpt.] Yes. To establish agency by estoppel, the appearance of authority must be shown to have been created by the manifestations of the alleged principal and not solely by the supposed agent. Where a party seeks to impose liability upon an alleged principal on a contract made by an alleged agent, as here, the party must assume the obligation of proving the agency relationship. It is not the burden of the alleged principal to disprove it. Here, Hoddeson's (P) evidence did not substantiate the existence of any basic express authority or project any question implicating implied authority. The law cannot permit apparent authority to be established by the mere proof that a dishonest person in fact exercised it. Nevertheless, the rule that those who bargain without inquiry with an apparent agent do so at the risk and peril of an absence of the agent's authority has a patently impracticable application to the customers who patronize modern department stores. Accordingly, while the judgment is reversed, the interests of justice recommend the allowance of a new trial.

▶ ANALYSIS

In *Hoddeson*, the court noted that the duty of a store proprietor does encompass the exercise of reasonable care and diligence to protect a customer from loss occasioned by the deceptions of an apparent salesman, although the lack of such care was not shown on the evidence in the instant case.

■=■

Quicknotes

ASSUMPSIT An oral or written promise by one party to perform or pay another.

EXPRESS AUTHORITY Authority that is delegated pursuant to expressly stated words.

IMPLIED AUTHORITY Inferred power granted, but not expressly given, to an agent to act on behalf of the principal in order to effectuate the principal's objective.

■=■

Atlantic Salmon A/S v. Curran

Wholesale sellers of salmon (P) v. Agent of partially disclosed principal (D)

32 Mass. App. Ct. 488, 591 N.E.2d 206 (1992).

NATURE OF CASE: Appeal of a judgment in favor of the agent of a salmon purchaser in a suit by the salmon wholesaler for recovery of contractual costs.

FACT SUMMARY: Atlantic Salmon A/S (Atlantic) (P) and Salmonor A/S (Salmonor) (P) sued Curran (D) for $153,788.50 and $101,759.65, respectively, owing on a contract which Curran (D) had purportedly made as the agent of Boston International Seafood Exchange, but which in fact Curran (D) had made with another company (Marketing Designs, Inc.) as a partially disclosed principal.

> ## 🏛 RULE OF LAW
> It is the duty of an agent, in order to avoid personal liability on a contract entered into on behalf of the principal, to disclose not only that he or she is acting in a representative capacity, but also the identity of the principal.

FACTS: Atlantic and Salmonor (P), salmon wholesalers, had for several years dealt with a salmon exporter known as "Boston International Seafood Exchange, Inc." or "Boston Seafood Exchange, Inc." Payment checks to the plaintiffs were imprinted with the name "Boston International Seafood Exchange, Inc." and signed by Curran (D), using the designation "Treas.," intending thereby to convey the impression that he was treasurer. Wire transfers and payments were also made in the same manner. Curran (D) also gave the plaintiffs business cards which listed him as "marketing director" of "Boston International Seafood Exchange, Inc." Subsequently, a new corporation named "Marketing Designs, Inc.," was organized, then dissolved. Atlantic (P) was owed $153,788.50 and Salmonor (P) owed $101,759.65 for salmon sold to a business known as "Boston International Seafood Exchange" during the period that such company was actually owned by "Marketing Designs, Inc." Curran (D) had made checks, imprinted with the name "Boston International Seafood Exchange, Inc," to plaintiffs as payment for the salmon. Curran never informed the plaintiffs of the existence of "Marketing Designs, Inc.," and they did not know of it until after the commencement of the present litigation. Atlantic and Salmonor (P) sued Curran (D) for the amount owing on the Boston International Seafood Exchange contract. The trial court awarded judgment for Curran (D). Atlantic and Salmonor (P) appealed.

ISSUE: Is it the duty of an agent, in order to avoid personal liability on a contract entered into on behalf of the principal, to disclose not only that he or she is acting in a representative capacity, but also the identity of the principal?

HOLDING AND DECISION: [Judge not stated in casebook excerpt.] Yes. It is the duty of an agent, in order to avoid personal liability on a contract entered into on behalf of the principal, to disclose not only that he or she is acting in a representative capacity, but also the identity of the principal. Here, it is not sufficient that the plaintiffs may have had the means, through a search of the records of the Boston city clerk, to determine the identity of Curran's (D) principal. Actual knowledge is the test. It is not enough that the other party has the means of determining such information. The agent must either bring forward actual knowledge or, what is the same thing—that which to a reasonable person is equivalent to knowledge, or the agent will be bound. There is no hardship to the agent in this rule since the agent always has the power to relieve itself from personal liability by fully disclosing the principal and contracting only in the latter's name. Here, the agent, Curran (D), did not bring forth such information, but in fact had contracted with Atlantic and Salmonor (P) at prior times directly. Reversed.

▶ ANALYSIS

In *Atlantic Salmon*, the court noted that if the other party to a transaction has notice that the agent is or may be acting for a principal, but has no notice of the principal's identity, the principal for whom the agent is acting is a partially disclosed principal. In the instant case, although Atlantic and Salmonor (P) had notice that Curran (D) was purporting to act for a corporate principal, Atlantic and Salmonor (P) had no notice of the identity of the principal. Hence, since the corporate principal was only a partially disclosed principal, Curran (D) was a party to the contract.

■=■

Quicknotes

AGENT An individual who has the authority to act on behalf of another.

PRINCIPAL A person or entity that authorizes another (the agent) to act on its behalf and subject to its authority to the extent that the principal may be held liable for the actions of the agent.

■=■

Humble Oil & Refining Co. v. Martin

Filling station owner (D) v. Injured bystander (P)

148 Tex. 175, 222 S.W.2d 995 (1949).

NATURE OF CASE: Appeal from judgment awarding damages for personal injury.

FACT SUMMARY: Martin (P), injured when a car rolled out of a service station owned by Humble (D), sought to hold Humble (D) liable for the station operator's negligence.

🏛 RULE OF LAW
A party may be liable for a contractor's torts if he exercises substantial control over the contractor's operations.

FACTS: Martin (P) and his two children (P) were injured when they were struck by a vehicle that rolled out of a service station owned by Humble Oil and Refining Co. (D) and operated by Schneider. Martin (P) sued both Love (D), the owner of the vehicle that struck him, and Humble (D). The evidence showed that Humble (D) exercised substantial control over the details of the station's operation. The trial court rendered judgment against both Love (D) and Humble (D), and the appellate court affirmed. Humble (D) appealed, contending that it was not responsible for the torts of its independent contractors.

ISSUE: May a party be liable for a contractor's torts if he exercises substantial control over the contractor's operations?

HOLDING AND DECISION: [Judge not stated in casebook excerpt.] Yes. A party may be liable for a contractor's torts if he exercises substantial control over the contractor's operations. A party is not normally liable for the torts of his contractors. However, when that party so substantially controls the manner of the contractor's operations, the contractor relationship breaks down and a master-servant relationship is formed. Here, Schneider was obligated to perform any duty Humble (D) might impose on him. Humble (D) paid some of Schneider's operating expenses, and also controlled the station's hours. The evidence showed that Humble (D) mandated much of the day-to-day operations of the station, certainly enough to justify the trial court's finding of a master-servant relationship rather than a contractor relationship. Affirmed.

▌ *ANALYSIS*

According to the Restatement (Second) of Agency, a master-servant relationship is one in which the servant has agreed to work and also to be subject to the master's control. An independent contractor, on the other hand, agrees to work, but is not under the principal's control insofar as the manner in which the job is accomplished. In general, liability will not be imputed to the principal for the tortious conduct of an independent contractor. Under the theory of "apparent agency," the mere appearance a master-servant-type relationship may subject the principal to liability.

■━■

Quicknotes

INDEPENDENT CONTRACTOR A party undertaking a particular assignment for another who retains control over the manner in which it is executed.

MASTER-SERVANT RELATIONSHIP Relationship where a particular individual agrees to render his personal services to another for valuable consideration.

NEGLIGENCE Conduct falling below the standard of care that a reasonable person would demonstrate under similar conditions.

■━■

Hoover v. Sun Oil Company

Injured motorist (P) v. Filling station owner (D)

58 Del. 553, 212 A.2d 214 (Del. Super. 1965).

NATURE OF CASE: Summary judgment for the defense in action seeking damages for personal injury.

FACT SUMMARY: Hoover (P) sought to hold franchisor Sun Oil (D) responsible after he was injured in a fire at a service station franchise operated by Barone (D).

RULE OF LAW

A franchisee is considered an independent contractor of the franchisor if the franchise retains control of inventory and operations.

FACTS: Barone (D) operated as a franchisee of Sun Oil Co. (D). The agreement called for a certain level of compliance by Barone (D) with Sun (D) standards, but Barone (D) was left in control of day-to-day operations of the station, and made all inventory decisions. He (D) carried primarily Sun (D) products, but was allowed to carry products by other companies as well. Hoover (P) suffered burns when a fire started while his vehicle was being filled by an employee at the station. He sued Sun (D) and Barone (D). Sun (D) moved for summary judgment, contending that it could not be liable under any form of vicarious liability. The trial court granted the motion, and Hoover (P) appealed.

ISSUE: Will a franchisee be considered an independent contractor of the franchisor if he retains control of inventory and operations?

HOLDING AND DECISION: [Judge not stated in casebook excerpt.] Yes. A franchisee is considered an independent contractor of the franchisor if the franchisee retains control of inventory and operations. The test in such a situation is whether the franchisor retains the right to control the details of the day-to-day operations of the franchisee. A franchisor's control or influence over the results alone, are insufficient to establish a principal-agent relationship. Here, while Sun (D) obviously had some control over the operation of Barone's (D) business, Barone (D) retained full control over his operations, including what inventory to stock. This clearly falls on the contractor side of the issue. Motion granted.

▎ ANALYSIS

It is difficult in cases dealing with the issue here to find one single determinant of whether one will be considered an agent or a contractor. Different courts focus on different factors. A franchise agreement that would lead to a result of no vicarious liability in one jurisdiction could well lead to the opposite conclusion in another jurisdiction.

Quicknotes

AGENT An individual who has the authority to act on behalf of another.

FRANCHISEE A party, whom a supplier of goods or services agrees to permit to sell the good or service or to otherwise conduct business on behalf of the franchise.

FRANCHISOR A supplier of goods or services, who agrees to permit a re-seller to sell the good or service or to otherwise conduct business on behalf of the franchise.

INDEPENDENT CONTRACTOR A party undertaking a particular assignment for another who retains control over the manner in which it is executed.

PRINCIPAL A person or entity who authorizes another (the agent) to act on its behalf and subject to its authority to the extent that the principal may be held liable for the actions of the agent.

SUMMARY JUDGMENT Judgment rendered by a court in response to a motion made by one of the parties, claiming that the lack of a question of material fact in respect to an issue warrants disposition of the issue without consideration by the jury.

VICARIOUS LIABILITY The imputed liability of one party for the unlawful acts of another.

Murphy v. Holiday Inns, Inc.

Injured guest (P) v. Hotel (D)

216 Va. 490, 219 S.E.2d 874 (1975).

NATURE OF CASE: Appeal from summary judgment dismissing personal injury action.

FACT SUMMARY: Murphy (P) sought to hold Holiday Inns, Inc. (D) liable when she slipped and fell at a motel operated by a franchisee.

🏛 RULE OF LAW
If a franchise contract so regulates the activities of a franchisee as to vest the franchisor with control within the definition of agency, a principal-agent relationship arises even if the parties expressly deny it.

FACTS: Murphy (P) suffered personal injuries as a result of a fall at a Holiday Inn. She filed an action seeking damages against the parent/franchisor corporation, Holiday Inns, Inc. (D). Holiday Inns (D) moved for summary judgment. In support thereof, it introduced evidence that it provided to its franchisees the right to use its name and mandated certain standards, but apart from that and the collection of its franchise fee, left the details of management to the franchisees. The trial court granted the motion, and Murphy (P) appealed.

ISSUE: Does a principal-agent relationship arise where a franchise contract so regulates the activities of a franchisee as to vest the franchisor with control within the definition of agency?

HOLDING AND DECISION: [Judge not stated in casebook excerpt.] Yes. If a franchise contract so regulates the activities of a franchisee as to vest the franchisor with control within the definition of agency, a principal-agent relationship arises even if the parties expressly deny it. It is the element of continuous subjection to the will of the principal that distinguishes an agent from contractors and other types of fiduciaries, and the agency agreement from other agreements. A franchise agreement can be structured so as to make the franchisee the agent of the franchisor, if the latter retains control over the everyday functioning of the franchise. However, there is nothing inherent in the franchise contract that leads to such a result. The relationship does not depend upon what the parties themselves call it, but rather in law what it actually is. Here, Holiday Inns (D) introduced uncontroverted evidence that its franchisee exercised control over the details of its operation, and this demonstrated that an agency relationship did not exist. Affirmed.

▶ ANALYSIS

According to the Restatement (Second) of Agency § 1, an agency relationship is of a consensual, fiduciary nature. The court here made passing reference to this notion, but focused on control. The Restatement defines agency as "the fiduciary relation which results from the manifestation of consent by one person to another that the other shall act on his behalf and subject to his control, and consent by the other so to act."

Quicknotes

AGENT An individual who has the authority to act on behalf of another.

FRANCHISEE A party, whom a supplier of goods or services agrees to permit to sell the good or service or to otherwise conduct business on behalf of the franchise.

FIDUCIARY RELATIONSHIP Person holding a legal obligation to act for the benefit of another.

PRINCIPAL A person or entity who authorizes another (the agent) to act on its behalf and subject to its authority to the extent that the principal may be held liable for the actions of the agent.

RESTATEMENT (SECOND) OF AGENCY, § 1 Agency is a fiduciary relation resulting from consent of one person to have another act on his behalf.

SUMMARY JUDGMENT Judgment rendered by a court in response to a motion made by one of the parties, claiming that the lack of a question of material fact in respect to an issue warrants disposition of the issue without consideration by the jury.

Miller v. McDonald's Corp.

Restaurant patron (P) v. Franchisor (D)

945 P.2d 1107 (Ore. App. 1997).

NATURE OF CASE: Appeal from summary judgment for defendant in tort action.

FACT SUMMARY: Miller (P) argued that McDonald's Corporation (D) was liable for injuries she sustained while eating at a McDonald's franchise owned by 3K Restaurants.

RULE OF LAW
For purposes of determining tort liability, a jury may find that an agency relationship exists between a franchisor and a franchisee where the franchisor retains significant control over the daily operations of the franchisee's business and insists on uniformity of appearance and standards designed to cause the public to think that the franchise is part of the franchisor's business.

FACTS: Miller (P) suffered injuries when she bit into a heart-shaped sapphire stone while eating a Big Mac sandwich that she had purchased at a McDonald's Corp. (McDonald's) (D) restaurant, which in fact was owned by 3K Restaurants (3K), a McDonald's franchisee. Miller (P) brought suit against McDonald's (D). The license agreement under which 3K operated its restaurant required it to operate in a manner consistent with the "McDonald's System." The agreement described the way in which 3K was to operate the restaurant in considerable detail. It expressly required 3K to operate in compliance with McDonald's (D) prescribed standards, policies, practices, and procedures, and 3K had to follow McDonald's (D) specifications and blueprints for the equipment and layout of the restaurant. In short, through its agreement, McDonald's (D) sought to ensure uniformity of appearance, food, service, and standards in all McDonald's (D) restaurants, whether franchised or not. In addition, to ensure compliance with the agreement, McDonald's (D) periodically sent field consultants to the restaurant to inspect its operations. Notwithstanding these efforts, the agreement provided that 3K was not an agent of McDonald's (D) for any purpose, but rather was an independent contractor. Miller (P) claimed that she went to the restaurant, believing that McDonald's (D) owned, controlled, and managed it. As far as she could tell, the restaurant's appearance was similar to that of other McDonald's (D) restaurants that she had patronized, and nothing disclosed to her that any entity other than McDonald's (D) was involved in its operation. The trial court granted summary judgment to McDonald's (D) on the ground that it did not own or operate the restaurant. The appellate court granted review.

ISSUE: For purposes of determining tort liability, may a jury find that an agency relationship exists between a

franchisor and a franchisee where the franchisor retains significant control over the daily operations of the franchisee's business and insists on uniformity of appearance and standards designed to cause the public to think that the franchise is part of the franchisor's business?

HOLDING AND DECISION: [Judge not stated in casebook excerpt.] Yes. For purposes of determining tort liability, a jury may find that an agency relationship exists between a franchisor and a franchisee where the franchisor retains significant control over the daily operations of the franchisee's business and insists on uniformity of appearance and standards designed to cause the public to think that the franchise is part of the franchisor's business. The kind of actual agency relationship that would make McDonald's (D) vicariously liable for 3K's negligence requires that McDonald's (D) had the right to control the method by which 3K performed its obligations under the agreement. Here, a jury could find that McDonald's (D) retained sufficient control over 3K's daily operations, that an actual agency relationship existed, and that McDonald's (D) had the right to control 3K in the precise part of its business that allegedly resulted in Miller's (P) injuries. That is sufficient to raise an issue of actual agency. Here, too, there is an issue of apparent agency. The crucial issue in that regard is whether the putative principal (McDonald's (D)) holds the third party (3K) out as an agent and whether the plaintiff (Miller (P)) relies on that holding out. In cases from other jurisdictions, the centrally imposed uniformity is the fundamental basis for the courts' conclusion that there was an issue of fact whether the franchisors held the franchisees out as the franchisors' agents. Likewise, here, there is an issue of fact about whether McDonald's (D) held 3K out as its agent. Because there are numerous factors indicating centrally imposed uniformity, McDonald's (D) does not seriously dispute that a jury could find that it held 3K out as its agent. Rather, it argues that there is insufficient evidence that Miller (P) justifiably relied on that holding out, and argues that Miller (P) would have to prove that she went to the restaurant because she believed that McDonald's (D) operated both it and the other McDonald's restaurants that she had previously patronized. McDonald's (D) argument both demands a higher level of sophistication about the nature of franchising than the general public can be expected to have and ignores the effect of its own efforts to lead the public to believe that McDonald's (D) restaurants are part of a uniform national system of restaurants with common products and common standards of quality. A jury could find from Miller's (P) affidavit that she believed that all McDonald's (D) restaurants were the same because she believed that one

Continued on next page.

entity owned and operated all of them or, at the least, exercised sufficient control that the standards that she experienced at one would be the same as she experienced at others. A jury could find that it was McDonald's (D) very insistence on uniformity of appearance and standards, designed to cause the public to think of every McDonald's (D), franchised or unfranchised, as part of the same system, that makes it difficult or impossible for Miller (P) to tell whether her previous experiences were at restaurants that McDonald's (D) owned or franchised. Reversed.

▶ *ANALYSIS*

In determining whether McDonald's (D) was vicariously liable for 3K's alleged negligence because 3K was McDonald's (D) apparent agent, the court relied on Restatement (Second) of Agency, § 267. That section indicates that: "One who represents that another is his servant or other agent and thereby causes a third person justifiably to rely upon the care or skill of such apparent agent is subject to liability to the third person for harm caused by the lack of care or skill of the one appearing to be a servant or other agent as if he were such."

■≡■

Quicknotes

AGENCY A fiduciary relationship whereby authority is granted to an agent to act on behalf of the principal in order to effectuate the principal's objective.

FRANCHISEE A party, whom a supplier of goods or services agrees to permit to sell the good or service or to otherwise conduct business on behalf of the franchise.

FRANCHISOR A supplier of goods or services, who agrees to permit a re-seller to sell the good or service or to otherwise conduct business on behalf of the franchise.

SUMMARY JUDGMENT Judgment rendered by a court in response to a motion made by one of the parties, claiming that the lack of a question of material fact in respect to an issue warrants disposition of the issue without consideration by the jury.

TORT A legal wrong resulting in a breach of duty by the wrongdoer, causing damages as a result of the breach.

VICARIOUS LIABILITY The imputed liability of one party for the unlawful acts of another.

■≡■

Ira S. Bushey & Sons, Inc. v. United States

Drydock owner (P) v. Federal government (D)

398 F.2d 167 (2d Cir. 1968).

NATURE OF CASE: Appeal of a judgment in favor of a drydock owner in its damages suit against the Government for injury to the drydock by a government employee.

FACT SUMMARY: When a drunken Coast Guard seaman turned wheels on a drydock wall, damaging a drydock owned by Ira S. Bushey & Sons (P), the latter sued the Government (D) for compensation.

🏛 RULE OF LAW
Conduct of an employee may be within the scope of employment even if the specific act does not serve the employer's interests.

FACTS: While the U.S. Coast Guard vessel Tamaroa was being overhauled in a floating drydock, Lane, a Coast Guard seaman returning drunk from shore leave late at night, turned some wheels on the drydock wall, thus flooding the lock, partially sinking the Tamaroa, and damaging the drydock which was owned by Ira S. Bushey & Sons (P). Access from the shore to the ship was provided by a route past the security guard at the gate, through the yard, up a ladder to the top of one drydock wall and along the wall to a gangway leading to the fantail deck, where men returning from leave reported at a quartermaster's shack. Bushey (P) sued the Government (D) and was granted compensation by the federal district court. The Government (D) appealed, arguing that Seaman Lane's conduct was not within the scope of his employment.

ISSUE: May conduct of an employee be within the scope of employment even if the specific act does not serve the employer's interests?

HOLDING AND DECISION: (Friendly, J.) Yes. Conduct of an employee may be within the scope of employment even if the specific act does not serve the employer's interests. Lane's conduct was not so "unforeseeable" as to make it unfair to charge the Government (D) with responsibility. What is reasonably foreseeable in the context of respondeat superior is quite a different thing from the foreseeable unreasonable risk of harm that spells negligence. The foresight that should impel the prudent person to take precautions is not the same measure as that by which he should perceive the harm likely to flow from his long-run activity in spite of all reasonable precautions on his own part. The proper test here bears far more resemblance to that which limits liability for workers' compensation than to the test for negligence. The employer should be held to expect risks, to the public also, which arise out of, and in the course of, his employment of labor. Here, it was foreseeable that crew members crossing the drydock might do damage, negligently or even intentionally, such as pushing a Bushey (P) employee or kicking property into the water. Moreover, the proclivity of seamen to find solace for solitude by copious resort to the bottle while ashore has been noted in opinions too numerous to warrant citation. Once all this is granted, "it is immaterial that Lane's precise action was not to be foreseen." The risk that seamen going and coming from the Tamaroa might cause damage to the drydock is enough to make it fair that the enterprise bear the loss. Affirmed.

▶ ANALYSIS

In the *Bushey* case, the court notes that people do not disregard their personal qualities when they go to work. Into the job they carry their intelligence, skill, habits of care and rectitude. Just as inevitably, they take along their tendencies to carelessness and camaraderie, as well as emotional make-up. All these expressions of human nature are incidents inseparable from working together. "They involve risks of injury and these risks are inherent in the working environment."

Quicknotes

RESPONDEAT SUPERIOR Rule that the principal is responsible for tortious acts committed by its agents in the scope of their agency or authority.

SCOPE OF EMPLOYMENT Those duties performed pursuant to a person's occupation or employment.

Manning v. Grimsley

Injured spectator (P) v. Baseball club (D)

643 F.2d 20 (1st Cir. 1981).

NATURE OF CASE: Appeal from a defense verdict in a suit by an injured baseball spectator against the pitcher and his employer.

FACT SUMMARY: When Manning (P), while attending an Orioles baseball game, continuously heckled the Orioles' pitcher, Ross Grimsley (D), Grimsley (D) pitched a speed ball directly into the mesh screen in front of Manning (P). The ball went through the screen, injuring Manning (P), whereupon Manning (P) sued both Grimsley (D) and the Baltimore Baseball Club (D), his employer, for battery and negligence.

🏛 RULE OF LAW
To recover damages from an employer for injuries from an employee's assault, the plaintiff must establish that the assault was in response to the plaintiff's conduct which was presently interfering with the employee's ability to perform his duties successfully.

FACTS: Manning (P) attended a professional baseball game at Fenway Park in Boston between the Baltimore Baseball Club (the Orioles) (D) and the Boston Red Sox. Ross Grimsley (D) was a pitcher employed by the Baltimore Baseball Club (D). Manning (P) and other spectators were seated behind a wire mesh fence in the right field bleachers. The spectators, including Manning (P), continuously heckled Grimsley (D). At the end of the third inning, Grimsley (D) faced the bleachers and hecklers, wound up, and pitched an 80 mile an hour ball at a 90 degree angle directly into the wire mesh screen. The ball passed through the wire mesh fence and hit Manning (P). Manning (P) sued both Grimsley (D) and his employer the Baltimore Baseball Club (D) for battery and negligence. The trial court rendered judgment in favor of both defendants, and Manning (P) appealed.

ISSUE: To recover damages from an employer for injuries from an employee's assault, must the plaintiff establish that the assault was in response to the plaintiff's conduct which was presently interfering with the employee's ability to perform his duties successfully?

HOLDING AND DECISION: [Judge not stated in casebook excerpt.] Yes. To recover damages from an employer for injuries from an employee's assault, the plaintiff must establish that the assault was in response to the plaintiff's conduct which was presently interfering with the employee's ability to perform his duties successfully. Constant heckling by fans at a baseball park, as here, is "conduct." The jury could reasonably have found that such conduct on the part of Manning (P) had either the affirmative purpose to rattle or the effect of rattling the employee, Grimsley (D), so that he could not perform his duties, namely pitching, successfully. Moreover, the jury could reasonably have found that Grimsley's (D) assault on Manning (P) was not a mere retaliation for past annoyance, but a response to continuing conduct which was "presently interfering" with his ability to pitch in the game if called upon to play. Thus, the battery count against the Baltimore Club (D), as Grimsley's (D) employer, should have been submitted to the jury. From the evidence that Grimsley (D) was an expert pitcher, that on several occasions immediately following the heckling he looked directly at the hecklers, not just into the stands, and that the ball traveled at a right angle to the direction in which he had been pitching and in the direction of the hecklers, the jury could reasonably have inferred that Grimsley (D) intended (1) to throw the ball in the direction of the hecklers, (2) to cause them imminent apprehension of being hit, and (3) to respond to conduct presently affecting his ability to warm up and, if the opportunity came, to play in the game itself. Vacated and remanded.

▶ ANALYSIS

The Restatement of Torts 2d § 13 provides that an actor is subject to liability to another for battery if, intending to cause a third person to have an imminent apprehension of a harmful conduct the actor causes the other to suffer a harmful conduct.

▬▬▬

Quicknotes

BATTERY Unlawful contact with the body of another person.

NEGLIGENCE Conduct falling below the standard of care that a reasonable person would demonstrate under similar conditions.

▬▬▬

Arguello v. Conoco, Inc.

Minority consumers (P) v. Gasoline distributor (D)

207 F.3d 803 (5th Cir. 2000).

NATURE OF CASE: Appeal by civil rights claimants from a summary judgment in favor of an oil company.

FACT SUMMARY: When several Conoco (D) stores subjected Hispanic and African-American consumers, including Denise Arguello (P), to various forms of racial discrimination, the latter brought suit against Conoco (D), alleging racial discrimination in violation of federal legislation while patronizing the Conoco (D) facilities.

RULE OF LAW
To impose liability under civil rights legislation for the discriminatory actions of a third party, the plaintiff must demonstrate an agency relationship between the defendant and the third party.

FACTS: Several Hispanic and African-American consumers, including Denise Arguello (P), were subjected to various forms of racial discrimination while purchasing gasoline and other services from Conoco (D) outlets. The discrimination took the form of refusal of service, racial epithets, and extremely rude treatment by the store clerks clearly based on the race of the consumers who had come to utilize the facilities. The incidents took place at two types of facilities: (1) Conoco-branded stores which were independently owned, and (2) Conoco-owned stores whose clerks were Conoco (D) employees. Arguello (P) and the other racial minority consumers filed suit against Conoco (D), alleging that they were subjected to racial discrimination in violation of Federal legislation while patronizing the Conoco (D) facilities. The federal district court granted a summary judgment in favor of Conoco (D) on all the claims. Arguello (P) and the other consumers appealed.

ISSUE: To impose liability under civil rights legislation for the discriminatory actions of a third party, must the plaintiff demonstrate an agency relationship between the defendant and the third party?

HOLDING AND DECISION: [Judge not stated in casebook excerpt.] Yes. To impose liability under civil rights legislation for the discriminatory actions of a third party, the plaintiff must demonstrate an agency relationship between the defendant and the third party. To establish an agency relationship between Conoco (D) and the branded stores, Arguello (P) must show that Conoco (D) had given consent for the branded stores to act on its behalf and that the branded stores were subject to the control of Conoco (D). The Conoco-branded stores were independently owned, but entered into Petroleum Marketing Agreements (PMAs) which allowed them to market and sell Conoco brand gasoline and supplies in their stores,

although Conoco (D) did not control the daily operations of these stores, including personnel decisions. Here, the PMAs expressly stated that each branded store was an independent business and that its clerks were not employees of Conoco (D). The PMAs further stated that Conoco (D) and the marketer were "completely separate entities" and not partners, general partners, "nor agents of each other in any sense whatsoever and neither has the power to obligate or bind the other." Thus, there was no agency. As to the Conoco-owned stores, however, the employees of these stores were acting within the scope of their employment for Conoco (D) when they engaged in the statutorily discriminatory practices because these clerks were performing authorized duties for Conoco (D) such as conducting sales. These clerks also used their authority to conduct credit card transactions and use the gas station intercom to commit the discriminatory acts in question. Summary judgment is affirmed as to liability of Conoco (D) for the actions of its branded stores because of lack of an agency relationship. On the other hand, Conoco's (D) summary judgment is reversed as to liability for the actions of the employee clerks of the Conoco-owned stores on the basis of an agency relationship. Hence, affirmed in part and reversed in part.

ANALYSIS

In the *Arguello* case, the court noted that, as to the discriminatory actions of the clerks in the branded stores, Conoco (D) could not be held to have ratified their actions by not suspending or firing them since an employer must be aware of an agent's actions before it can ratify such actions.

Quicknotes

AGENCY A fiduciary relationship whereby authority is granted to an agent to act on behalf of the principal in order to effectuate the principal's objective.

DISCRIMINATION Unequal treatment of a class of persons.

SUMMARY JUDGMENT Judgment rendered by a court in response to a motion made by one of the parties, claiming that the lack of a question of material fact in respect to an issue warrants disposition of the issue without consideration by the jury.

Majestic Realty Associates, Inc. v. Toti Contracting Co.

Owner of damaged property (P) v. Demolition company and municipality (D)

30 N.J. 425, 153 A.2d 321 (1959).

NATURE OF CASE: Appeal from a defense judgment in a property damage suit by a building owner against the employer of an independent contractor.

FACT SUMMARY: When a building owned by Majestic Realty Associates, Inc. (P) and occupied by its tenant, Bohen's Inc. (P) was extensively damaged by demolition work on adjoining buildings performed by Toti Contracting Company (D), Majestic (P) and Bohen's Inc. (P) sued Toti (D) and the Parking Authority of the City of Paterson, New Jersey (D), who had hired Toti (D) to perform the demolition.

🏛 **RULE OF LAW**
Although a person who engages a contractor, who conducts an independent business using its own employees, is not ordinarily liable for negligence of the contractor in the performance of the contract, such person is liable when the contractor performs inherently dangerous work.

FACTS: The Parking Authority of the City of Paterson, New Jersey (D), contracted with Toti Contracting Company (D) to demolish several buildings, including one which adjoined a building owned by Majestic Realty Associates, Inc. (P) and occupied by its tenant, Bohen's Inc. (P). In the process of leveling the adjacent buildings, Toti (D) first removed the roofs, then the front and south sidewalls and all of the interior partitions and floors. To accomplish the demolition, Toti (D) used a 3500-pound metal ball, suspended from a street crane. During the demolition, Toti (D) caused extensive damage to the building owned by Majestic (P) and occupied by Bohen's Inc. (P). Toti's (D) president said at the time, "I goofed." Both Majestic (P) and Bohen's Inc. (P) sued Toti (D) and the Parking Authority (D). The trial court entered judgment for Toti (D) and the Parking Authority (D). Majestic (P) and Bohen's Inc. (P) appealed, and the Appellate Division reversed.

ISSUE: Although a person who engages a contractor, who conducts an independent business using its own employees, is not ordinarily liable for negligence of the contractor in the performance of the contract, is such person liable when the contractor performs inherently dangerous work?

HOLDING AND DECISION: [Judge not stated in casebook excerpt.] Yes. Although a person who engages a contractor, who conducts an independent business using its own employees, is not ordinarily liable for negligence of the contractor in the performance of the contract, such person is liable when the contractor performs inherently dangerous work. Inherently dangerous work, which in New York may also be equated with nuisance, is an activity which can be carried on safely only by the exercise of special skill and care, and which involves grave risk of danger to persons or property if negligently done. There is no doubt that the line between work which is ordinary, usual and commonplace, and that which is inherently dangerous because its very nature involves a peculiar and high risk of harm to members of the public or adjoining proprietors of land unless special precautions are taken, "is somewhat shadowy." In demolishing the walls of the building in question, Toti (D) used a large metal ball, weighing 3500 pounds, suspended from a crane which was stationed in the street. Every time the ball would strike a wall, debris and dirt would fly and the Majestic (P) building "rocked." The razing of buildings by demolition is an activity which necessarily involves a peculiar risk of harm, and the razing of buildings in a busy, built-up section of a city is inherently dangerous. Affirmed.

▌ *ANALYSIS*

The *Majestic* court noted that it is important to distinguish an operation which may be classified as inherently dangerous from one that is ultra-hazardous. The latter is described by the Restatement, Torts § 520 as one which (a) necessarily involves a serious risk of harm to the person, land, or chattels of others which cannot be eliminated by the exercise of the utmost care, and (b) is not a matter of common usage. The distinction is important because liability is absolute where the work is ultra-hazardous.

■▬■

Quicknotes

INHERENTLY DANGEROUS ACTIVITY An activity that is dangerous at all times so that precautions must be taken to avoid injury.

VICARIOUS LIABILITY The imputed liability of one party for the unlawful acts of another.

■▬■

Reading v. Regem

British soldier (P) v. British government (D)

King Bench, 2 K.B. 268, 2 All E.R. 27, W.N. 205 (1948).

NATURE OF CASE: Petition for the return of money.

FACT SUMMARY: When military authorities took possession of bribe money obtained by Reading (P) while an army sergeant, Reading (P) filed a petition for its return.

🏛 RULE OF LAW
An agent who takes advantage of the agency to make a profit dishonestly is accountable to the principal for the wrongfully obtained proceeds.

FACTS: During the period that Reading (P) was a sergeant in the Royal Army Medical Corps, he was found to have accepted bribes. Military authorities took possession of the bribe money. Reading (P) brought suit against the Crown (D), arguing that these moneys were his and should be returned to him. The Crown (D) responded that the bribes were received by Reading (P) by reason of his military employment; hence, the money should be retained by the Crown (D).

ISSUE: Is an agent who takes advantage of the agency to make a profit dishonestly, accountable to the principal for the wrongfully obtained proceeds?

HOLDING AND DECISION: [Judge not stated in casebook excerpt.] Yes. An agent, who takes advantage of the agency to make a profit dishonestly, is accountable to the principal for the wrongfully obtained proceeds. It matters not that the master has not lost any profit nor suffered any damage, nor does it matter that the master could not have done the act itself. If the servant has unjustly enriched himself by virtue of his service without the master's sanction, such servant should not to be allowed to keep the money. It should belong to the master because the servant obtained it solely by reason of the position the servant occupied as a servant of the master. Here, although there was not a fiduciary relationship because Reading (D) was not acting in the course of his employment when he accepted the bribes, agency is not an essential ingredient of the instant cause of action. The uniform of the Crown (D) and the position of Reading (D) as a servant of the Crown (D) were the only reasons why he was able to get the money; that is sufficient to make him liable to hand it over to the Crown (D). Petition dismissed with costs.

▶ ANALYSIS

The *Reading* court noted that it was unnecessary in this case to draw a distinction between law and equity since here the real cause of action was a claim for the restitution of moneys which, in justice, ought to be paid over.

Quicknotes

AGENCY A fiduciary relationship whereby authority is granted to an agent to act on behalf of the principal in order to effectuate the principal's objective.

BRIBERY The offering, giving, receiving, or soliciting of something of value for the purpose of influencing the action of an official in the discharge of his public or legal duties.

■■■

General Automotive Manufacturing Co. v. Singer

Employer (P) v. Salesman (D)

19 Wis.2d 528, 120 N.W.2d 659 (1963).

NATURE OF CASE: Appeal from judgment awarding damages for breach of fiduciary duty.

FACT SUMMARY: Singer (D), a consultant and representative of General Automotive (P), solicited customers on his own behalf.

🏛 RULE OF LAW
An agent who draws business away from his principal for his own enrichment is liable to the principal for his profits therefrom.

FACTS: Singer (D) was hired by General Automotive Manufacturing (P), a small machine shop, to both solicit customers and to assist in the manufacturing of ordered goods. During the period of his employment, Singer (D) would sometimes solicit side business of the same type done by Automotive (P). After Singer's (D) employment ended, Automotive (P) became aware of these activities. It sued Singer (D) to recover his profits from these ventures. A jury awarded Automotive (P) approximately $64,000, and Singer (D) appealed.

ISSUE: Is an agent who draws business away from his principal for his own enrichment liable to the principal for his profits therefrom?

HOLDING AND DECISION: [Judge not stated in casebook excerpt.] Yes. An agent who draws business away from his principal for his own enrichment is liable to the principal for his profits therefrom. An agent has a fiduciary relationship to his principal. A fiduciary owes a high degree of loyalty to the principal. Part of this duty of loyalty is not to do anything to the principal's economic detriment. An agent who "moonlights" or otherwise engages in activities that draw profits away from the principal does precisely this. Here, Singer (D) was hired partly to obtain customers for Automotive (P). By drawing potential customers for his own account, Singer (D) clearly worked to the detriment of Automotive (P), and he is therefore liable for the profits he realized. Affirmed.

▶ ANALYSIS

The issue here is a common one in the business world. Whether an employee's side work constitutes a breach of fiduciary duty depends on numerous variables. Most important of these are the position of the employee (usually, the higher up the employee, the higher the fiduciary duty), and the closeness of the side work to the type of economic activity of the principal.

Quicknotes

AGENT An individual who has the authority to act on behalf of another.

DUTY OF LOYALTY A director's duty to refrain from self-dealing or to take a position that is adverse to the corporation's best interests.

FIDUCIARY DUTY A legal obligation to act for the benefit of another.

PRINCIPAL A person or entity who authorizes another (the agent) to act on its behalf and subject to its authority to the extent that the principal may be held liable for the actions of the agent.

Town & Country House & Home Service, Inc. v. Newbery

Cleaning service company (P) v. Former employee (D)

3 N.Y.2d 554, 170 N.Y.S.2d 328, 147 N.E.2d 724 (1958).

NATURE OF CASE: Appeal from order holding former employees liable for unfair competition against their former employer.

FACT SUMMARY: Certain employees of Town & Country (P) left, formed a competing company, and utilized customer lists they had obtained from their former employer.

RULE OF LAW
Former employees may not use confidential customer lists belonging to their former employer to solicit new customers.

FACTS: Town & Country House & Home Service, Inc. (P) operated a home cleaning service catering to affluent households. Newbery (D) and several other employees (D) resigned and formed a competing company. Using customer lists they had obtained while in Town & Country's (P) employ, they began soliciting accounts of their own. Town & Country (P) sued for unfair competition. The trial court dismissed, but the appellate division reversed, holding that the employees (D) had conspired to engage in unfair competition and breach of fiduciary duties. An appeal was taken.

ISSUE: May former employees use confidential customer lists belonging to their former employer to solicit new customers of their own?

HOLDING AND DECISION: [Judge not stated in casebook excerpt.] No. Former employees may not use confidential customer lists belonging to their former employer to solicit new customers. A customer list is, insofar as it contains information not readily available to the general public, a trade secret. The law does not permit another to use a trade secret that he obtained through employment with the one possessing the secret. Therefore, while there was nothing illegitimate about the employees (D) forming their own competing company, they crossed the line when they used Town & Country's (P) confidential customer list in soliciting business. Town & Country (P) is entitled to an injunction prohibiting further solicitation, and recoupment of profits obtained from use of the list. Affirmed in part, reversed in part.

ANALYSIS

When an employee leaves a company to form a competitor, the customers of the former employer are a natural place to start looking for accounts. Needless to say, the former employer will not take kindly to this. Most states have some sort of prohibition against this type of activity, although total prohibition is not always the case.

Quick Reference Rules of Law

Fenwick v. Unemployment Compensation Commission

Beauty salon manager (P) v. State unemployment agency (D)

133 N.J.L. 295, 44 A.2d 172 (1945).

NATURE OF CASE: Appeal from judgment characterizing business relationship as a partnership.

FACT SUMMARY: The Unemployment Compensation Commission (UCC) (D) determined that a written agreement fixing compensation between Chesire and her employer, Fenwick (P), owner of the United Beauty Shoppe, did not make her a partner in the shop.

> 🏛 **RULE OF LAW**
> A partnership is an association of two or more persons to carry on as co-owners a business for profit.

FACTS: Fenwick (P) hired Chesire as a cashier and receptionist for his beauty salon. She was employed at a salary of fifteen dollars per week until December 1938, when she requested a raise. Fenwick (P) agreed to pay her a higher wage if the income from the shop warranted it. To that end, an agreement was drawn up by a local attorney. The agreement stated that Chesire and Fenwick (P) associated themselves as a "partnership" for the operation of the shop; however, Chesire would make no capital investment, would have no control over the management of the shop, and would not be liable for any losses of the business. The agreement further provided that her salary would remain the same, but she would receive a year-end bonus of 20% of the net profits of the shop, if the business warranted it, and that the partnership could be terminated by either party upon ten days' notice. The relationship was terminated on January 1, 1942. The UCC (D) sought to determine whether Chesire was an employee or partner for the year of 1939 for the purpose of assessing Fenwick's (P) liability under an unemployment compensation statute. The UCC (D) held that the agreement was nothing more than an agreement to fix compensation. The state supreme court, however, found that the parties were partners. The UCC (D) appealed.

ISSUE: Is a partnership an association of two or more persons to carry on as co-owners a business for profit?

HOLDING AND DECISION: [Judge not stated in casebook excerpt.] Yes. A partnership is an association of two or more persons to carry on as co-owners a business for profit. Although the agreement between Fenwick (P) and Chesire was termed a "partnership" agreement, the essential element of co-ownership was lacking. The agreement was merely one in which Fenwick (P) agreed to share the profits from a business he owned with Chesire. In determining whether a partnership exists, factors to be considered include: the intentions of the parties as evidenced through the language of any written agreements, the right

to share in profits, the obligation to share in losses, the ownership and control of the partnership property, control over management of the business, and the rights of the parties on dissolution. Fenwick (P) contributed all the capital, managed the business, and took over all assets on dissolution. Chesire got nothing from the agreement other than a new wage scale, and risked nothing from it. Ownership was conclusively with Fenwick (P). Reversed.

▶ *ANALYSIS*

This case stands for the proposition that courts will look beyond the mere language of an agreement to determine the true nature of a business association. Similarly, the absence of a written agreement will not preclude a finding that a partnership did exist. Although profit sharing is often strong evidence that a partnership was intended, it is never conclusive.

■═■

Quicknotes

PARTNERSHIP A voluntary agreement entered into by two or more parties to engage in business and to share any attendant profits and losses.

■═■

Martin v. Peyton

Creditor (P) v. Alleged partner (D)

246 N.Y. 213, 158 N.E. 77 (1927).

NATURE OF CASE: Appeal from judgment holding a business relationship was a not partnership.

FACT SUMMARY: Martin (P), a creditor of the brokerage firm Knauth, Nachod, & Kuhne (KN&K), claimed that investments made by Peyton (D) and his associates (D) in KN&K made them partners in the firm.

RULE OF LAW
The absence of an explicit partnership agreement does not preclude the creation of a partnership.

FACTS: In the spring of 1921, Knauth, Nachod, & Kuhne (KN&K) was having financial difficulties and obtained a loan from Peyton (D) for $500,000 to use as collateral to secure bank advances. When this money was insufficient to cure KN&K's financial woes, it was suggested that Peyton (D) and his associates, Perkins (D) and Freeman (D), become partners to assist KN&K in its recovery. They refused the suggestion. Instead, they drew up an agreement whereby Peyton (D), Perkins (D), and Freeman (D) would loan KN&K $2,500,000 worth of securities and would be given in return KN&K's more speculative securities, 40% of KN&K's profits until the loan was repaid, and an option to join KN&K if they desired. The agreement further provided that Peyton (D), Perkins (D), and Freeman (D) were to be designated as "trustees" and kept advised and consulted on important KN&K matters, that each member of KN&K must assign his interest in the firm to the trustees, and that no loans to firm members or distributions of profits were to be made. Martin (P), a creditor of KN&K, filed suit against Peyton (D), Perkins (D), and Freeman (D), claiming that their investments in KN&K made them partners in the firm and they were therefore liable for KN&K's debts. The trial court found that Peyton (D), Perkins (D) and Freeman (D) were creditors, not partners, and Martin (P) appealed.

ISSUE: Does the absence of an explicit partnership agreement preclude the creation of a partnership?

HOLDING AND DECISION: [Judge not stated in casebook excerpt.] No. The absence of an explicit partnership agreement does not preclude the creation of a partnership. However, the existence of an intention to form an association to carry on as co-owners a business for profit must be proven. The agreements between Peyton (D), Perkins (D), and Freeman (D) and KN&K do not prove that this was their intent. The documents were merely a loan of securities with provisions to insure their collateral. Given the financial troubles KN&K was suffering from, it is entirely understandable that the agreement would contain provisions allowing Peyton (D), Perkins (D) and Freeman (D) to closely monitor their investment. Although the option provision of the agreement was somewhat unusual, it alone is not enough to prove that a present partnership was created. Affirmed, with costs.

ANALYSIS

Two types of business associations available in most states today but not available in the 1920s would likely have been attractive options for KN&K: the Limited Liability Company (LLC) and the Limited Liability Partnership (LLP). Like a corporation, an LLC provides liability protection for its members while still allowing for hands-on management. The rules governing LLPs vary by state but generally provide limited liability for debts of the partnership due to negligence but not for contractual obligations.

Quicknotes

PARTNERSHIP A voluntary agreement entered into by two or more parties to engage in business and to share any attendant profits and losses.

Southex Exhibitions, Inc. v. Rhode Island Builders Association, Inc.

Business (P) v. Purported business partner (D)

279 F.3d 94 (1st Cir. 2002).

NATURE OF CASE: Appeal from a judgment holding that no partnership existed.

FACT SUMMARY: Southex Exhibitions, Inc. (Southex) (P), as the successor-in-interest of Sherman Exposition Management, Inc. (SEM), sought damages from Rhode Island Builder's Association, Inc. (RIBA) (D) for breach of an agreement which it contended was a partnership agreement since the agreement used the word "partners."

> ## RULE OF LAW
> The existence of a partnership normally must be determined under a totality-of-the-circumstances test.

FACTS: In 1974, the Rhode Island Builder's Association, Inc. (RIBA)(D) entered into an agreement with Sherman Exposition Management, Inc. (SEM), a professional show owner and producer, for productions of RIBA (D) home shows. The preamble to the agreement stated that both entities would participate in the shows as "sponsors and partners." The term of the agreement was fixed at five years, renewable by mutual agreement. In contemporaneous conversations relating to the meaning of the term "partners," SEM's president informed RIBA's (D) representative that he "wanted no ownership of the show" and described SEM simply as the "producer" of the RIBA (D) shows. Subsequently, Southex Exhibitions, Inc. (Southex) (P) acquired SEM's interest under the agreement. RIBA (D) later expressed dissatisfaction with Southex's (P) performance, and refused to renew the agreement. Southex (P) brought suit against RIBA (D), alleging that the 1974 agreement established a partnership between RIBA (D) and Southex's (P) predecessor-in-interest (i.e., SEM) and that RIBA (D) had breached its fiduciary duties to its co-partner, Southex (P), by its wrongful dissolution of their partnership and its subsequent appointment of another producer. The trial court rendered judgment for RIBA (D). Southex (P) appealed.

ISSUE: Must the existence of a partnership normally be determined under a totality-of-the-circumstances test?

HOLDING AND DECISION: [Judge not stated in casebook excerpt.] Yes. The existence of a partnership normally must be determined under a totality-of-the-circumstances test. Here, the original 1974 agreement was simply entitled "Agreement," rather than "Partnership Agreement." Second, rather than an agreement for an identifiable duration, it prescribed a fixed, albeit renewable, term. Third, rather than undertake to share operating costs with RIBA (D), SEM not only agreed to advance all monies required to produce the shows, but to indemnify RIBA (D) for all show-related losses as well. State law normally presumes that partners share equally, or at least proportionately, in partnership losses. Similarly, although RIBA (D) involved itself in some management decisions, SEM was responsible for the lion's share. Further, Southex (P) not only entered into contracts, but conducted business with third parties. As a matter of fact, their mutual association was never given a name. It is also noteworthy that Southex (P) never filed either a federal or state partnership tax return. Similarly, the evidence as to whether either SEM or RIBA (D) contributed any corporate property was highly speculative, particularly since their mutual endeavor simply involved a periodic event, namely, an annual home show, with neither generated, nor necessitated, ownership interests in significant tangible properties, aside from cash receipts. Affirmed.

ANALYSIS

In *Southex*, the court noted that even though the Uniform Partnership Act explicitly identifies profit sharing as particularly probative indicia of partnership formation, and that some courts have even held that the absence of profit sharing compels a finding that no partnership existed, it does not necessarily follow that evidence of profit sharing compels a finding of partnership formation.

Quicknotes

TOTALITY OF THE CIRCUMSTANCES TEST Standard, which focuses on all the circumstances of a particular case, instead of individual factors.

Young v. Jones

Investor (P) v. Bank (D)

816 F. Supp. 1070 (D.S.C. 1992), *aff'd sub nom Young v. Federal Deposit Insurance Corporation*,
103 F.3d 1180 (4th Cir.), *cert. denied*, 522 U.S. 928 (1997).

NATURE OF CASE: Action for damages alleging partnership by estoppel.

FACT SUMMARY: Young (P), a Texas investor who lost $550,000 after relying on a falsified financial audit statement attached to an audit letter by Price Waterhouse–Bahamas (D), sought to recover damages from Price Waterhouse–U.S. (D).

> 🏛 **RULE OF LAW**
> A person who represents himself, or permits another to represent him, to anyone as a partner in an existing partnership or with others not actual partners, is liable to persons to whom such a representation is made who has given credit to the actual or apparent partnership.

FACTS: Young (P), an investor from Texas, deposited $550,000 in a South Carolina Bank on the basis of an unqualified audit letter issued by Price Waterhouse–Bahamas (PW-Bahamas) (D) regarding the financial statement of Swiss American Fidelity and Insurance Guaranty (SAFIG). The letterhead used for the SAFIG audit identified the Bahamian accounting firm only as "Price Waterhouse," and the audit letter also bore a Price Waterhouse trademark and signature. The financial statement turned out to have been falsified, and Young (P) lost the deposited money. Young (P) filed suit to recover the lost funds and investment potential alleging that PW-Bahamas (D) knew that the letter would induce third parties to rely to their detriment on the financial statement. Young (P) asserted that PW-Bahamas (D) and PW-U.S. (D) operated as a partnership, or in the alternative, operated as partners by estoppel, and therefore PW-U.S. (D) should be held liable for the negligent acts of PW-Bahamas (D). PW-Bahamas (D) and PW-U.S. (D) denied that a partnership existed between the two and submitted documents establishing that the two were separately organized.

ISSUE: Is a person who represents himself, or permits another to represent him, to anyone as a partner in an existing partnership or with others not actual partners, liable to persons to whom such a representation is made who has given credit to the actual or apparent partnership?

HOLDING AND DECISION: [Judge not stated in casebook excerpt.] Yes. A person who represents himself, or permits another to represent him, to anyone as a partner in an existing partnership or with others not actual partners, is liable to any such person to whom such a representation is made who has, on the faith of the representation, given credit to the actual or apparent partnership. Although Young (P) alleges that Price Waterhouse holds itself out as an international accounting firm, he can point to nothing concrete that should hold the various affiliated entities liable for the acts of others. There is no evidence that Young (P) relied on any act or statement by any PW-U.S. (D) partner indicating the existence of a partnership with PW-Bahamas (D). Even if there were, there has been no evidence presented that any member of PW-U.S. (D) had anything to do with SAFIG's falsified financial statement or any other act related to the lost investment. The allegations of negligence against PW-Bahamas (D) cannot serve to hold members of PW-U.S. (D) liable as partners by estoppel.

▌ *ANALYSIS*

Perhaps Young (P) would have been more successful had he argued for liability on an agency theory. Provisions of the Uniform Partnership Act (U.P.A.) state that every partner is an agent of the partnership and potentially liable for the unauthorized torts and contracts of a partner. Although PW-U.S. (D) would still have argued that the Bahamian group was a separate entity, the U.P.A. sections on acts involving third parties are extremely favorable to such third parties when they have been injured.

■=■

Quicknotes

ESTOPPEL An equitable doctrine precluding a party from asserting a right to the detriment of another who justifiably relied on the conduct.

PARTNERSHIP A voluntary agreement entered into by two or more parties to engage in business and to share any attendant profits and losses.

■=■

Meinhard v. Salmon

Partner (P) v. Partner (D)

249 N.Y. 458, 164 N.E. 545 (1928).

NATURE OF CASE: Appeal from judgment enforcing fiduciary rights arising from a joint venture.

FACT SUMMARY: Meinhard (P) filed suit against Salmon (D), his coadventurer in a joint venture, after Salmon (D) usurped an opportunity that should have been offered to the venture.

🏛 RULE OF LAW
Joint adventurers owe one another the highest fiduciary duty of loyalty while the enterprise is ongoing.

FACTS: In April 1902, Salmon (D) entered into a joint venture with Meinhard (P) to lease a hotel in New York City from Louisa Gerry for a term of twenty years. Under the terms of the agreement, Meinhard (P) provided the majority of the funding for the lease, while Salmon (D) managed and operated the property, although both partners were responsible for any losses. In January 1922, as the old lease was near its end, Elbridge Gerry, who had become owner of the property, approached Salmon (D) with an offer for a new lease. The new lease covered a larger tract of property for a period of twenty years, but contained covenants for renewal potentially expanding the deal to a maximum of eighty years. The new lease was signed between Gerry and the Midpoint Realty Company, which was owned and controlled exclusively by Salmon (D). Salmon (D) did not tell Meinhard (P) of the new lease until the deal had already been completed. Meinhard (P) then demanded that the lease be held in trust as an asset of the venture to be shared, but Salmon (D) refused. Meinhard (P) subsequently filed suit to enforce his share, and the trial judge ruled that he was entitled to 25%. Following cross-appeals, the appellate division enlarged Meinhard's (P) equitable interest to 50% of the whole lease. Salmon (D) appealed.

ISSUE: Do joint adventurers owe to one another the highest fiduciary duty of loyalty while the enterprise is ongoing?

HOLDING AND DECISION: (Cardozo, C.J.) Yes. Joint adventurers owe to one another the highest fiduciary duty of loyalty while the enterprise is ongoing. Salmon (D) appropriated to himself, in secrecy and silence, an opportunity that should have belonged to the joint venture. The subject matter of the new lease was an extension and enlargement on the old one. Salmon's (D) conduct excluded his coadventurer Meinhard (P) from any chance to compete or enjoy the opportunity that had come to him alone by virtue of their venture. Salmon (D) need only have advised Meinhard (P) of the opportunity when it arose and then either of them would have been free to compete for the project. The judgment of the appellate court should be generally affirmed, but modified to provide for a trust attaching to shares of stock on the lease, with Salmon (D) receiving one share more than Meinhard (P) so that he may retain management control over the new lease.

DISSENT: (Andrews, J.) The joint venture entered into by Salmon (D) and Meinhard (P) was for a limited scope, object, and duration of time. It was designed to exploit a particular lease and contained no mention of the venture continuing beyond the date of its termination. Had this been a general partnership between the two, then the majority's result would have been correct. However, given the limited nature of the venture, Salmon (D) did not act unfairly.

▶ ANALYSIS

Judge Cardozo, in his majority opinion, indicated that the fiduciary duty owed to co-venturers is equal to that owed a partner. The dissent, on the other hand, drew a distinction between the fiduciary duties required by the two. The Uniform Partnership Act and Revised Uniform Partnership Act have roughly incorporated Cardozo's approach.

■■■

Quicknotes

COVENANT A written promise to do, or to refrain from doing, a particular activity.

FIDUCIARY DUTY A legal obligation to act for the benefit of another.

JOINT VENTURE Venture undertaken based on an express or implied agreement between the members, common purpose and interest, and an equal power of control.

■■■

Perretta v. Prometheus Development Company, Inc.

Limited partner (P) v. General partner (D)

520 F.3d 1039 (9th Cir. 2008).

NATURE OF CASE: Appeal from judgment for defendants in action for breach of fiduciary duty by partners.

FACT SUMMARY: Limited partners (P) in Prometheus Income Partners, LP (Partnership) contended that Prometheus Development Co., Inc. (PDC) (D), the general partner, breached its fiduciary duty of loyalty by voting to ratify an unfair self-interested merger, and that a partnership agreement provision permitting an interested partner to count its votes in the total required for ratification would be "manifestly unreasonable."

> ## 🏛 RULE OF LAW
> A partnership agreement provision that permits an interested partner to count its votes in the total required for ratification of a self-interested transaction is "manifestly unreasonable," so that ratification obtained with the interested partner's vote is invalid.

FACTS: Prometheus Development Co., Inc. (PDC) (D), the general partner of Prometheus Income Partners, LP (Partnership), desired to cash out the Partnership's unaffiliated limited partners (P) in a merger with PIP Partners-General, LLC (PIP Partners), an entity owned by PDC's (D) owners, and which owned 18.2% of the limited partnership units in the Partnership. To this end, PDC (D) issued a proxy statement that, among other things, alerted the limited partners that the interests of PDC (D) and its affiliates were adverse to those of the unaffiliated limited partners (P), and which asserted that PIP Partners would vote its units neutrally, meaning that it would vote its units for or against the proposal in the same proportion as the total number of units voted by unaffiliated partners. The partnership agreement required an absolute majority of limited partner interests entitled to vote to ratify a merger. During the vote, 73.6% of the total partnership units owned by unaffiliated limited partners (P) were actually voted, but only 46% of those were voted to approve the merger. Not counting the votes of PIP Partners, an absolute majority of the votes in favor of the merger would not have been achieved; with those votes counted, the merger was approved by 50.7% of the units outstanding. A class of unaffiliated limited partners (P) brought suit for breach of fiduciary against PDC (D), arguing that PDC (D) had breached its duty of loyalty by setting an "unfairly low price" in a self-interested transaction. PDC (D) countered that its actions, which concededly were self-interested, had been properly ratified by the disinterested partners, which inoculated it from a breach of fiduciary claim. The unaffiliated limited partners (P) argued, however, that ratification was not proper because an absolute majority would not have been reached if PIP Partners' votes had not been

counted. The trial court ruled for PDC (D), and the court of appeals granted review.

ISSUE: Is a partnership agreement provision that permits an interested partner to count its votes in the total required for ratification of a self-interested transaction "manifestly unreasonable," so that ratification obtained with the interested partner's vote is invalid?

HOLDING AND DECISION: [Judge not stated in casebook excerpt.] Yes. A partnership agreement provision that permits an interested partner to count its votes in the total required for ratification of a self-interested transaction is "manifestly unreasonable," so that ratification obtained with the interested partner's vote is invalid. A partner has a duty of loyalty to refrain from dealing with the partnership in a way that is adverse to the partnership. This does not mean all self-interested transactions violate the duty of loyalty, since the question is not whether the self-interested partner is benefited, but whether the partnership or other partners are harmed. While a partner who seeks a business advantage over another partner bears the burden of showing complete good faith and fairness to the other, the self-interested partner may satisfy this burden by having the other disinterested partners ratify its actions. Upon a showing of proper ratification by the partners, any claim against the self-interested partner for a violation of the duty of loyalty is extinguished. Thus, to successfully defend against a breach of fiduciary claim here, PDC (D) must prove that the merger was properly ratified. Under state law, a self-interested transaction must be approved unanimously by the other partners unless the partnership agreement provides otherwise. Under the Partnership's partnership agreement, a majority vote of all votes entitled to vote (not just those actually voting) must be achieved for valid ratification. Here, a majority vote would not be achieved unless the votes of PIP Partners could be counted. This raises the question of whether ratification must be made by a vote of the majority of the unaffiliated limited partner units or all limited partner units, including interested limited partner units. Here, the voting provisions of the partnership agreement do not forbid the limited partners from ratifying the actions of an interested general partner, and the plain language of the agreement does not limit the ability of an interested general partner to participate in ratifying its own self-interested transactions. However, under state law, provisions to vary or permit ratification of violations of the duty of loyalty are permitted only if they are "not manifestly unreasonable." Thus, it must be determined whether the partnership agreement's

Continued on next page.

ratification provision is "manifestly unreasonable." While there is some authority that a provision permitting an interested partner to vote to ratify a self-interested transaction is not manifestly unreasonable, such authority is unpersuasive in the face of state policy requiring "thorough and relentless" scrutiny of self-interested transactions. This policy is codified in other areas of the law, such as those relating to corporations or the rescission of a merger of a limited partnership. Moreover, allowing an interested partner to participate in a ratification election subverts the very purpose of ratification itself, even where, as here, the interested partner votes "neutrally" since the neutral vote does not account for those outstanding disinterested units not voted. For these reasons, a partnership agreement provision that permits an interested partner to count its votes in a ratification vote is "manifestly unreasonable." Accordingly, the ratification here was invalid because it was not obtained from a majority of the disinterested interests entitled to vote. Because the ratification fails, PDC (D) has the burden of showing that its conduct did not violate the duty of loyalty, i.e., that its conduct was undertaken in complete good faith and fairness to the other limited partners. [Reversed and remanded.]

▶ ANALYSIS

The Delaware Court of Chancery in *R.S.M. Inc. v. Alliance Capital Mgmt. Holdings L.P.,* 790 A.2d 478 (Del. Ch. 2001) articulated why permitting an interested partner to participate in a ratification election subverts the very purpose of ratification itself. The court observed that when unitholders have the contractual opportunity to protect themselves against an unfair vote simply by voting no, it would be paternalistic and inefficient for courts to exercise a supervening judgment to protect the unitholders from their own erroneous investment decision. It is at best highly doubtful the court is in a better position than unitholders to determine the economic utility of transactions put to them; moreover, it seems a misallocation of judicial resources to have courts reassess the fairness of transactions that minority unitholders could have blocked themselves. Allowing an interested party to vote, however, only interferes with the unaffiliated partners' self-protection. The interested party has no need to "protect itself" from its own decision, and its contention that the decision also benefits the unaffiliated partners, unaccompanied by those partners' affirmative agreement, need not be taken at face value.

Quicknotes

BREACH OF FIDUCIARY DUTY The failure of a fiduciary to observe the standard of care exercised by professionals of similar education and experience.

GOOD FAITH COMPLIANCE A sincere or unequivocal intention to fulfill an obligation or to comply with specifically requested conduct.

Meehan v. Shaughnessy

Attorney (P) v. Former law firm (D)

404 Mass. 419, 535 N.E.2d 1255 (1989).

NATURE OF CASE: Appeal from judgment ordering recovery of fees and rejecting breach-of-duty counterclaim.

FACT SUMMARY: Meehan (P) and Boyle (P) commenced an action to determine their rights and liabilities after terminating their relationship with Parker Coulter (D), their former law firm, to start a firm of their own.

RULE OF LAW
A partner has an obligation to provide true and full information of all things affecting the partnership to any partner.

FACTS: Meehan (P) and Boyle (P), partners of the law firm Parker, Coulter, Daley & White (D), decided in June 1984 to terminate their relationship with Parker Coulter (D) and start their own firm beginning in January 1985. In preparing to establish their new firm, they decided on who from Parker Coulter (D) they wanted to invite to join them and which clients they would seek to remove to their new firm. Although they originally planned to give notice to Parker Coulter (D) on December 1, 1984, rumors of their departure began to circulate as early as July, and Meehan (P) was approached on several occasions by different partners regarding the rumors. On each occasion Meehan (P) denied that he was leaving, but after being approached by partner Shaughnessy (D) on November 30, Meehan (P) and Boyle (P) decided to distribute their notice that afternoon. The partners of Parker Coulter (D) subsequently asked Boyle (P) to identify the cases he intended to take with him. Boyle (P) did not return the list until two weeks later by which time he had obtained authorizations from the majority of clients whose cases he planned to take with him, unbeknownst to Parker Coulter (D). Shortly after leaving Parker Coulter (D), Boyle (P) and Meehan (P) commenced an action against Parker Coulter (D) to recover amounts claimed owed to them under the partnership agreement. Parker Coulter (D) counterclaimed that Meehan (P) and Boyle (P) had violated their fiduciary duties, breached the partnership agreement, and tortiously interfered with their advantageous business and contractual relationships by engaging in improper conduct in withdrawing cases and clients from Parker Coulter (D) and inducing Parker Coulter (D) employees to join the new firm. The superior court judge rejected all of Parker Coulter's (D) claims and found that Meehan (P) and Boyle (P) were entitled to recover amounts owed to them under the partnership agreement. Parker Coulter (D) appealed.

ISSUE: Does a partner have an obligation to render on demand true and full information of all things affecting the partnership to any partner?

HOLDING AND DECISION: [Judge not stated in casebook excerpt.] Yes. A partner has an obligation to provide true and full information of all things affecting the partnership to any partner. Although fiduciaries may plan to compete with the entity to which they owe allegiance, in the course of such arrangements they must not otherwise violate their fiduciary duties. Meehan (P) and Boyle (P) were entitled to make logistical arrangements such as signing a lease, obtaining financing, and drawing up lists of clients in preparing to establish their new firm. Meehan (P) and Boyle (P) committed no breach of their duties to Parker Coulter (D) during their last several months with the firm with regard to their handling of cases or changes in workload. However, they did breach their fiduciary duties by unfairly acquiring consent from clients to remove cases from Parker Coulter (D). Through their preparation for obtaining clients' consent, their secrecy concerning which clients they intended to take, and the substance and method of their communications with clients, Meehan (P) and Boyle (P) obtained an unfair advantage over their former partners in breach of their fiduciary duties. Reversed and remanded.

ANALYSIS

Many partnership agreements contain provisions that expressly prescribe procedures to be followed when a partner leaves to start a new firm or transfers to another firm. Such clauses are becoming increasingly common as attorneys move more and more frequently among firms. Even where such provisions do exist, such changes are inevitably uncomfortable and some periods of secrecy unavoidable.

Quicknotes

COUNTERCLAIM An independent cause of action brought by a defendant to a lawsuit in order to oppose or deduct from the plaintiff's claim.

FIDUCIARY DUTY A legal obligation to act for the benefit of another, including subordinating one's personal interests to that of the other person.

UNIFORM PARTNERSHIP ACT § 20 Partners have an obligation to provide true and full information of all things affecting the partnership to any partner.

Lawlis v. Kightlinger & Gray

Former partner (P) v. Law firm (D)

562 N.E.2d 435 (Ind. App. 1990).

NATURE OF CASE: Appeal from an adverse summary judgment in a suit for damages for breach of contract.

FACT SUMMARY: Although Lawlis (P) successfully battled his problem with alcohol abuse, the law firm of Kightlinger & Gray (D) voted to expel him from his senior partnership position.

🏛 RULE OF LAW
When a partner is involuntarily expelled from a business, his expulsion must have been in good faith for dissolution to occur without violating the partnership agreement.

FACTS: Lawlis (P) was a partner in the law firm of Kightlinger & Gray (Firm) (D) for ten years, until 1982. In that year, he became an alcohol abuser. The Firm (D) agreed to allow Lawlis (P) to continue as a partner while he sought treatment, stipulating that there was to be no second chance. Lawlis (P) was, however, given a second chance when he later resumed the consumption of alcohol. Although remaining a partner of the Firm (D), Lawlis's (P) workload was greatly reduced. Because he had not consumed alcohol since his second trip to the clinic, Lawlis (P) believed his previous status should be restored. The Firm (D), however, voted to sever his relationship with the Firm (D), allowing him a weekly draw and retaining his status as a senior partner to facilitate his transition to other employment. When Lawlis (P) refused to agree to this arrangement, the Firm (D) voted to expel him. Lawlis (P) filed suit for damages for breach of contract. Summary judgment was for the Firm (D). Lawlis (P) appealed.

ISSUE: When a partner is involuntarily expelled from a business, must his expulsion have been in good faith for dissolution to occur without violating the partnership agreement?

HOLDING AND DECISION: [Judge not stated in casebook excerpt.] Yes. When a partner is involuntarily expelled from a business, his expulsion must have been in good faith for dissolution to occur without violating the partnership agreement. Where the remaining partners in a firm deem it necessary to expel a partner under a no-cause expulsion clause in a partnership agreement, the expelling partners are deemed to have acted in good faith if their conduct does not cause a wrongful withholding of money or property legally due the expelled partner. That the Firm (D) in this case recommended a step-down severance over six months rather than immediate severance, as permitted under the partnership agreement, demonstrates a compassionate, not greedy, purpose. Affirmed.

▶ ANALYSIS

Potential damage to partnership business may be a consideration where no-cause expulsion of a partner from a law firm takes place. Under the partnership agreement in existence in the instant case, a two-thirds majority of the senior partners could, at any time, expel any partner from the partnership. Lawlis (P) was the only partner who voted against his own expulsion.

■■■

Quicknotes

FIDUCIARY RELATIONSHIP Person holding a legal obligation to act for the benefit of another.

■■■

Putnam v. Shoaf

Former partner (P) v. Transferee (D)

620 S.W.2d 510 (Ct. App. of Tenn., Western Section, at Jackson 1981).

NATURE OF CASE: Appeal from a denial of intervener's share of a judgment.

FACT SUMMARY: Putnam's estate (P) intervened in a suit, alleging that it was entitled to a one-half interest in the judgment paid to a partnership after Putnam (P) had transferred her interest in the partnership by quit claim to Shoaf (D).

🏛 RULE OF LAW
A co-partner owns no personal specific interest in any specific property or asset of the partnership, and may only convey an undivided interest in the value or deficit of the partnership.

FACTS: Mrs. Putnam (P) sold her interest in a partnership to the Shoafs (D) when the business was operating at a loss. When the Shoafs (D) became partners, the services of an old bookkeeper were terminated, and a new bookkeeper took over. It was later discovered that the old bookkeeper had been embezzling. This led to suits being filed by the company against the bookkeeper and the banks that had honored checks forged by the bookkeeper. Mrs. Putnam (P) was allowed to intervene, claiming an interest in any funds paid by the banks. A judgment was paid into court by the banks and Mrs. Putnam's estate (P) sought to recover one-half of the judgment from the Shoafs (D).

ISSUE: Does a co-partner own no personal specific interest in any specific property or asset of the partnership, and only convey an undivided interest in the value or deficit of the partnership?

HOLDING AND DECISION: [Judge not stated in casebook excerpt.] Yes. A co-partner owns no personal specific interest in any specific property or asset of the partnership and may only convey an undivided interest in the value or deficit of the partnership. The partnership owns the property or the asset. The partner's asset is an undivided interest; i.e. her pro rata share of the net value of the partnership. All Mrs. Putnam (P) had to convey was her interest in the partnership. She therefore had no specific interest in any possible lawsuits which she could separately convey or retain. At the time of the conveyance, Mrs. Putnam (P) intended to convey her interest in a share of the profits and losses of the company. The transfer agreement cannot be reformed because of the parties' mutual ignorance of the embezzlement. Affirmed.

▌ *ANALYSIS*

The court in this case analogized the facts of this case to a hypothetical discovery of oil on the partnership-owned real property after transfer of a partnership interest. The partnership owned the property. The transferor would not have transferred his partnership interest if he had known of the existence of oil on the partnership property, but she would not be successful in seeking a share of the value of the oil later discovered.

■=■

Quicknotes

CHOSE IN ACTION The right to recover, or the item recoverable, in a lawsuit.

EMBEZZLEMENT The fraudulent appropriation of property lawfully in one's possession.

INTERVENOR A party, not an initial party to the action, who is admitted to the action in order to assert an interest in the subject matter of a lawsuit.

PARTNERSHIP A voluntary agreement entered into by two or more parties to engage in business and to share any attendant profits and losses.

PROPERTY INTEREST An owner's interest and rights in property.

QUITCLAIM DEED A deed whereby the grantor conveys whatever interest he or she may have in the property without any warranties or covenants as to title.

■=■

National Biscuit Company v. Stroud

Food distributor (P) v. Grocery partner (D)

249 N.C. 467, 106 S.E.2d 692 (1959).

NATURE OF CASE: Suit to recover for goods sold.

FACT SUMMARY: Stroud (D) advised National Biscuit (P) that he would not be responsible for any bread which the company (P) sold to his partner. Nevertheless, National Biscuit (P) continued to make deliveries.

🏛 RULE OF LAW
The acts of a partner, if performed on behalf of the partnership and within the scope of its business, are binding upon all co-partners.

FACTS: Stroud (D) and Freeman entered into a general partnership to sell groceries under the name of Stroud's Food Center. Both partners apparently had an equal right to manage the business. The partnership periodically ordered bread from National Biscuit Company (P). Eventually, however, Stroud (D) notified National (P) that he would not be responsible for any additional bread which the company (D) sold to Stroud's Food Center. Nevertheless, National (P) sent, at Freeman's request, additional bread of a total value of $171.04. On the day of the last delivery, Stroud (D) and Freeman dissolved their partnership. Most of the firm's assets were assigned to Stroud (D), who agreed to liquidate the assets of the partnership and to discharge its liabilities. National (P) eventually sued Stroud (D) to recover the value of the bread which had been delivered but never paid for. Stroud (D) denied liability for the price of the bread, contending that his notice to the company (P) that he would not be responsible for further deliveries had relieved him of any obligation to pay for the bread. The trial court rendered judgment in favor of National (P), and Stroud (D) appealed.

ISSUE: May a partner escape liability for debts incurred by a co-partner merely by advising the creditor, in advance, that he will not be responsible for those debts?

HOLDING AND DECISION: [Judge not stated in casebook excerpt.] No. The acts of a partner, if performed on behalf of the partnership and within the scope of its business, are binding upon all co-partners. According to the appropriate provisions of the Uniform Partnership Act, all partners are jointly and severally liable for all obligations incurred on behalf of the partnership. If a majority of the partners disapprove of a transaction before it is entered into, then they may escape liability for whatever obligations that transaction ultimately incurs. But Freeman and Stroud (D) were equal partners, with neither possessing the power to exercise a majority veto over the acts of the other. Freeman's acts were entered into on behalf of the partnership, were within the scope of its ordinary business, and probably

conferred a benefit upon both Freeman and Stroud (D) as partners. Under these circumstances, it is proper to hold Stroud (D) liable for the price of the bread delivered by National (P) even after Stroud's (D) notice that he would not be held responsible for additional shipments. Affirmed.

▶ ANALYSIS

The rule adopted by the Uniform Partnership Act is consistent with traditional principles of agency law. In the absence of a contrary provision in the parties' partnership agreement, each partner acts as the agent of the partnership and of each other partner. Of course, only acts which are performed on behalf of the partnership and are consistent with its purposes are binding on other partners. However, even an act which was outside the scope of a partner's duties may bind his co-partners if they ratify it.

■■■

Quicknotes

AGENT An individual who has the authority to act on behalf of another.

NORTH CAROLINA UNIFORM PARTNERSHIP ACT All partners are jointly and severally liable for the acts and obligations of the partnership.

PRINCIPAL A person or entity who authorizes another (the agent) to act on its behalf and subject to its authority to the extent that the principal may be held liable for the actions of the agent.

■■■

Summers v. Dooley

Partner (P) v. Partner (D)

94 Idaho 87, 481 P.2d 318 (1971).

NATURE OF CASE: Claim for reimbursement of partnership funds.

FACT SUMMARY: In Summers's (P) suit against his partner Dooley (D) for reimbursement of his expenditure of $11,000 for the purpose of hiring an employee, Dooley (D) contended that because he did not approve of hiring the additional employee, the majority of partners did not consent to his hiring, and that Summers (P) should not be reimbursed for his unilateral hiring decision.

> ### 🏛 RULE OF LAW
> Business differences in a partnership must be decided by a majority of the partners provided no other agreement between the partners speaks to the issues.

FACTS: Summers (P) and Dooley (D) entered into a partnership for the purpose of operating a trash collection business. The business was operated by the two men and when either of them was unable to work, the non-working partner provided a replacement at his own expense. Dooley (D) became unable to work, and Summers (P), at his own expense, hired an employee to take Dooley's (D) place. Four years later, Summers (P) approached Dooley (D) regarding the hiring of an additional employee, but Dooley (D) refused. Summers (P), on his own, then hired another person and paid him out of his own pocket. Dooley (D) objected and refused to pay for the new person out of partnership funds. Summers (P) kept the man employed, but filed an action against Dooley (D) for reimbursement of Summers's (P) expenditures of $11,000 in hiring the extra employee. Dooley (D) argued that the majority of partners had not approved of the hiring, and that Summers (P) should not be reimbursed for his unilateral hiring decision. The trial court denied Summers (P) relief, and he appealed.

ISSUE: Must business differences in a partnership be decided by a majority of the partners provided no other agreement between the partners speaks to the issues?

HOLDING AND DECISION: [Judge not stated in casebook excerpt.] Yes. Business differences in a partnership must be decided by a majority of the partners provided no other agreement between the partners speaks to the issues. Here, the record shows that although Summers (P) requested Dooley's (D) acquiescence in the hiring of the extra employee, such requests were not honored. In fact, Dooley (D) made it clear that he was "voting no" with regard to the hiring of an additional employee. An application of Idaho law to the factual situation presented here indicates that the trial court was correct in its disposal of the issue since a majority of the partners did not consent to the hiring of the extra man. Dooley (D) continually voiced objection to the hiring. He did not sit idly by and acquiesce to Summers' (P) actions. Thus, it would be unfair to permit Summers (P) to recover for an expense which was incurred individually, not for the benefit of the partnership, but rather for the benefit of one partner. Affirmed.

▌ ANALYSIS

The rule that any difference arising as to ordinary matters connected with the partnership business may be decided by a majority of the partners is subject to any agreement between them. Partnership agreements often contain provisions vesting management in a managing partner or management committee. The same result, however, may be reached without explicit agreement on the basis of course of conduct.

■=■

Quicknotes

L C. § 53-318(8) Any difference as to ordinary partnership matters may be decided by a majority of the partners.

■=■

Day v. Sidley & Austin

Former partner (P) v. Law firm (D)

394 F. Supp. 986 (D.D.C. 1975), *aff'd sub nom. Day v. Avery,* 548 F.2d 1018
(D.C. Cir. 1976), *cert. denied,* 431 U.S. 908 (1977).

NATURE OF CASE: Motion for summary judgment in action for damages.

FACT SUMMARY: Day (P), a former partner in the law firm of Sidley & Austin (D), filed suit following approval of Sidley & Austin's (D) merger with another firm and the changes that resulted from the merger.

🏛 RULE OF LAW
Partners have a fiduciary duty to make a full and fair disclosure to other partners of all information that may be of value to the partnership.

FACTS: Day (P) was a senior partner at the Washington office of the law firm Sidley & Austin (D) from 1963 to 1972. He was a senior underwriting partner entitled to a certain percentage of the firm's profits and was privileged to vote on certain matters as specified in the partnership agreement. Day (P) was not a member of Sidley & Austin's (D) executive committee, which managed day-to-day business. In early 1972, the executive committee began exploring the idea of a merger with another firm. Each partner, including Day (P), voiced approval of the merger idea. Several other meetings of the underwriting partners were held before the final agreement was drawn up, but Day (P) chose not to attend any of them. The final amended Partnership Agreement, dated October 16, 1972, was executed by all Sidley & Austin (D) partners, including Day (P). Day (P) resigned from the firm effective December 31, 1972, claiming that the changes that occurred after the merger in the Washington office made continued service with Sidley & Austin (D) intolerable. He contended that the firm had made several active misrepresentations about the merger proposal which amounted to fraud and breach of fiduciary duty owed to him as a partner. Sidley and Austin (D) filed a motion for summary judgment asserting that Day's (P) factual allegations failed to support a cause of action.

ISSUE: Do partners have a fiduciary duty to make a full and fair disclosure to other partners of all information that may be of value to the partnership?

HOLDING AND DECISION: [Judge not stated in casebook excerpt.] Yes. Partners have a fiduciary duty to make a full and fair disclosure to other partners of all information that may be of value to the partnership. Sidley & Austin (D) did not breach any fiduciary duty owed to Day (P). No court has recognized a fiduciary duty to disclose the type of information handled by the executive committee involving the merger, the concealment of which does not produce any profit for the offending partners or any financial loss for the partnership as a whole. Day's (P) breach of contract claims also fail to support a cause of action for which a legal remedy is available. Day (P) had no reasonable expectation that no changes would be made in the office since the firm's partnership agreement gave complete authority to the executive committee to decide questions of firm policy. As an able and experienced attorney, it should have been clear to Day (P) that the differences and misunderstandings that developed with his former partners were the type of business risks that, although not uncommon, are not resolvable by judicial proceedings. Sidley & Austin's (D) alleged activities did not amount to illegality, and any personal humiliation was a risk he assumed when he joined the partnership. Sidley & Austin's (D) motion for summary judgment was granted.

▶ ANALYSIS

Courts are extremely reluctant to become involved in claims such as this one where a partnership agreement clearly defines the parties' rights as relating to one another. As the court pointed out, the primary and perhaps only injury Day (P) suffered was a bruised ego. A court is more likely to intervene when a third party is involved who was not privy to the standard operating procedures of the partnership, or a less savvy plaintiff than a seasoned attorney, like Day (P).

■■■

Quicknotes

FIDUCIARY DUTY A legal obligation to act for the benefit of another.

FRAUD A false representation of facts with the intent that another will rely on the misrepresentation to his detriment.

MISREPRESENTATION A statement or conduct by one party to another that constitutes a false representation of fact.

PARTNERSHIP A voluntary agreement entered into by two or more parties to engage in business and to share any attendant profits and losses.

■■■

Owen v. Cohen

Partner (P) v. Partner (D)

19 Cal. 2d 147, 119 P.2d 713 (1941).

NATURE OF CASE: Action for dissolution of a partnership and sale of its assets.

FACT SUMMARY: Owen (P), who had entered into an oral agreement with Cohen (D) whereby they contracted to become partners in the operation of a bowling alley business, sought judicial dissolution of the partnership.

🏛 RULE OF LAW
A court may order the dissolution of a partnership where there are disagreements of such a nature and extent that all confidence and cooperation between the parties has been destroyed or where one of the parties by his misbehavior materially hinders a proper conduct of the partnership business.

FACTS: Owen (P) and Cohen (D) entered into an oral agreement to become partners in operating a bowling alley business. For the purpose of securing necessary equipment, Owen (P) advanced close to $7,000 to the partnership, with the understanding that the amount was to be considered a loan to the partnership to be repaid out of the business's profits as soon as it could reasonably do so. The bowling alley opened on March 15, 1940, and until June 28, 1940, when Owen (P) commenced an action to dissolve the partnership, the business operated at a profit. Shortly after the business was begun, strong differences arose between the partners regarding the management of the partnership affairs and their respective rights and duties under their agreement. At the date of Owen's (P) filing of his complaint, his loan to the partnership had not been repaid, and the court appointed a receiver to control and manage the business during the court proceedings. The trial court found that Cohen (D) constantly attempted to become the dominating figure in the partnership and humiliated Owen (P) in front of the bowling alley's employees and customers. He also disagreed with the fixed salary the partners had agreed to take for themselves and began appropriating small sums from the partnership's funds to his own use without Owen's (P) knowledge or consent. The court ordered the partnership dissolved and the assets sold by the receiver with the proceeds of the sale used to pay the costs of the receiver, the debt to Owen (P) and other partnership debts, and the remainder split between the partners with costs to Owen (P). Cohen (D) appealed, asserting that the evidence did not show that their relationship had deteriorated to the point of warranting dissolution of the business.

ISSUE: May a court order the dissolution of a partnership where there are disagreements of such a nature and extent that all confidence and cooperation between the parties has been destroyed or where one of the parties by his misbehavior materially hinders a proper conduct of the partnership business?

HOLDING AND DECISION: [Judge not stated in casebook excerpt.] Yes. A court may order the dissolution of a partnership where there are disagreements of such a nature and extent that all confidence and cooperation between the parties has been destroyed or where one of the parties by his misbehavior materially hinders a proper conduct of the partnership business. Where there are only minor differences and grievances that involve no permanent mischief, a court should not issue a decree to dissolve a partnership. However, one partner cannot constantly minimize and deprecate the importance of the other without undermining the basic status upon which a successful partnership rests. The trial court had ample evidence to support a finding that the differences between Owen (P) and Cohen (D) were of an extremely serious nature. Affirmed.

⦙ ANALYSIS

Section 32 of the Uniform Partnership Act defines the circumstances under which a partner can apply for dissolution by a court. Besides a deteriorated personal relationship between the partners, additional reasons for seeking dissolution include disappointing economic returns or other changes in circumstances which no longer make the partnership satisfying. However, for a judicially ordered dissolution to be granted, the court will require proof of any allegations.

▄▅▆

Quicknotes

DISSOLUTION Annulment or termination of a formal or legal bond, tie or contract.

RECEIVERSHIP Proceeding or condition whereby a receiver is appointed in order to maintain the holdings of a corporation, individual or other entity that is insolvent.

UNIFORM PARTNERSHIP ACT § 32 A partnership may be dissolved on application whenever a partner is guilty of prejudicing the business or breaches the partnership agreement.

▄▅▆

Collins v. Lewis

Partner (P) v. Partner (D)

283 S.W.2d 258 (Tex. Civ. App. 1955).

NATURE OF CASE: Suit seeking dissolution of a partnership and other relief.

FACT SUMMARY: Lewis (D) persuaded Collins (P) to enter into a partnership for the operation of a cafeteria. The venture failed to make money, allegedly because of Collins's (P) lack of cooperation.

RULE OF LAW
A partner who has not fully performed the obligations required by the partnership agreement may not obtain an order dissolving the partnership.

FACTS: After entering into a long-term lease of space in a building then under construction, Collins (P) and Lewis (D) established a partnership. Collins (P) agreed to advance money to equip a cafeteria which Lewis (D) agreed to manage, Collins's (P) investment to be repaid out of the profits of the business. Delays and rising costs required a larger initial investment than the parties had anticipated, and Collins (P) eventually threatened to discontinue his funding of the venture unless it began to generate a profit. Eventually, Collins (P) sued Lewis (D), seeking dissolution of the partnership, the appointment of a receiver, and foreclosure of a mortgage upon Lewis's (D) interest in the partnership's assets. Lewis (D) filed a cross-action in which he alleged that Collins (P) had breached his contractual obligation to provide funding for the enterprise. The trial court denied Collins's (P) petition for appointment of a receiver, and a jury, after finding that the partnership's lack of success was attributable to Collins's (P) conduct, returned a verdict denying the other relief sought by Collins (P). From the judgment entered pursuant to that verdict, Collins (P) appealed.

ISSUE: Does a partner always have the right to obtain dissolution of the partnership?

HOLDING AND DECISION: [Judge not stated in casebook excerpt.] No. A partner who has not fully performed the obligations required by the partnership agreement may not obtain an order dissolving the partnership. In this case, the jury specifically found that Collins's (P) conduct prevented the cafeteria venture from succeeding. It was because Collins (P) withheld the funds which were needed to cover the expenses incurred by the business, thus requiring Lewis (D) to expend the cafeteria's receipts in order to meet those expenses, that the business showed no profit. In refusing to pay these costs, Collins (P) breached his contractual obligations, and he is therefore precluded from obtaining either dissolution or foreclosure. If Collins (P) is adamant in his desire to be released from

the partnership, his only recourse is to take unilateral action to end the relationship and subjecting himself to a suit for the recovery of whatever damages Lewis (D) may sustain. Affirmed.

ANALYSIS

Sometimes partnerships are created for a specific period of time, e.g., 15 years. Or, they may be established for an indefinite but determinable period of time, as is the case with partnerships that are to continue until the death of one of the partners. For good cause, partnerships may also be dissolved by judicial decree. However, this last method of termination is comparatively rare. Even partners who are locked in an irreconcilable dispute usually manage to agree to some plan which enables one or all of them to exit gracefully, because whatever settlement the feuding individuals can work out is likely to prove more economical than court-ordered dissolution, a procedure which typically results in the partnership property being disposed of for considerably less than its actual value.

Quicknotes

DISSOLUTION Annulment or termination of a formal or legal bond, tie or contract.

FORECLOSURE An action to recover the amount due on a mortgage of real property where the owner has failed to pay their debt, terminating the owner's interest in the property which must then be sold to satisfy the debt.

PARTNERSHIP A voluntary agreement entered into by two or more parties to engage in business and to share any attendant profits and losses.

RECEIVER An individual who is appointed in order to maintain the holdings of a corporation, individual or other entity that is insolvent.

Page v. Page

Partner (P) v. Partner (D)

55 Cal.2d 192, 10 Cal. Rptr. 643, 359 P.2d 41 (1961).

NATURE OF CASE: Appeal from a judgment declaring a partnership to be for a term rather than at-will.

FACT SUMMARY: After the business started by two brothers had suffered losses for the eight years it was in operation, Page (P) dissolved the partnership by express notice to Page (D), who then contended that the partnership was for a definite term.

🏛 RULE OF LAW
A partnership may be dissolved by the express will of any partner when no definite term or particular undertaking is specified.

FACTS: Two brothers, Page (P) and Page (D), entered into an oral partnership agreement to run a linen supply business. The business was unprofitable for the first eight years. After it appeared the business might become profitable due to the establishment of Vandenberg Air Force Base in its vicinity, Page (P) sought a declaratory judgment that the partnership was not for any definite term and therefore could be dissolved at the will of either partner. Page (D) contended that there was an implied agreement to continue the partnership for a term, namely the time it would take the partnership to repay its indebtedness from partnership profits. The trial court agreed with this contention. Page (P) appealed.

ISSUE: May a partnership be dissolved by the express will of any partner when no definite term or particular undertaking is specified?

HOLDING AND DECISION: (Traynor, J.) Yes. A partnership may be dissolved by the express will of any partner when no definite term or particular undertaking is specified. In this instance, Page (D) failed to prove any facts from which an agreement to continue the partnership for a term may be implied. All partnerships are ordinarily entered into with the hope that they will be profitable, but that alone does not make them all partnerships for a term and obligate the partners to continue in the partnerships until all of the losses over a period of many years have been recovered. However, the power to dissolve a partnership-at-will by the express will of any partner must, like any other power held by a fiduciary, be exercised in good faith. Reversed.

▌ *ANALYSIS*

A partner may not dissolve a partnership to gain the benefits of the business for himself, unless he fully compensates his co-partner for his share of the prospective business opportunity. However, in the above case there was no showing of bad faith or that the improved profit situation was more than temporary. Further, a partner-at-will is not bound to remain in a partnership, regardless of whether the business is profitable or unprofitable.

■■■

Quicknotes

BAD FAITH Conduct that is intentionally misleading or deceptive.

■■■

Prentiss v. Sheffel

Minority partner (D) v. Partnership (P)

20 Ariz. App. 411, 513 P.2d 949 (1973).

NATURE OF CASE: Appeal from an order confirming a purchase by the majority partners of assets sold upon dissolution.

FACT SUMMARY: After freezing Prentiss (D) out of the partnership's management and affairs, Sheffel (P) and a third partner filed for dissolution, purchasing partnership assets at a judicially supervised sale.

> 🏛 **RULE OF LAW**
> Majority partners in a partnership-at-will may purchase the partnership assets at a judicially supervised sale.

FACTS: Sheffel (P) and another partner (P) formed a partnership with Prentiss (D) for the purpose of acquiring and operating a shopping center. After numerous unresolved disputes arose between the parties, Sheffel (P) and the other partner (P) excluded Prentiss (D) from the partnership's management and affairs. When the majority partners (P) sought dissolution of the partnership, Prentiss (D) counterclaimed, seeking a winding up of the partnership and the appointment of a receiver. The trial court, finding that the partners had a partnership-at-will which was dissolved as a result of the freeze-out or exclusion of Prentiss (D), ordered a partition and distribution of the partnership assets. Prentiss (D) appealed the trial court's ruling allowing Sheffel (P) and the other partner (P) to purchase the partnership assets at the judicially supervised sale.

ISSUE: May majority partners of a partnership-at-will purchase the partnership assets at a judicially supervised dissolution sale?

HOLDING AND DECISION: [Judge not stated in casebook excerpt.] Yes. Majority partners in a partnership-at-will may purchase the partnership assets at a judicially supervised dissolution sale. Although Prentiss (D) was excluded from management of the partnership, the trial court found no indication that such exclusion was done for the wrongful purpose of obtaining the partnership assets in bad faith. Rather, it was merely the result of the inability of the partners to harmoniously function in a partnership relationship. Moreover, the participation of the majority partners (P) in the sale increased the final sale price, thus considerably enhancing Prentiss's (D) 15% interest in the partnership. Affirmed.

> ▶ *ANALYSIS*

Regardless of the size of the investment in the partnership, every partner has the right to actively participate, on an equal basis, in the management of the partnership. However, partners share in the partnership's profits and losses in proportion to the percentage of their interest in the partnership. The trial court had established that Prentiss (D) was unable to pay his pro rata share of the deficits when asked to do so.

■══■

Quicknotes

FREEZE-OUT Merger whereby the majority shareholder forces minority shareholders into the sale of their securities.

■══■

Pav-Saver Corporation v. Vasso Corporation

Partner (P) v. Partner (D)

143 Ill. App. 3d 1013, 97 Ill. Dec. 760, 493 N.E.2d 423 (1986).

NATURE OF CASE: Appeal from a judgment finding wrongful termination of a partnership agreement.

FACT SUMMARY: When the partnership between Pav-Saver Corporation (PSC) (P) and Vasso (D) was wrongfully terminated by PSC (P), the head of Vasso (D) took over PSC (P) and continued to operate the business.

> ### 🏛 RULE OF LAW
> When a wrongful dissolution occurs, partners who have not wrongfully caused the dissolution shall have the right to continue the business in the same name and to receive damages for breach of the agreement.

FACTS: Pav-Saver Corporation (PSC) (P) owned the trademark and certain patents for the design and marketing of concrete paving machines. Dale, inventor of the concrete paver and majority shareholder of PSC (P), formed a partnership with Meersman, owner and sole shareholder of Vasso Corporation (D), in order to manufacture and sell the paving machines. The partnership was to be permanent and not to be terminated or dissolved except upon mutual approval of both parties. When Meersman was subsequently informed that the partnership was being terminated by PSC (P), he moved into an office at PSC (P), physically ousted Dale, and assumed day-to-day management of the business. PSC (P) then filed suit for a court-ordered dissolution of the partnership, return of its patents and trademark, and an accounting. The trial court ruled that PSC (P) had wrongfully terminated the partnership and that Vasso (D) was entitled to continue the partnership business and to possess the trademark and patents. Liquidated damages were awarded to Vasso (D). Both parties appealed.

ISSUE: When a wrongful dissolution occurs, do partners who have not wrongfully caused the dissolution have the right to continue the business in the same name and to receive damages for breach of the agreement?

HOLDING AND DECISION: [Judge not stated in casebook excerpt.] Yes. When a wrongful dissolution occurs, partners who have not wrongfully caused the dissolution shall have the right to continue the business in the same name and to receive damages for breach of the agreement. Wrongful termination invokes the provisions of the Uniform Partnership Act. Thus, although the partnership agreement between PSC (P) and Vasso (D) provided for a return of the trademark and patents, such return is not mandated by the statute where wrongful termination has occurred. In this case, the business could not continue

without the patents and the trademark. Moreover, there is no evidence tending to prove that the amount of liquidated damages as determined by the agreement's formula was unreasonable. Under the terms of the partnership agreement, what might have been a penalty appears to be a fairly bargained for, judicially enforceable, liquidated damages provision. Affirmed.

CONCURRENCE AND DISSENT: (Stouder, J.) It is clear that the parties agreed that the partnership only be allowed the use of the patents during the term of the agreement. The agreement having been terminated, the right to use the patents should be terminated. Since liquidated damages depends on return of the patents, the part of the judgment allowing Vasso (D) continued use of the patents should be vacated.

▶ ANALYSIS

Where a wrongful withdrawal has occurred, the aggrieved partner or partners have the option, under the Revised Uniform Partnership Act, to continue the business or to dissolve it. Should they elect to continue the business, they have the right to possess the partnership property. However, they must compensate the withdrawing partner for her share of the property, minus any damages caused by the wrongful withdrawal.

Quicknotes

DISSOLUTION Annulment or termination of a formal or legal bond, tie or contract.

LIQUIDATED DAMAGES An amount of money specified in a contract representing the damages owed in the event of breach.

UNIFORM PARTNERSHIP ACT § 38 When dissolution is caused, the partner(s) that did not cause the dissolution is entitled to damages for breach of the partnership agreement and may continue the business.

Kovacik v. Reed

Investor (P) v. Superintendent (D)

49 Cal. 2d 166, 315 P.2d 314 (1957).

NATURE OF CASE: Suit for an accounting and to recover one-half the losses sustained by the parties' joint venture.

FACT SUMMARY: Kovacik (P) asked Reed (D) to be his superintendent on several remodeling jobs; when the jobs were unprofitable, Kovacik (P) asked Reed (D) to share equally in the losses and Reed (D) refused.

🏛 RULE OF LAW
In a joint venture in which one party contributes funds and the other labor, neither party is liable to the other for contribution for any loss sustained.

FACTS: Kovacik (P) asked Reed (D) to be his superintendent on several remodeling jobs. Kovacik (P) told Reed (D) that he had approximately $10,000 to invest and that if Reed (D) would superintend and estimate the jobs, he would share the profits with him on a 50-50 basis. They did not discuss the apportionment in the event of any losses. Reed (D) accepted the proposal and began working. Several months later Kovacik (P) informed Reed (D) that the venture lost money, and demanded Reed (D) contribute to the losses. Reed (D) refused and Kovacik (P) filed suit for an accounting and to recover from Reed (D) one-half the losses. The trial court concluded the parties were to "share equally all their joint venture profits and losses" and, following an accounting, awarded plaintiff $4,340, representing one-half the losses found to have been incurred by Kovacik (P). Reed (D) appealed.

ISSUE: In a joint venture, in which one party contributes funds and the other labor, is either party liable to the other for contribution for any loss sustained?

HOLDING AND DECISION: [Judge not stated in casebook excerpt.] No. In a joint venture, in which one party contributes funds and the other labor, neither party is liable to the other for contribution for any loss sustained. The general rule is that in the absence of an agreement to the contrary the law presumes partners and joint venturers intended to participate equally in profits and losses of the common enterprise, irrespective of the amounts contributed, each sharing in the loss in the same proportion as he would in the profits. However, that presumption applies only in cases in which each party had contributed capital or was to receive compensation to be paid to them before computation of the losses or profits. This was not such a case. Reversed.

▶ ANALYSIS

The court also stated that the party who contributed money or other capital to the venture was not entitled to recovery from the party who contributed his labor. The rationale for the rule is that in the event of a loss, each party would lose his investment, one, money and the other, labor. Another basis for the rule is that each party valued his contributions to be equal and thus have sustained equivalent losses.

Quicknotes

CONTRIBUTION The right of a person or party who has compensated a victim for his injury to seek reimbursement from others who are equally responsible for the injury in proportional amounts.

JOINT VENTURE Venture undertaken based on an express or implied agreement between the members, common purpose and interest, and an equal power of control.

G & S Investments v. Belman

Partnership (P) v. Partner's estate (D)

145 Ariz. 258, 700 P.2d 1358 (Ct. App., Div. 2, 1984).

NATURE OF CASE: Appeal from judgment for plaintiffs.

FACT SUMMARY: G & S (P) were partners with Nordale and wanted to dissolve the partnership pursuant to the buyout provision in their agreement due to Nordale's wrongful conduct, but then continued the partnership after Nordale died.

RULE OF LAW
A partnership buyout agreement is valid and binding even if the purchase price is less than the value of the partner interest, since partners may agree among themselves by contract as to their rights and liabilities.

FACTS: G & S Investments (P) sought a judicial dissolution of their limited partnership with Nordale after he began using cocaine and started making irrational and bad business decisions. Nordale died after the filing of the complaint, and G & S (P) filed a supplemental complaint invoking their right to continue the partnership and acquire Nordale's interest. The trial court entered judgment in favor of G & S (P), finding that it had the right to continue the partnership and that the estate was owed $4,867. Belman (D), as executor of Nordale's estate, claimed that the mere filing of the complaint acted as a dissolution of the partnership, requiring the liquidation of the assets and distribution of the net proceeds to the partners, and appealed. Belman (D) also claimed that the term "capital account" in the partnership agreement was ambiguous because it was not clear whether the cost basis or the fair market value of the partnership's assets should be used in determining the capital account.

ISSUE: Is a partnership buyout agreement valid and binding even if the purchase price is less than the value of the partner interest, since partners may agree among themselves by contract as to their rights and liabilities?

HOLDING AND DECISION: [Judge not stated in casebook excerpt.] Yes. A partnership buyout agreement is valid and binding even if the purchase price is less than the value of the partner interest, since partners may agree among themselves by contract as to their rights and liabilities. Nordale's conduct was in contravention of the partnership agreement. His conduct affected the carrying on of the business and made it impracticable to continue in partnership with him. The Articles of Partnership provided that upon the death, retirement, insanity, or resignation of one of the general partners the surviving or remaining partners may continue the partnership business, and that they must purchase the interest of the retiring or resigning partner. Such buyout agreements are valid and binding.

Modern business practices allow parties to be bound by a contract they enter into willingly, absent fraud or duress. The words "capital account" are not ambiguous and clearly mean the partner's capital account as it appears on the books of the partnership, and not the fair market value. Affirmed.

ANALYSIS

The court in this case relied on a decision in an earlier case. In the case of *Cooper v. Isaacs*, 448 F.2d 1202 (D.C. Cir. 1971), the court had rejected the contention that the mere filing of a complaint acted as a dissolution of a partnership. Dissolution was found to occur only when decreed by the court or when brought about by other acts.

Quicknotes

ARTICLES OF PARTNERSHIP A written agreement specifying the terms of a partnership.

CAPITAL In tax, is often used synonymously with basis; in accounting, refers to an account that represents the equity (ownership) interests of the owners, i.e., the amounts they would obtain if the business were liquidated.

COST BASIS The value paid for an asset.

DISSOLUTION Annulment or termination of a formal or legal bond, tie or contract.

DURESS Unlawful threats or other coercive behavior by one person that causes another to commit acts that he would not otherwise do.

FAIR MARKET VALUE The price of particular property or goods that a buyer would offer and a seller accept in the open market, following full disclosure.

FRAUD A false representation of facts with the intent that another will rely on the misrepresentation to his detriment.

PARTNERSHIP A voluntary agreement entered into by two or more parties to engage in business and to share any attendant profits and losses.

Holzman v. De Escamilla

Bankruptcy trustee (P) v. General partner (D)

86 Cal. App. 2d 858, 195 P.2d 833 (1948).

NATURE OF CASE: Appeal from a finding that defendants were general partners and were personally liable to creditors.

FACT SUMMARY: Hacienda Farms was formed as a limited partnership with Russell (D) and Andrews (D) acting as limited partners.

> 🏛 **RULE OF LAW**
> If a limited partner participates in or exercises control over the partnership business, he becomes a general partner.

FACTS: De Escamilla (D) was the only general partner of Hacienda Farms. Russell (D) and Andrews (D) were limited partners. However, Russell (D) and Andrews (D) exerted control over business operations and decisions. Hacienda Farms went bankrupt and Holzman (P), the trustee, sought to hold Russell (D) and Andrews (D) personally liable for partnership debts. The court found that, by taking an active interest in the business, Russell (D) and Andrews (D) had lost their limited partnership protection. The court found them liable.

ISSUE: May a party participate in or exercise control over a partnership business while retaining his status as a limited partner?

HOLDING AND DECISION: [Judge not stated in casebook excerpt.] No. Limited partnership protection is lost if there is participation in or control over the business. These are the actions of general partners. Where a limited partner assumes such duties his protection ceases. He becomes personally liable for partnership debts just as though he were a general partner. Judgment affirmed.

▌ *ANALYSIS*

A limited partner is considered similar to the shareholder of a corporation. To encourage and facilitate investments in partnerships, most states have accorded limited partners personal immunity from partnership debts. Their potential loss is limited to the capital contributed to the partnership. To preserve this immunity, the limited partner must not assume any active interest in partnership affairs.

■■■

Quicknotes

GENERAL PARTNERSHIP A voluntary agreement entered into by two or more parties to engage in business whereby each of the parties is to share in any profits and losses therefrom equally and each is to participate equally in the management of the enterprise.

LIMITED PARTNERSHIP A voluntary agreement entered into by two or more parties whereby one or more general partners are responsible for the enterprise's liabilities and management and the other partners are only liable to the extent of their investment.

■■■

CALIFORNIA CIVIL CODE, § 2483 Limited partner shall not become liable as a general partner unless he takes part in the control of the business.

The Nature of the Corporation

Quick Reference Rules of Law

Southern-Gulf Marine Co. No. 9, Inc. v. Camcraft, Inc.

Ship buyer (P) v. Ship manufacturer (D)

410 So. 2d 1181 (La. App. 1982), *cert. denied*, 412 So. 2d 1115 (La. 1982).

NATURE OF CASE: Appeal from a granting of a defendant's motion for peremptory exception of no cause of action.

FACT SUMMARY: Camcraft (D) sought to get out of a contract with Southern-Gulf (P), because Southern-Gulf (P) had not been incorporated when the contract was signed.

🏛 RULE OF LAW
Where a party has contracted with what he acknowledges to be a corporation, he is estopped from denying the existence or the legal validity of such a corporation.

FACTS: Before Southern-Gulf (P) was incorporated, its president, Barrett (P), entered into a contract with Camcraft (D), which was to build a ship for Southern-Gulf (P). Subsequently, Barrett (P) informed Camcraft (D) by letter that Southern-Gulf (P) had been incorporated in the Cayman Islands, rather than in Texas as originally planned. Camcraft's (D) president signed a written acceptance and agreement to the letter. When Camcraft (D) defaulted on its obligation, Southern-Gulf (P) brought suit, seeking to sequester the vessel involved and demanding specific performance and damages. Camcraft (D) filed a motion for peremptory exception of no cause of action based upon the legal status of Southern-Gulf (P). The trial court sustained the motion. Southern-Gulf (P) appealed.

ISSUE: Where a party has contracted with what he acknowledges to be a corporation, is he estopped from denying its corporate existence?

HOLDING AND DECISION: [Judge not stated in casebook excerpt.] Yes. Where a party has contracted with what he acknowledges to be a corporation, he is estopped from denying the existence or the legal validity of such a corporation. The record discloses nothing indicating that the substantial rights of Camcraft (D) were affected by Southern-Gulf's (P) de facto status. Southern-Gulf (P) relied upon the contract and secured financing. Likewise, Camcraft (D) relied on the contract and began construction of the vessel. Camcraft (D) is thus estopped from denying the corporate existence of Southern-Gulf (P). In addition, Camcraft (D) apparently had no objection to Southern-Gulf's (P) altered status as a Cayman rather than de facto corporation. However, as the trial judge did not reach this consideration, it may be raised on remand. Reversed and remanded.

▶ ANALYSIS

The court of appeals also noted that the evidence indicated that Southern-Gulf's (P) legal status should not be grounds for avoidance of the contract. What most likely happened here is that the vessel appreciated in value above the contract price between the time of the contract and the agreed delivery-date. However, allowing Camcraft (D) to escape liability for its obligations under the contract would not accord with justice and fair dealing.

Quicknotes

CORPORATION A distinct legal entity characterized by continuous existence; free alienability of interests held therein; centralized management; and limited liability on the part of the shareholders of the corporation.

ESTOPPEL An equitable doctrine precluding a party from asserting a right to the detriment of another who justifiably relied on the conduct.

SPECIFIC PERFORMANCE An equitable remedy whereby the court requires the parties to perform their obligations pursuant to a contract.

Walkovszky v. Carlton

Injured pedestrian (P) v. Cab company owner (D)

18 N.Y.2d 414, 276 N.Y.S.2d 585, 223 N.E.2d 6 (1966).

NATURE OF CASE: Action to recover damages for personal injury.

FACT SUMMARY: Walkovszky (P), run down by a taxicab owned by Seon Cab Corporation (D), sued Carlton (D), a stockholder of ten corporations, including Seon (D), each of which had only two cabs registered in its name.

RULE OF LAW
Whenever anyone uses control of the corporation to further his own rather than the corporation's business, he will be liable for the corporation's acts. Upon the principle of respondeat superior, the liability extends to negligent acts as well as commercial dealings. However, where a corporation is a fragment of a larger corporate combine which actually conducts the business, a court will not "pierce the corporate veil" to hold individual shareholders liable.

FACTS: Walkovszky (P) was run down by a taxicab owned by Seon Cab Corporation (D). In his complaint, Walkovszky (P) alleged that Seon (D) was one of ten cab companies of which Carlton (D) was a shareholder and that each corporation had but two cabs registered in its name. The complaint, by this, implied that each cab corporation carried only the minimum automobile liability insurance required by law ($10,000). It was further alleged that these corporations were operated as a single entity with regard to financing, supplies, repairs, employees, and garaging. Each corporation and its shareholders were named as defendants because the multiple corporate structures, Walkovszky (P) claimed, constituted an unlawful attempt to "defraud members of the general public."

ISSUE: Did Walkovszky's (P) complaint state a sufficient cause of action so as to recover against each cab corporation, Carlton (D) as shareholder, and each corporation's shareholders?

HOLDING AND DECISION: (Fuld, J.) No. While the law permits the incorporation of a business for the purpose of minimizing personal liability, this privilege can be abused. Courts will disregard the corporate form ("pierce the corporate veil") to prevent fraud or to achieve equity. General rules of agency—respondeat superior—will apply to hold an individual liable for a corporation's negligent acts. The court here had earlier invoked the doctrine in a case where the owner of several cab companies (and whose name was prominently displayed on the cabs) actually serviced, inspected, repaired, and dispatched them. However, in such instances, it must be shown that the stockholder was conducting the business in his individual capacity. In this respect, Walkovszky's (P) complaint is deficient. The corporate form may not be disregarded simply because the assets of the corporation, together with liability insurance, are insufficient to assure recovery. If the insurance coverage is inadequate, the remedy lies with the legislature and not the courts. It is not fraudulent for the owner of a single cab corporation to take out no more than minimum insurance. Fraud goes to whether Carlton (D) and his associates (D) were shuttling their funds in and out of the corporations without regard to formality and to suit their own convenience. Reversed.

DISSENT: (Keating, J.) The corporations formed by Carlton (D) were intentionally undercapitalized for the purpose of avoiding responsibility for acts that were bound to arise as a result of the operation of a large taxi fleet. During the course of the corporations' existence, all income was continually drained out of the corporations for the same purpose. Given these circumstances, the shareholders (D) should all be held individually liable to Walkovszky (P) for the injuries he suffered. Carlton (D) was incorrect in claiming that, because the minimum amount of insurance required by the statute was obtained, the corporate veil could not and should not be pierced despite the fact that the assets of the corporation that owned the cab were trifling compared with the business to be done and the risks of loss, which were certain to be encountered. In requiring the minimum liability insurance of $10,000, the legislature did not intend to shield those individuals who organized corporations with the specific intent of avoiding responsibility to the public, where the operation of the corporate enterprise yielded profits sufficient to purchase additional insurance. Moreover, it is reasonable to assume that the legislature believed that those individuals and corporations having substantial assets would take out insurance far in excess of the minimum in order to protect those assets from depletion. In addition, it cannot be lightly inferred from the legislature's failure to increase the minimum insurance requirements that the legislature acquiesced in the shareholders' (D) scheme to avoid liability and responsibility to the public. Thus, the court should hold that a participating shareholder of a corporation vested with a public interest, organized with capital insufficient to meet liabilities, which are certain to arise in the ordinary course of the corporation's business, may be held personally responsible for such liabilities. Under such a holding, the only types of corporate enterprises that will be discouraged as a result of a decision allowing the individual shareholder to be sued will be those such as the one in question, designed solely to abuse the corporate privilege at the expense of the public interest.

Continued on next page.

▶ *ANALYSIS*

Courts, in justifying disregard of the corporate entity so as to pierce the corporate veil, advance an estoppel argument. If the entity is not respected by the shareholders, they cannot complain if the court, likewise, disregards the corporate arrangement—this is to prevent abuse of the form. Since the corporate veil may be dismissed even in instances where there has been no reliance on a company's seeming healthiness, as in tort claims, whether or not creditors have been misled is not of primary importance. Rather, a court will look at the degree to which the corporate shell has been perfected and the corporation's use as a mere business conduit of its shareholders.

■═■

Quicknotes

CORPORATE VEIL Refers to the shielding from personal liability of a corporation's officers, directors or shareholders for unlawful conduct engaged in by the corporation.

ESTOPPEL An equitable doctrine precluding a party from asserting a right to the detriment of another who justifiably relied on the conduct.

NEGLIGENCE Conduct falling below the standard of care that a reasonable person would demonstrate under similar conditions.

RESPONDEAT SUPERIOR Rule that the principal is responsible for tortious acts committed by its agents in the scope of their agency or authority.

■═■

Sea-Land Services, Inc. v. Pepper Source

Carrier (P) v. Dissolved corporation (D)

941 F.2d 519 (7th Cir. 1991).

NATURE OF CASE: Appeal from a grant of summary judgment for the plaintiff in an action for money owed.

FACT SUMMARY: When Sea-Land (P) could not collect a shipping bill because Pepper Source (PS) (D) had been dissolved, Sea-Land (P) sought to pierce the corporate veil to hold PS's (D) sole shareholder personally liable.

🏛 RULE OF LAW
The corporate veil will be pierced where there is a unity of interest and ownership between the corporation and an individual and where adherence to the fiction of a separate corporate existence would sanction a fraud or promote injustice.

FACTS: After Sea-Land (P), an ocean carrier, shipped peppers for the Pepper Source (PS) (D), it could not collect on the substantial freight bill because PS (D) had been dissolved. Moreover, PS (D) apparently had no assets. Unable to recover on a default judgment against PS (D), Sea-Land (P) filed another law suit, seeking to pierce the corporate veil and hold Marchese (D), sole shareholder of PS (D) and other corporations, personally liable. PS (D) then took the necessary steps to be reinstated as a corporation in Illinois. Sea-Land (P) moved for summary judgment, which the court granted. Marchese (D) and Pepper Source (D) appealed.

ISSUE: Will the corporate veil be pierced where there is a unity of interest and ownership between a corporation and an individual and where adherence to the fiction of a separate corporate existence would sanction a fraud or promote injustice?

HOLDING AND DECISION: (Bauer, C.J.) Yes. The corporate veil will be pierced where there is a unity of interest and ownership between a corporation and an individual and where adherence to the fiction of a separate corporate existence would sanction a fraud or promote injustice. There can be no doubt that the unity of interest and ownership part of the test is met here. Corporate records and formalities have not been maintained, funds and assets have been commingled with abandon, PS (D) was undercapitalized, and corporate assets have been moved and tapped and borrowed without regard to their source. The second part of the test is more problematic, however. An unsatisfied judgment, by itself, is not enough to show that injustice would be promoted. On remand, Sea-Land (P) is required to show the kind of injustice necessary to evoke the court's power to prevent injustice. Reversed and remanded.

▶ ANALYSIS

On remand, judgment for Sea-Land (P) required Marchese (D) to pay the shipping debt plus post-judgment interest. On appeal, the judgment was affirmed, *Sea-Land Services, Inc. v. Pepper Source*, 993 F.2d 1309 (7th Cir. 1993). The court in that case observed that Marchese (D) had received countless benefits at the expense of Sea-Land (P) and others, including loans and salaries paid in such a way as to insure that his corporations had insufficient funds with which to pay their debts.

■━▪

Quicknotes

COMMINGLED ASSETS The combining of money or property into a joint account or asset.

CORPORATE VEIL Refers to the shielding from personal liability of a corporation's officers, directors or shareholders for unlawful conduct engaged in by the corporation.

■━▪

Roman Catholic Archbishop of San Francisco v. Sheffield

Religious corporate sole (D) v. Purchaser of dog (P)

15 Cal. App. 3d 405, 93 Cal. Rptr. 338 (1971).

NATURE OF CASE: Appeal from denial of motion to dismiss and of motion for summary judgment.

FACT SUMMARY: The Roman Catholic Archbishop of San Francisco (the Archbishop) (D) contended that it was not the alter ego of a Swiss monastery with which Sheffield (P) had contracted for a St. Bernard dog.

🏛 RULE OF LAW
(1) Where a parent corporation controls several subsidiaries, the corporate veil of one subsidiary may not be pierced to satisfy the liability of another.
(2) The alter ego theory may not be applied where the unsatisfied creditor-plaintiff will merely not be able to collect if the corporate veil is not pierced.

FACTS: While traveling through Switzerland, Sheffield (P) entered into an agreement with a monastery operated by a Roman Catholic order (The Canons Regular of St. Augustine (D)) whereby the monastery would send him a St. Bernard dog in exchange for several installment payments. When the monastery breached the agreement, Sheffield (P) filed suit in California court against the Roman Catholic Church d.b.a., the Roman Catholic Archbishop of San Francisco (the Archbishop) (D), a corporation sole; the Bishop of Rome, the Holy See, the Canons Regular of St. Augustine; and Father Cretton. The complaint alleges that defendants the Archbishop (D) and the Canons Regular of St. Augustine (D) were controlled and dominated by the Roman Catholic Church (D), the Bishop of Rome (D) and the Holy See (D), that there existed a "unity of interest and ownership between all and each of the defendants," that the Archbishop (D) and the Canons Regular (D) were a "mere shell and naked framework which defendants Roman Catholic Church, The Bishop of Rome, and the Holy See, have used and do now use as a mere conduit for the conduit of their ideas, business, property, and affairs," and that all defendants were "alter egos" of each other. The Archbishop (D) presented evidence that it was not a party to the disputed transaction, and that the archbishop (D) was a separate and distinct legal entity from the monastery (D). Sheffield (P) presented evidence that "the Roman Catholic Church, governed by the Pope through the Code of Canon Law, Roman Congregations, and other ecclesiastical organs, is but [one] worldwide entity; not a composite of 'entirely separate' entities as claimed by [the Archbishop]. The Roman Catholic Church considers itself to be a hierarchial society, with spiritual and temporal headquarters in Rome. The Pope possesses supreme spiritual authority over all Catholics throughout the world, and, both in law and practice, exercises considerable temporal control over the persons and property of clerics, religious, dioceses, and religious congregations throughout the world." The trial court denied the Archbishop's (D) motion to dismiss and motion for summary judgment.

ISSUE:
(1) Where a parent corporation controls several subsidiaries may the corporate veil of one subsidiary be pierced to satisfy the liability of another?
(2) May the alter ego theory be applied where the unsatisfied creditor-plaintiff will merely not be able to collect if the corporate veil is not pierced?

HOLDING AND DECISION: [Judge not stated in casebook excerpt.]
(1) No. Where a parent corporation controls several subsidiaries, the corporate veil of one subsidiary may not be pierced to satisfy the liability of another. The terminology "alter ego" or "piercing the corporate veil" refers to situations where there has been an abuse of corporate privilege, because of which the equitable owner of a corporation will be held liable for the actions of the corporation. If anything, Sheffield's (P) evidence shows that both the Archbishop (D) and the Canons Regular of St. Augustine (D) are controlled by the Pope (D). But the issue is not whether the Pope (D) or any other entity in Rome may be held liable for the actions of the Canons Regular of St. Augustine (D), but whether the Archbishop (D) may be held liable. This evidence may raise a triable issue of fact as to whether the Canons Regular of St. Augustine (D) is an alter ego of the Pope (D), but it does not show that the Swiss organization is an alter ego of the Archbishop (D) or vice versa. The Archbishop's (D) uncontroverted evidence indicates that the Archbishop (D) had no dealings with the Canons Regular (D), thus negating any possibility that the Archbishops (D) so controlled and dominated that organization so as to be liable for its actions under the alter ego doctrine. The alter ego theory makes a "parent" liable for the actions of a "subsidiary" which it controls, but it does not mean that where a "parent" controls several subsidiaries each subsidiary then becomes liable for the actions of all other subsidiaries. There is no respondent superior between the subagents.
(2) No. The alter ego theory may not be applied where the unsatisfied creditor-plaintiff will merely not be able to collect if the corporate veil is not pierced. A requirement

Continued on next page.

for application of the alter ego theory is that the failure to pierce the corporate veil would lead to an inequitable result. That requirement is not satisfied here. Sheffield (P) argues that (1) the Archbishop (D) would not be injured by a judgment against it, as Canon Law allows the Archbishop (D) to seek indemnity from the Canons Regular of St. Augustine (D), and (2) if he can't sue the Archbishop (D), he would have to discontinue his cause of action, as suing in Switzerland or Italy would be prohibitive. It is not sufficient that Sheffield (P) will not be able to collect if the corporate veil is not pierced. "In almost every instance where a plaintiff has attempted to invoke the doctrine he is an unsatisfied creditor. The purpose of the doctrine is not to protect every unsatisfied creditor, but rather to afford him protection, where some conduct amounting to bad faith makes it inequitable . . . for the equitable owner of a corporation to hide behind its corporate veil." Reversed.

▶ *ANALYSIS*

This case suggests that Sheffield (P) may have been able to collect from the Pope (the Bishop of Rome) (D), or the Vatican (D), under the theory that the parent corporation was the alter ego of its subsidiary, the Canons Regular of St. Augustine (D). Of course, Sheffield (P) would have to show that the subsidiary was not only influenced and governed by the parent, but that there was such a unity of interest and ownership that the individuality, or separateness, of such person and corporation had ceased, and the facts were such that an adherence to the fiction of the separate existence of the subsidiary would, under the particular circumstances, sanction a fraud or promote injustice—a very high threshold to overcome.

■══■

Quicknotes

ALTER EGO Other self; under the "alter ego" doctrine, the court disregards the corporate entity and holds the individual shareholders liable for acts done knowingly and intentionally in the corporation's name.

CORPORATE VEIL Refers to the shielding from personal liability of a corporation's officers, directors or shareholders for unlawful conduct engaged in by the corporation.

LIABILITY Any obligation or responsibility.

SUBSIDIARY A company, a majority of whose shares are owned by another corporation and which is subject to that corporation's control.

SUMMARY JUDGMENT Judgment rendered by a court in response to a motion made by one of the parties, claiming that the lack of a question of material fact in respect to an issue warrants disposition of the issue without consideration by the jury.

■══■

In re Silicone Gel Breast Implants Products Liability Litigation

Class action members (P) v. Corporation (D)

887 F. Supp. 1447 (N.D. Ala. 1995).

NATURE OF CASE: Appeal from summary judgment dismissing plaintiff's piercing claim in some cases included in multidistrict products liability litigation.

FACT SUMMARY: When parent corporation Bristol-Myers (D) sought summary judgment on plaintiffs' veil-piercing claim in multidistrict litigation involving a products liability of a subsidiary corporation (D), the lower court found that summary judgment would be proper in some jurisdictions, but not in others.

> ## 🏛 RULE OF LAW
> In a corporate control claim seeking to pierce the corporate veil to abrogate limited liability and reach the parent corporation, summary judgment could be proper if the evidence presented could lead to but one result.

FACTS: Plaintiffs from many states claimed that they had been injured by breast implants produced by Medical Equipment Corporation (MEC) (D), a wholly-owned subsidiary of Bristol-Myers Squibb Co. (D). Although Bristol-Myers (D) itself had never manufactured or distributed breast implants, plaintiffs claimed that Bristol-Myers (D) could be held liable by piercing MEC's (D) corporate veil. The corporation MEC (D) was owned by a single shareholder, Bristol-Myers (D), which, as a parent corporation, was expected to exercise some control over its subsidiary. Bristol-Meyers (D) contended that a finding of fraud or like misconduct was necessary to pierce the corporate veil in Delaware.

ISSUE: In a corporate control claim seeking to pierce the corporate veil to abrogate limited liability and reach the parent corporation, may veil-piercing ever be resolved by summary judgment?

HOLDING AND DECISION: (Pointer, C.J.) Yes. In a corporate control claim seeking to pierce the corporate veil to abrogate limited liability and reach the parent corporation, summary judgment could be proper if the evidence presented could lead to but one result. Because a jury could find that MEC (D) was but the alter ego of Bristol-Myers (D), summary judgment must be denied. When a corporation is so controlled as to be the alter ego of mere instrumentality of its stockholder, the corporate form may be disregarded in the interest of justice. Many jurisdictions that require a showing of fraud, injustice, or inequity in a contract case do not do so in a tort situation. The totality of the circumstances must be evaluated in determining whether a corporation is so controlled as to be the alter ego or mere instrumentality of its stockholders. Delaware courts do not necessarily require a showing of fraud if a subsidiary is found to be the mere instrumentality or alter ego of its sole shareholder. Therefore, Bristol-Myers (D) is not entitled to dismiss the claims by summary judgment.

▶ ANALYSIS

While limited liability is the rule, in many cases where a plaintiff seeks to reach the assets of the parent to satisfy a judgment, piercing the corporate veil of the subsidiary occurs. Factors the courts consider include: whether the parent and subsidiary have common directors, officers, or common business departments; whether the parent and subsidiary file consolidated financial statements and tax returns; whether the parent finances the subsidiary; and whether the subsidiary operates with grossly inadequate capital. While the standards vary from state to state, all jurisdictions require a show of substantial domination.

■=■

Quicknotes

CLASS ACTION A suit commenced by a representative on behalf of an ascertainable group that is too large to appear in court, who shares a commonality of interests and who will benefit from a successful result.

CORPORATE VEIL Refers to the shielding from personal liability of a corporation's officers, directors or shareholders for unlawful conduct engaged in by the corporation.

■=■

Frigidaire Sales Corporation v. Union Properties, Inc.

Manufacturer (P) v. Limited partners (D)

88 Wash. 2d 400, 562 P.2d 244 (1977).

NATURE OF CASE: Appeal in action to attach liability to limited partners.

FACT SUMMARY: Frigidaire Sales Corporation (P) attempted to hold the limited partners of Commercial Investors generally liable after Commercial breached its contract with Frigidaire (P).

🏛 RULE OF LAW
Limited partners do not incur general liability for the limited partnership's obligations simply because they are officers, directors, or shareholders of the corporate general partner.

FACTS: Frigidaire (P) entered into a contract with Commercial Investors, a limited partnership. Mannon (D) and Baxter (D) were limited partners of Commercial and also officers, directors, and shareholders of Union Properties (D), the only general partner of Commercial. Mannon (D) and Baxter (D) controlled Commercial by exercising day-to-day control and management of Union (D). Commercial breached the contract and Frigidaire (P) filed suit against Union (D), Mannon (D), and Baxter (D), asserting that they should incur general liability for the limited partnership's obligations because they exercised day-to-day control and management of Commercial. Mannon (D), and Baxter (D) argued that Commercial was controlled by Union (D), a separate legal entity, and not by them in their individual capacities. The trial court declined to hold Mannon (D) and Baxter (D) generally liable, and Frigidaire (P) appealed.

ISSUE: Do limited partners incur general liability for the limited partnership's obligations simply because they are officers, directors, or shareholders of the corporate general partner?

HOLDING AND DECISION: [Judge not stated in casebook excerpt.] No. Limited partners do not incur general liability for the limited partnership's obligations simply because they are officers, directors, or shareholders of the corporate general partner. In Washington, parties may form a limited partnership with a corporation as the sole general partner. To hold that Mannon (D) and Baxter (D) incurred general liability for the limited partnership's obligations would require the court to totally ignore the corporate entity of Union (D), when Frigidaire (P) knew it was dealing with that corporate entity. Although Mannon (D) and Baxter (D) controlled Commercial through their control of Union (D), they scrupulously separated their actions on behalf of Commercial from their personal actions and the corporations were clearly separate entities.

Frigidaire (P) knew that Union (D) was the sole general partner of Commercial and that Mannon (D) and Baxter (D) were only limited partners. If Frigidaire (P) had not wished to rely on the solvency of Union (D) as the only general partner, it could have insisted that Mannon (D) and Baxter (D) personally guarantee contractual performance. When the shareholders of a corporation, who are also the corporation's officers and directors, conscientiously keep the affairs of the corporation separate from their personal affairs, and no fraud or manifest injustice is perpetrated upon third persons who deal with the corporation, the corporation's separate entity should be respected. Affirmed.

▶ ANALYSIS

The court's opinion does not preclude a finding of general liability of limited partners where there is a showing of fraud or deception. Other courts have been less lenient in protecting limited partners and have held them generally liable if their actions constituted control of the corporation. In some states, on the other hand, a corporate entity is not permitted to be a general partner because such arrangements are viewed as shams.

■═■

Quicknotes

GENERAL PARTNERSHIP A voluntary agreement entered into by two or more parties to engage in business whereby each of the parties is to share in any profits and losses therefrom equally and each is to participate equally in the management of the enterprise.

LIMITED PARTNERSHIP A voluntary agreement entered into by two or more parties whereby one or more general partners are responsible for the enterprise's liabilities and management and the other partners are only liable to the extent of their investment.

■═■

Cohen v. Beneficial Industrial Loan Corp.

Shareholder (P) v. Corporation (D)

337 U.S. 541 (1949).

NATURE OF CASE: Motion to require security in shareholder derivative action.

FACT SUMMARY: Cohen (P), a shareholder filing a derivative action, challenged the constitutionality of a New Jersey statute requiring an unsuccessful plaintiff to indemnify the corporation for its reasonable expenses in defending the action.

🏛 RULE OF LAW
A statute holding an unsuccessful plaintiff liable for the reasonable expenses of a corporation in defending a derivative action and entitling the corporation to require security for such payment is constitutional.

FACTS: Cohen (P) owned 100 of the more than two million shares of the Beneficial Industrial Loan Corporation (D), a Delaware corporation. Cohen's (P) shares never had a market value of more than $5,000. In 1943, Cohen's decedent (P) brought a derivative action in U.S. district court in New Jersey, alleging that since 1929 certain managers and directors of Beneficial (D) had engaged in a continuing and successful conspiracy to enrich themselves at the expense of the corporation. Specific charges of mismanagement and fraud extended over a period of eighteen years and the assets allegedly wasted or diverted exceeded $100,000,000. Cohen (P) had demanded that Beneficial (D) institute proceedings for its recovery, but by their control of the corporation the directors and managers prevented it from doing so, and the derivative action was filed. In 1945, New Jersey enacted a statute that required a plaintiff having less than a 5% or $50,000 interest in a corporation to be liable for the reasonable expenses and attorney's fees of the defense if he was unsuccessful in his suit and entitling the corporation to indemnity before the case could be prosecuted. Beneficial (D) moved to require such security, seeking a bond of $125,000, and Cohen's decedent (P) challenged the statute as unconstitutional. The district court declined to fix the amount of indemnity, the court of appeals reversed, and the Supreme Court granted review.

ISSUE: Is a statute holding an unsuccessful plaintiff liable for the reasonable expenses of a corporation in defending a derivative action and entitling the corporation to require security for such payment constitutional?

HOLDING AND DECISION: (Jackson, J.) Yes. A statute holding an unsuccessful plaintiff liable for the reasonable expenses of a corporation in defending a derivative action and entitling the corporation to require security for such payment is constitutional. A stockholder who brings suit on a cause of action derived from the corporation assumes a position of a fiduciary character. The Constitution does not oblige the state to place its litigating and adjudicating processes at the disposal of such a representative, at least without imposing standards of responsibility, liability, and accountability which it considers will protect the interests the representative elects himself to represent. It cannot be said that the state makes such unreasonable use of its power as to violate the Constitution when it provides liability and security for payment of reasonable expenses if the litigation is adjudged to be unsustainable. Although it is perhaps not the optimal determinant of liability for litigation, nothing forbids the state using the amount of financial interest in the corporation of the litigant as a measure of his accountability. Such a measure will undoubtedly prevent a number of the harassment suits the statute was designed to target. Furthermore, the statute should be applied in a federal diversity case and can not be disregarded as a mere procedural device. Affirmed.

▶ ANALYSIS

Many states have imposed similar statutes to New Jersey's in an attempt to curb lawsuits brought simply to harass a corporation or pressure it into an undesirable settlement. Without such statutory protection, an individual who purchased just one share of stock could wreak havoc upon a corporation if they were so determined. Additional protection is offered in many jurisdictions by requiring court approval before a derivative action can be settled.

Quicknotes

FIDUCIARY DUTY A legal obligation to act for the benefit of another, including subordinating one's personal interests to that of the other person.

INDEMNIFICATION Reimbursement for losses sustained or security against anticipated loss or damages.

SHAREHOLDER'S DERIVATIVE ACTION Action asserted by a shareholder in order to enforce a cause of action on behalf of the corporation.

Eisenberg v. Flying Tiger Line, Inc.

Shareholder (P) v. Corporation (D)

451 F.2d 267 (2d Cir. 1971).

NATURE OF CASE: Appeal from dismissal of action by stockholder to enjoin a merger.

FACT SUMMARY: Eisenberg (P), a shareholder of Flying Tiger Line (D), filed suit against Flying Tiger (D) to overturn reorganization and merger that he alleged was intended to dilute his voting rights.

🏛 **RULE OF LAW**
A cause of action that is determined to be personal, rather than derivative, cannot be dismissed because the plaintiff fails to post security for the corporation's costs.

FACTS: In July 1969, Flying Tiger (D) organized a wholly owned Delaware subsidiary, the Flying Tiger Corporation (FTC), which in turn organized a wholly owned subsidiary, FTL Air Freight Corporation (FTL). The three corporations then entered into a plan of reorganization under which Flying Tiger (D) merged into FTL, FTL took over operations, and Flying Tiger (D) shares were converted into an identical number of FTL shares. The plan was approved by the necessary two-thirds vote at the annual meeting on September 15. The effect of the merger was that business operations were confined to a wholly owned subsidiary of a holding company whose shareholders were the former shareholders of Flying Tiger (D). Eisenberg (D) filed a class action on behalf of himself and other shareholders contending that the merger was a complex plan to deprive minority shareholders of any vote or influence over the affairs of the new company and seeking to overturn the reorganization. Flying Tiger (D) moved for an order to compel Eisenberg (P) to comply with a New York law that required a plaintiff suing derivatively on behalf of a corporation to post security for the corporation's costs. The trial judge granted the motion, Eisenberg (P) failed to comply, and his action was dismissed. Eisenberg (P) appealed, arguing that his class action was representative, not derivative, and that the statute requiring security was not applicable.

ISSUE: Can a cause of action that is determined to be personal, rather than derivative, be dismissed because the plaintiff fails to post security for the corporation's costs?

HOLDING AND DECISION: (Kaufman, J.) No. A cause of action that is determined to be personal, rather than derivative, cannot be dismissed because the plaintiff fails to post security for the corporation's costs. The essence of Eisenberg's (P) claim is that the reorganization deprived him and fellow stockholders of their right to vote on Flying Tiger's (D) affairs. This was in no sense a right that ever belonged to Flying Tiger (D) itself. Eisenberg (P) argues that the right belongs to stockholders per se, and that his action therefore cannot be deemed derivative. Although there has been much debate over the precise definition of a derivative suit, the current codification deems a suit derivative only if it is brought in the right of a corporation to procure a judgment in its favor. Such a definition clearly supports Eisenberg's (P) argument that his suit is not derivative and therefore no security need be posted. Reversed.

▶ **ANALYSIS**

Some actions may have both direct and derivative components. A recovery of damages in a derivative action is paid to the corporation, while a recovery in a direct action is paid to the shareholders. However, a court in its discretion may order that a judgment in a derivative action be paid to shareholders who may have been indirectly harmed by the wrongdoing, if it is determined that recovery by the corporation would constitute a windfall to controlling shareholders or would not adequately compensate the injured shareholders.

■═■

Quicknotes

CLASS ACTION A suit commenced by a representative on behalf of an ascertainable group that is too large to appear in court, who shares a commonality of interests and who will benefit from a successful result.

PROXY STATEMENT A statement, containing specified information by the Securities and Exchange Commission, in order to provide shareholders with adequate information upon which to make an informed decision regarding the solicitation of their proxies.

SHAREHOLDER'S DERIVATIVE ACTION Action asserted by a shareholder in order to enforce a cause of action on behalf of the corporation.

■═■

Grimes v. Donald

Shareholder (P) v. Corporation (D)

673 A.2d 1207 (Del. 1996).

NATURE OF CASE: Appeal from dismissal of a shareholder's derivative and direct suits.

FACT SUMMARY: Grimes (P), a shareholder, unsuccessfully sought a declaration of the invalidity of certain agreements made between Donald (D), the Chief Executive Officer (CEO), and the Board of Directors of DSC Communications Corporation, alleging excessive compensation and abdication of directorial duty by the Board of Directors of the corporation.

🏛 RULE OF LAW
If a shareholder demands that the board of directors take action and that demand is rejected, the board rejecting the demand is entitled to the presumption that the rejection was made in good faith unless the stockholder can allege sufficient facts to overcome the presumption.

FACTS: DSC, a Delaware corporation with headquarters in Texas, designs, manufactures, and services telecommunication systems. Employment agreements made with Donald (D) gave him the right to declare a constructive termination without cause in the event of unreasonable interference, as perceived in good faith by Donald (D), through the Board or a substantial stockholder of the company. Grimes (P), a shareholder, wrote to the Board, demanding that they abrogate the agreements as excessive compensation. The Board refused and Grimes (P) filed suit, seeking a declaration of the invalidity of these agreements made between the Board of Directors and Donald (D), and requesting damages from Donald (D) and other members of the Board. Grimes (P) alleged that the Board had breached its fiduciary duties by abdicating authority, failing to exercise due care, and committing waste. Donald (P) claimed that the Board had made a business decision which was entitled to protection under the business judgment rule. The Chancellor dismissed the abdication claim, which was a direct claim. Contending that demand was excused, Grimes (P) later filed a derivative suit alleging waste, excessive compensation and due care claims. The Chancellor held that Grimes (P) had waived his right to argue that demand was excused with respect to those claims because he had already made demand that the agreements be abrogated as unlawful. Grimes (P) appealed.

ISSUE: If a shareholder demands the board of directors take action and that demand is rejected, is the board rejecting the demand entitled to the presumption that the rejection was made in good faith unless the stockholder can allege sufficient facts to overcome the presumption?

HOLDING AND DECISION: [Judge not stated in casebook excerpt.] Yes. If a shareholder demands that the board of directors take action and that demand is rejected, the board rejecting the demand is entitled to the presumption that the rejection was made in good faith unless the stockholder can allege sufficient facts to overcome the presumption. Demand having been made as to the propriety of the agreement, it cannot be excused as to the claim that the agreement constituted waste, excessive compensation or was the product of a lack of due care. Since Grimes (P) made a pre-suit demand with respect to all claims arising out of the agreements, he was required to plead with particularity why the Board's refusal to act on the derivative claims was wrongful. The complaint failed to include particularized allegations which would raise a reasonable doubt that the Board's decision to reject the demand was the product of a valid business judgment. An abdication claim can be stated by a stockholder as a direct claim, as distinct from a derivative claim, but here the complaint failed to state a claim upon which relief could be granted. Affirmed.

▶ ANALYSIS

The court in this case discussed the difference between derivative and direct claims. To pursue a direct action, the stockholder-plaintiff must allege more than an injury resulting from a wrong to the corporation. The plaintiff must state a claim for an injury which is separate and distinct from that suffered by other shareholders.

■■■

Quicknotes

BUSINESS JUDGMENT RULE Doctrine relieving corporate directors and/or officers from liability for decisions honestly and rationally made in the corporation's best interests.

CORPORATION A distinct legal entity characterized by continuous existence; free alienability of interests held therein; centralized management; and limited liability on the part of the shareholders of the corporation.

FIDUCIARY DUTY A legal obligation to act for the benefit of another, including subordinating one's personal interests to that of the other person.

SHAREHOLDER'S DERIVATIVE ACTION Action asserted by a shareholder in order to enforce a cause of action on behalf of the corporation.

■■■

Marx v. Akers

Shareholder (P) v. Corporation (D)

644 N.Y.S.2d 121, 666 N.E.2d 1034 (1996).

NATURE OF CASE: Appeal from ruling by Appellate Division dismissing complaint for failure to make a demand on the board and failure to state a cause of action.

FACT SUMMARY: Marx (P), shareholder of IBM (D), brought a derivative action against the corporation alleging that the directors violated their fiduciary duty by voting for unreasonably high compensation for company executives.

🏛 RULE OF LAW
Demands on boards of directors are futile if a complaint alleges with particularity that: (1) a majority of the directors are interested in the transaction; (2) the directors failed to inform themselves to a degree reasonably necessary about the transaction; or (3) the directors failed to exercise their business judgment in approving the transaction.

FACTS: Marx (P), a shareholder of IBM (D), commenced a derivative action against IBM (D) alleging that Akers (D), a former chief executive officer of IBM, and other directors violated their fiduciary duty and engaged in self-dealing by awarding excessive compensation to other directors on the board. IBM (D) moved to dismiss the complaint for failure to state a cause of action and failure to serve a demand on IBM's board to initiate a lawsuit based on these allegations. The Supreme Court dismissed the complaint stating that Marx (P) failed to show that demand would have been futile, and the Appellate Division affirmed. Marx (P) appealed.

ISSUE: Is a demand on the board of directors futile if a complaint alleges with particularity that: (1) a majority of the directors are interested in the transaction; (2) the directors failed to inform themselves to a degree reasonably necessary about the transaction; or (3) the directors failed to exercise their business judgment in approving the transaction?

HOLDING AND DECISION: [Judge not stated in casebook excerpt.] Yes. Demands on boards of directors are futile if a complaint alleges with particularity that: (1) a majority of the directors are interested in the transaction; (2) the directors failed to inform themselves to a degree reasonably necessary about the transaction; or (3) the directors failed to exercise their business judgment in approving the transaction. Directors are self-interested in a transaction if they receive a direct financial benefit from the transaction that is different from the benefit to the shareholders generally. Voting oneself a raise excuses a demand. However, the inquiry must still be made as to whether this is a sufficient basis to support a cause of action. Courts have repeatedly held that a cause of action will not stand alone on the basis of excessive salary raises unless wrongdoing, oppression, or abuse of a fiduciary position is also demonstrated. The evidence presented is not ample to support Marx's (P) allegations of wrongdoing, so the Appellate Division's order should stand. Affirmed.

▶ ANALYSIS

In setting forth the instances in which demand will be excused, the court rejected both the "Delaware rule" and the "universal demand rule" proposed by the American Law Institute and adopted by eleven states. Although a universal demand requirement would decrease the number of cases such as this one, it would also be a waste of time in many circumstances. On the other hand, until the standards excusing demand are tested and clarified, there will still be an increase in the number of cases on this issue.

■═■

Quicknotes

BUSINESS JUDGMENT RULE Doctrine relieving corporate directors and/or officers from liability for decisions honestly and rationally made in the corporation's best interests.

FIDUCIARY DUTY A legal obligation to act for the benefit of another, including subordinating one's personal interests to that of the other person.

SHAREHOLDER'S DERIVATIVE ACTION Action asserted by a shareholder in order to enforce a cause of action on behalf of the corporation.

■═■

Auerbach v. Bennett

Shareholder (P) v. Corporate directors (D)

47 N.Y.2d 619, 419 N.Y.S.2d 920, 393 N.E.2d 994 (1979).

NATURE OF CASE: Appeal from summary judgment terminating shareholder derivative action.

FACT SUMMARY: A shareholder (P) of General Telephone and Electronics Corporation (GTE) (D) challenged the decision by a board-appointed special litigation committee to terminate a shareholder's derivative action.

> ## RULE OF LAW
> A court may properly inquire as to the adequacy and appropriateness of a special litigation committee's investigative procedures and methodologies, but may not consider factors under the domain of business judgment.

FACTS: With the assistance of special counsel and Arthur Andersen & Co. (D), GTE's (D) audit committee conducted an investigation into GTE's (D) world-wide operations. The audit committee subsequently released its report, which stated that evidence had been found that, in the period from 1971 to 1975, GTE (D) had made payments abroad and in the United States constituting bribes and kickbacks totaling more than $11,000,000, and that some directors (D) had been involved. Auerbach (P), a shareholder, instituted a derivative action on behalf of GTE against GTE's directors (D), Arthur Andersen (D), and GTE (D), alleging breach of corporate duties and seeking damages as reimbursement for the wrongful payments. The board of directors then adopted a resolution creating a special litigation committee to investigate the derivative action and determine what position GTE (D) should take. The committee comprised three disinterested directors who had joined the board after the alleged transactions had occurred. The committee concluded that Arthur Andersen (D) had acted in accordance with generally accepted auditing standards and in good faith and that no proper interest of GTE (D) or its shareholders would be served by continuing the claim against it. The committee also found that the claims against the individual directors (D) were without merit. GTE's (D) general counsel filed for and was granted summary judgment. Another shareholder, Wallenstein (P), was substituted as plaintiff and appealed.

ISSUE: May a court inquire as to the adequacy and appropriateness of a special litigation committee's investigative procedures and methodologies?

HOLDING AND DECISION: (Jones, J.) Yes. A court may properly inquire as to the adequacy and appropriateness of a special litigation committee's investigative procedures and methodologies, but may not consider factors under the domain of business judgment. The business judgment doctrine recognizes that courts are ill-equipped to evaluate what are and essentially must be business judgments. However, the rule shields the deliberations and conclusions of a special committee only if its members possess disinterested independence and do not stand in a dual relation that would prevent an unprejudicial exercise of judgment. In this case there is nothing in the record to raise a triable issue of fact as to the independence and disinterested status of the three directors on the special litigation committee, or as to the sufficiency and appropriateness of the investigative procedures they employed. The derivative suit was brought against only four members of the fifteen-member board, and the three members of the special litigation committee joined the board after the alleged transactions occurred. To disqualify an entire board would be to render a corporation powerless to make an effective business judgment with respect to prosecution of a derivative action. The decision of the disinterested special litigation committee forecloses further judicial inquiry. Affirmed.

DISSENT: (Cooke, C.J.) Summary judgment should not be granted prior to disclosure proceedings, because the continuation of this suit is so dependent upon the motives and actions of the board members (D) and the special litigation committee, who are in exclusive possession of much of the factual information concerning the case.

ANALYSIS

While the court did not make it impossible for a derivative action to survive a special litigation committee's decision to terminate it, it did make it extremely difficult. Other courts have been far less deferential to the business judgment of such committees. In Delaware and other jurisdictions, the court first determines whether the committee is disinterested, independent, and acting in good faith, and then applies its own business judgment in evaluating the evidence presented and the committee's recommendation.

■■■

Quicknotes

BUSINESS JUDGMENT RULE Doctrine relieving corporate directors and/or officers from liability for decisions honestly and rationally made in the corporation's best interests.

SHAREHOLDER'S DERIVATIVE ACTION Action asserted by a shareholder in order to enforce a cause of action on behalf of the corporation.

■■■

Zapata Corp. v. Maldonado

Corporation (D) v. Shareholder (P)

430 A.2d 779 (Del. 1981).

NATURE OF CASE: Appeal from dismissal of derivative action.

FACT SUMMARY: William Maldonado (P), a shareholder of the Zapata Corp. (D), sought to prevent the dismissal of his derivative action against Zapata (D) following the recommendation for dismissal by a corporation-appointed investigation committee.

🏛 RULE OF LAW

When assessing a special litigation committee's motion to dismiss a derivative action, a court must: (1) determine whether the committee acted independently, in good faith, and made a reasonable investigation; and (2) apply the court's own independent business judgment.

FACTS: In June 1975, Maldonado (P) instituted a derivative action against ten officers and/or directors of Zapata (D), alleging breaches of fiduciary duty. Maldonado (P) did not first demand that the board bring the action, believing that demand would be futile because all directors (D) were named as defendants and allegedly participated in the wrongful acts. By June 1979, four of the directors (D) named in the action were no longer on the board, and the remaining directors (D) appointed two new outside directors to the board. The board then created an independent investigation committee, comprised solely of the two new directors, to investigate Maldonado's (P) allegations and determine whether Zapata Corp. (D) should continue the litigation. The committee's determination was intended to be final and binding upon Zapata Corp. (D). In September 1979, the committee concluded that the action should be dismissed because it was not in Zapata Corp.'s (D) best interests. Zapata Corp. (D) filed a motion for dismissal or summary judgment, which was granted by the Court of Chancery.

ISSUE: Should a court automatically grant a special litigation committee's recommendation to dismiss a derivative action?

HOLDING AND DECISION: (Quillen, J.) No. When assessing a special litigation committee's motion to dismiss a derivative action, a court must: (1) determine whether the committee acted independently, in good faith, and made a reasonable investigation, with the burden of proof on the corporation; and (2) apply the court's own independent business judgment. A board has the power to choose not to pursue litigation when demand is made upon it, so long as the decision is not wrongful. Where demand has been excused, courts have struggled between allowing the independent business judgment of a board committee to prevail and yielding to unbridled plaintiff stockholder control. The test promulgated here allows for the balancing of these competing interests under appropriate court supervision. While courts should be mindful of judicial overreaching, the interests at stake necessitate the fresh view of a judicial outsider. Reversed and remanded.

▶ ANALYSIS

The approach set forth in this Delaware case has been adopted by many jurisdictions searching for a compromise between demand-required and demand-excused cases. New York courts, on the other hand, have applied a more deferential standard of review in cases challenging the recommendations of special litigation committees. New York courts apply only the first half of the *Zapata* test, relying on the business judgment of a committee so long as the committee members are disinterested, independent, and have conducted a reasonable investigation.

■▬■

Quicknotes

BUSINESS JUDGMENT RULE Doctrine relieving corporate directors and/or officers from liability for decisions honestly and rationally made in the corporation's best interests.

FIDUCIARY DUTY A legal obligation to act for the benefit of another, including subordinating one's personal interests to that of the other person.

SHAREHOLDER'S DERIVATIVE ACTION Action asserted by a shareholder in order to enforce a cause of action on behalf of the corporation.

■▬■

In re Oracle Corp. Derivative Litigation

Parties not identified.

824 A.2d 917 (Del. Ch. 2003).

NATURE OF CASE: Motion to terminate a derivative action.

FACT SUMMARY: Oracle Corp.'s special litigation committee moved to terminate a derivative action brought on Oracle's behalf, claiming it was independent.

🏛 RULE OF LAW
A special litigation committee does not meet its burden of demonstrating the absence of a material dispute of fact about its independence where its members are professors at a university that has ties to the corporation and to the defendants that are the subject of a derivative action that the committee is investigating.

FACTS: Shareholders of Oracle Corp. (Oracle) brought a derivative action asserting insider trading by four members of Oracle's board of directors. One of the insiders was Oracle's chairman, Ellison, one of the wealthiest men in the world. The suit alleged breaches of fiduciary duty by those directors as well as by the non-trading directors, whose indifference according to the plaintiff shareholders amounted to subjective bad faith. Oracle formed a special litigation committee (SLC) to investigate the charges in the derivative action and to determine whether to press the claims raised, terminate the action, or settle. Two Oracle board members, who joined the board after the alleged breaches, were named to the SLC. Both were professors at Stanford University. Both agreed to give up any SLC-related compensation if their compensation was deemed to impair their impartiality. The independence of the SLC's legal and analytic advisors was not challenged. The SLC's investigation was extensive, and the committee produced an extremely lengthy report that concluded that Oracle should not pursue any of the derivative action claims. The SLC based its opinion on Oracle's quarterly earnings cycle, and determined that none of the accused directors had possessed material, non-public information. In its report, the SLC took the position that its members were independent. In this regard, the report pointed out that the SLC members received no compensation from Oracle other than as directors, that neither were on the board at the time of the alleged wrongdoing, that they were willing to return their compensation, and that there were no other material ties between the defendants and the SLC members. However, the report failed to indicate that there were significant ties between Oracle, the trading defendants, and Stanford University (Stanford)—namely, in the form of very large donations, or potential donations, of which the SLC members were aware. In addition, one of the SLC members had been taught by one of the trading defendants,

and the two were both senior fellows and steering committee members of a Stanford research institute. The SLC contended that even together, these facts regarding the ties among Oracle, the trading defendants, Stanford, and the SLC members did not impair the SLC's independence. In so arguing, the SLC placed great weight on the fact that none of the trading defendants had the practical ability to deprive either SLC member of their current positions at Stanford. Nor, given their tenure, did Stanford itself have any practical ability to punish them for taking action adverse to Oracle or any of the defendants.

ISSUE: Does a special litigation committee meet its burden of demonstrating the absence of a material dispute of fact about its independence where its members are professors at a university that has ties to the corporation and to the defendants that are the subject of a derivative action that the committee is investigating?

HOLDING AND DECISION: (Strine, V. Chan.) No. A special litigation committee does not meet its burden of demonstrating the absence of a material dispute of fact about its independence where its members are professors at a university that has ties to the corporation and to the defendants that are the subject of a derivative action that the committee is investigating. In analyzing whether the SLC was independent, emphasis should not be placed exclusively on domination and control. Instead, the law should take into account human nature, human motivations, and the social nature of humans. Thus, a court would not only consider greed or avarice, but would also take into account envy, love, friendship, collegiality, and other like motivators. At bottom, the question of independence turns on whether a director is, for any substantial reason, incapable of making a decision with only the best interests of the corporation in mind. Thus, here, the issue is whether the SLC can independently make the difficult decision entrusted to it. In the context of human nature, the SLC has not met its burden to show the absence of a material factual question about its independence. This is the case because the ties among the SLC, the trading defendants, and Stanford are so substantial that they cause reasonable doubt about the SLC's ability to impartially consider whether the trading defendants should face suit. The SLC members were already being asked to consider whether the company should level extremely serious accusations of wrongdoing against fellow board members. As to one of the trading defendants, the SLC members faced the additional task of having to determine whether

Continued on next page.

to press serious charges against a fellow professor at their university. Even more daunting was that one of the SLC members had a long history with that defendant and served together with him on a university research institute. That SLC member would find it difficult to assess the trading defendant's conduct without pondering his own associations and mutual affiliations with him. This would likewise be true with regard to those trading defendants who were significant university benefactors. In addition, the SLC has not made a convincing argument that tenured faculty are indifferent to large contributors to their institutions, such that a tenured faculty member would not be worried about writing a report finding that a suit by the corporation should proceed against a large contributor and that there was credible evidence that he had engaged in illegal insider trading. To conclude otherwise, would rest on a narrow-minded understanding of the way that collegiality works in institutional settings. Finally, Ellison had publicly indicated that he would make very large contributions to Stanford, and it is implausible that the SLC members were not aware of his intentions. Motion to terminate denied.

▶ ANALYSIS

The Delaware Supreme Court has reaffirmed that the SLC has the burden of establishing its own independence by a yardstick that must be "like Caesar's wife"—"above reproach." Moreover, unlike the pre-suit demand context, the SLC analysis contemplates not only a shift in the burden of persuasion, but also the availability of discovery into various issues, including independence. Moreover, because the members of an SLC are vested with enormous power to seek dismissal of a derivative suit brought against their director-colleagues in a setting where pre-suit demand is already excused, the Court of Chancery must exercise careful oversight of the members of the SLC and the SLC's process.

■══■

Quicknotes

BAD FAITH Conduct that is intentionally misleading or deceptive.

BONA FIDE In good faith.

SHAREHOLDER An individual who owns shares of stock in a corporation.

SHAREHOLDER'S DERIVATIVE ACTION Action asserted by a shareholder in order to enforce a cause of action on behalf of the corporation.

■══■

A.P. Smith Mfg. Co. v. Barlow

Corporation (P) v. Shareholder (D)

13 N.J. 145, 98 A.2d 581, *appeal dismissed*, 346 U.S. 861 (1953).

NATURE OF CASE: Appeal from declaratory judgment affirming corporate authority.

FACT SUMMARY: Barlow (D) and other shareholders of A.P. Smith Mfg. (P) challenged its authority to make a donation to Princeton University.

☰ RULE OF LAW
State legislation adopted in the public interest can be constitutionally applied to preexisting corporations under the reserved power.

FACTS: A.P. Smith Mfg. (P) was a New Jersey corporation incorporated in 1896. Over the years it regularly made donations to various community organizations and public universities. In 1951, the board of directors adopted a resolution stating that it was in A.P. Smith Mfg.'s (P) best interest to donate $1,500 to Princeton University's annual fund. Shareholders (D) of A.P. Smith Mfg. (P) questioned the corporation's authority to make the contribution on two grounds: (1) its certificate of incorporation did not expressly authorize the donation and A.P. Smith (P) possessed no implied power to make it; and (2) the New Jersey statutes that would have expressly authorized the contribution did not constitutionally apply to A.P. Smith (P) because it was created long before their enactment. A.P. Smith Mfg. (P) sought a declaratory judgment following the shareholder's challenges. The court held that the donation was intra vires, and the shareholders (D) appealed.

ISSUE: Can state legislation adopted in the public interest be constitutionally applied to preexisting corporations under the reserved power?

HOLDING AND DECISION: [Judge not stated in casebook excerpt.] Yes. State legislation adopted in the public interest can be constitutionally applied to preexisting corporations under the reserved power. Fifty years before the incorporation of A.P. Smith Mfg. (P), the New Jersey legislature provided that every corporate charter thereafter granted would be subject to alteration and modification at the discretion of the legislature. A similar reserved power was incorporated into the state constitution. New Jersey courts have repeatedly recognized that where justified by the advancement of the public interest, the reserved power may be invoked to sustain later charter alterations even though they affect contractual rights between the corporation and its stockholders. Therefore, a statute enacted in 1930 encouraging and expressly authorizing reasonable charitable contributions is applicable to A.P. Smith Mfg. (P) and must be upheld as a lawful exercise of A.P. Smith Mfg.'s (P) implied and incidental powers under common law principles. Affirmed.

▶ ANALYSIS

The court was clearly swayed as much by philanthropic concerns and social policy as by statutory law. It dedicated a large portion of its opinion to discussing the economic and social importance of corporate contributions, particularly those made to universities. The opinion was quite prophetic as such donations have grown even more significantly in the forty-five years since the opinion was written.

Quicknotes

DECLARATORY JUDGMENT An adjudication by the courts which grants not relief but is binding over the legal status of the parties involved in the dispute.

INTRA VIRES "Within the power" refers to powers that are within the scope of authority of an individual or corporation.

Dodge v. Ford Motor Co.

Shareholder (P) v. Corporation (D)

204 Mich. 459, 170 N.W. 668 (1919).

NATURE OF CASE: Appeal from order compelling a dividend.

FACT SUMMARY: Shareholders Horace and John Dodge (P) filed suit against the Ford Motor Co. (D) after Henry Ford (D) decided not to pay any more special dividends and to instead reinvest the money in the business.

🏛 RULE OF LAW
A corporation's primary purpose is to provide profits for its stockholders.

FACTS: Ford Motor Co. (D) was incorporated in 1903 with Henry Ford (D) as the majority shareholder and the Dodge brothers (P) owning 10% of the common shares. Ford Motor Co. (D) grew rapidly, profits soared, and from 1911 to 1915 large regular and special dividends were paid to the shareholders. In 1915, the Dodges' (P) share of the regular dividend was $120,000 and their share of the special dividend was $1,000,000, with the prospect of even more increases in the future. In 1913, the Dodges (P) formed a separate auto company, which competed with Ford (D). In 1916, despite having profits of almost $174,000,000 and more than $50,000,000 cash on hand, Henry Ford (D) announced that in the future no special dividends would be paid, profits would be reinvested into the business, and the price of the company's cars would be reduced. After the announcement of the new dividend policy, John Dodge (P) met with Ford (D) to complain about the new policy and offered to sell his and his brother's shares to Ford (D) for $35,000,000. After Ford (D) rejected the buyout offer, the Dodges (P) filed suit, attacking both the dividend policy and Ford's (D) plans to expand manufacturing facilities. The trial court ruled in favor of the Dodges (P), and Ford (D) appealed.

ISSUE: Is a corporation's primary purpose to provide profits for its stockholders?

HOLDING AND DECISION: [Judge not stated in casebook excerpt.] Yes. A corporation's primary purpose is to provide profits for its stockholders. The powers of a corporation's directors are to be employed to that end and their discretion is to be exercised in the choice of means to attain that end. However, this discretion does not extend to a change in the end itself, to the reduction of profits, or to the nondistribution of profits among stockholders in order to devote them to other purposes. Given the Ford Motor Co.'s (D) clearly prosperous economic outlook, Ford (D) was not entitled to arbitrarily refuse to pay a dividend which had been established over several years. Although the courts should not interfere with the proposed expansion of

Ford Motor Co. (D), the evidence shows that there was a large and consistent daily, weekly, and monthly receipt of cash as well as a large balance on hand. Furthermore, the contemplated expenditures were not to be immediately made, but to be paid over a considerable period of time. The trial court was correct in ruling that a large sum of money should have been distributed to the shareholders. Affirmed, reversed in part on other grounds.

⏺ ANALYSIS

The court realized that Ford (D) was motivated by more than a desire to expand his company's manufacturing capabilities. Ford (D) clearly wanted to avoid funding his competition's new venture. Perhaps that is why he also refused the Dodge brothers' (P) buyout offer.

■=■

Quicknotes

COMMON STOCK A class of stock representing the corporation's ownership, the holders of which are entitled to dividends only after the holders of preferred stock are paid.

DIVIDEND The payment of earnings to a corporation's shareholders in proportion to the amount of shares held.

FIDUCIARY DUTY A legal obligation to act for the benefit of another, including subordinating one's personal interests to that of the other person.

SHAREHOLDER An individual who owns shares of stock in a corporation.

■=■

Shlensky v. Wrigley

Minority shareholder (P) v. Majority shareholder (D)

95 Ill. App.2d 173, 237 N.E.2d 776 (1968).

NATURE OF CASE: Appeal from dismissal.

FACT SUMMARY: Wrigley (D), the majority shareholder in the Chicago Cubs, refused to install lights at Wrigley Field in order to hold night games, and Shlensky (P), a minority shareholder, filed a derivative suit to compel the installation.

🏛 RULE OF LAW
A shareholder's derivative suit can only be based on conduct by the directors which borders on fraud, illegality, or conflict of interest.

FACTS: Wrigley (D) was the majority shareholder and a director of the Chicago Cubs baseball team. Shlensky (P), a minority shareholder, sought to bring a shareholders' derivative action to compel the directors to equip Wrigley Field (the Cub's home field) with lights so that night games could be played, and revenues could be increased. The trial court sustained Wrigley's (D) motion to dismiss over Shlensky's (P) contention that the refusal to install lights was a personal decision of Wrigley's (D) and not in the best interest of the shareholders.

ISSUE: Can a shareholders' derivative suit be based on conduct by the directors that does not border on fraud, illegality, or conflict of interest?

HOLDING AND DECISION: [Judge not stated in casebook excerpt.] No. Shlensky (P) is attempting to use the derivative suit to force a business judgment on the board of directors of the Chicago Cubs, but there is no showing of fraud, illegality, or conflict of interest. There are valid reasons for refusal to install lights in the stadium. Though Shlensky (P) alleges that night games haven't been considered due to Wrigley's (D) personal feelings about the sport, Wrigley (D) has suggested that night games in the Wrigley Field area would have a detrimental effect on the neighborhood. Additionally, there is no showing that night games would significantly increase revenues, or even that additional expenses wouldn't be required. Affirmed.

▶ ANALYSIS

Though the "business judgment rule" is typically stated as relating to the functions of directors, the rule is equally applicable to officers of the corporation while acting in their official capacities; and it may apply to controlling shareholders as well if these persons assert their more extraordinary management functions, e.g., mergers or sale of their complete interest.

Quicknotes

BUSINESS JUDGMENT RULE Doctrine relieving corporate directors and/or officers from liability for decisions honestly and rationally made in the corporation's best interests.

CONFLICT OF INTEREST Refers to ethical problems that arise, or may be anticipated to arise, between an attorney and his client if the interests of the attorney, another client or a third-party conflict with those of the present client.

FRAUD A false representation of facts with the intent that another will rely on the misrepresentation to his detriment.

SHAREHOLDER'S DERIVATIVE ACTION Action asserted by a shareholder in order to enforce a cause of action on behalf of the corporation.

CHAPTER 4

The Limited Liability Company

Quick Reference Rules of Law

Water, Waste & Land, Inc. d/b/a Westec v. Lanham

Creditor (P) v. LLC manager/member (D)

955 P.2d 997 (Colo. 1998).

NATURE OF CASE: Appeal from reversal of judgment against a member of a limited liability company (LLC) in his personal capacity.

FACT SUMMARY: Lanham (D), a member and manager of Preferred Income Investors, L.L.C. (the Company or P.I.I.), contended that the state's LLC Act displaced common law agency doctrines so that Water, Waste, & Land, Inc. d/b/a Westec (Westec) (P), which had performed work for the Company but not been paid for it, and did not have actual notice that the Company was an LLC, had constructive notice of that fact, and, therefore, could not hold Lanham (D) individually liable.

> ## RULE OF LAW
> An LLC statute's notice provision, which provides that the filing of the articles of organization serves as constructive notice of a company's status as a limited liability company, does not apply instead of common law agency principles where a third party sues a manager or member of an LLC under an agency theory.

FACTS: Water, Waste, & Land, Inc. d/b/a Westec (Westec) (P), after being contacted by Clark, a member and manager of Preferred Income Investors, L.L.C. (the Company or P.I.I.), performed work for the Company but was not paid for it. The business card that Clark had given Westec (P) had Lanham's (D) address on it. Lanham (D) was also a member and manager of the Company. However, the card, which had "P.I.I." on it, did not indicate that the Company was a limited liability company (LLC). Westec (P) filed a claim against Clark and Lanham (D) individually as well as against the Company. The trial court ruled, inter alia, that Clark was an agent of both Lanham (D) and the Company with authority to obligate Lanham (D) and the Company. The court also ruled that because Westec (P) understood Clark to be Lanham's (D) agent, Clark was not personally liable. Accordingly, the trial court entered judgment against Lanham (D) and the Company. On appeal, the intermediate appellate court held that the state's LLC act, which provides that the filing of articles of organization serves as constructive notice of the company's status as a limited liability company, governed. Therefore, that court reversed. The state's highest court granted review.

ISSUE: Does an LLC statute's notice provision, which provides that the filing of the articles of organization serves as constructive notice of a company's status as a limited liability company, apply instead of common law agency principles where a third party sues a manager or member of an LLC under an agency theory?

HOLDING AND DECISION: [Judge not stated in casebook excerpt.] No. An LLC statute's notice provision, which provides that the filing of the articles of organization serves as constructive notice of a company's status as a limited liability company, does not apply instead of common law agency principles where a third party sues a manager or member of an LLC under an agency theory. The appellate court's analysis assumed that the LLC act displaced certain common law agency doctrines, at least insofar as these doctrines otherwise would be applicable to suits by third parties seeking to hold the agents of a limited liability company liable for their personal actions as agents. These statutory notice provisions apply only where a third party seeks to impose liability on an LLC's members or managers simply due to their status as members or managers of the LLC. However, when a third party sues a manager or member of an LLC under an agency theory, the principles of agency law apply notwithstanding the LLC act's statutory notice rules. Under the common law of agency, an agent is liable on a contract entered on behalf of the principal where the principal is not fully disclosed. Whether a principal is partially or completely disclosed is a question of fact. Here, the trial court found that Westec (P) did not know Clark was acting as an agent for the Company or that the letters P.I.I. stood for Preferred Income Investors, a limited liability company. Such a factual finding is binding. The trial court's finding that Clark was an agent for Lanham (D) also should not have been disturbed by the intermediate appellate court. In light of the partially disclosed principal doctrine, the trial court's determination that Clark and Lanham (D) failed to disclose the existence as well as the identity of the limited liability company they represented was dispositive under the common law of agency. The issue, therefore, becomes whether the LLC act displaced this common law doctrine. For Lanham (D) to be relieved of liability, the statute would have to be read to establish a conclusive presumption that a third party who deals with the agent of a limited liability company always has constructive notice of the existence of the agent's principal. Such a construction, however, would exaggerate the plain meaning of the language in the statute. A plausible interpretation of the statute is that once the limited liability company's name is known to the third party, constructive notice of the company's limited liability status has been given, as well as the fact that managers and members will not be liable simply due to their status as

Continued on next page.

managers or members. Moreover, the broad interpretation urged by Lanham (D) would be an invitation to fraud, because it would leave the agent of a limited liability company free to mislead third parties into the belief that the agent would bear personal financial responsibility under any contract, when in fact, recovery would be limited to the assets of a limited liability company not known to the third party at the time the contract was made. It can be presumed, in this context that the legislature did not intend to create a safe harbor for deceit. Other LLC act provisions reinforce this conclusion. For example, the act requires limited liability companies to use the words "Limited Liability Company" or the initials "LLC" as part of their names, implying that the legislature intended to compel any entity seeking to claim the benefits of the LLC act to identify itself clearly as a limited liability company. If Lanham (D) and Clark had identified Preferred Income Investors, LLC, as the principal in the transaction, neither could be held individually liable. Reversed.

▌ ANALYSIS

The decision in this case is sound. As commentators have noted, it would be an unwarranted stretch to have LLC laws extend the insulation of limited liability beyond that traditionally provided by the corporate form. That means that participants in closely held enterprises will continue to be liable for their acts taken in the entity's name that are wrongful or violate regulatory provisions either under agency law or by a court piercing the entity's veil.

Quicknotes

AGENCY A fiduciary relationship whereby authority is granted to an agent to act on behalf of the principal in order to effectuate the principal's objective.

AGENT An individual who has the authority to act on behalf of another.

COMMON LAW A body of law developed through the judicial decisions of the courts as opposed to the legislative process.

CONSTRUCTIVE NOTICE Knowledge of a fact that is imputed to an individual who was under a duty to inquire and who could have learned of the fact through the exercise of reasonable prudence.

CORPORATE VEIL Refers to the shielding from personal liability of a corporation's officers, directors or shareholders for unlawful conduct engaged in by the corporation.

DOCTRINE Rule or theory of law.

FRAUD A false representation of facts with the intent that another will rely on the misrepresentation to his detriment.

INTER ALIA Among other things.

LIMITED LIABILITY An advantage of doing business in the corporate form by safeguarding shareholders from liability for the debts or obligations of the corporation.

LIMITED LIABILITY COMPANY A business entity combining the features of both a corporation and a general partnership; the LLC provides its shareholders and officers with limited liability, but it is treated as a partnership for taxation purposes.

PRINCIPAL A person or entity who authorizes another (the agent) to act on its behalf and subject to its authority to the extent that the principal may be held liable for the actions of the agent.

STATUTORY NOTICE Notification of a fact, or reason to know of the fact, that is accomplished by legislative enactment.

Elf Atochem North America, Inc. v. Jaffari

Joint venturer (P) v. Other joint venturer (D)

727 A.2d 286 (Del. 1999).

NATURE OF CASE: Appeal from dismissal for lack of jurisdiction under terms of a limited liability company (LLC) agreement.

FACT SUMMARY: Elf's (P) allegations of breach of contract, tortious interference with prospective business relations, and fraud were dismissed because, under the terms of the LLC agreement, all disputes were to be settled in California.

🏛 RULE OF LAW
Because the policy of the Uniform Limited Liability Company Act (ULLCA) is to give maximum effect to the principle of freedom of contract and to the enforceability of LLC agreements, the parties may contract to avoid the applicability of certain provisions of the Act.

FACTS: Elf (P), a manufacturer of solvent-based maskants to the aerospace industry, and Jaffari (D), who had developed an innovative, environmentally friendly alternative to the solvent-base maskants recently classified as hazardous by the Environmental Protection Agency, agreed to undertake a joint venture that would be carried out using a limited liability company as the vehicle. A Delaware LLC was formed and the parties entered into several agreements. The LLC was not a signatory to the agreement detailing the governance of the new company. The agreement contained an arbitration clause and a forum selection clause providing California courts would have jurisdiction over any claims arising out of, under, or in connection with, the agreement. Elf (P) later sued Jaffari (D) for breach of fiduciary duty when he withdrew funds for personal use, interfered with business opportunities, failed to make disclosures and threatened to violate environmental regulations. Elf (P) also alleged breach of contract, tortious interference, and fraud. The Court of Chancery dismissed, holding that Elf's (P) claims arose under the agreement and were subject to the provision mandating that all claims be settled in California. Elf (P) appealed, contending that the LLC was not a signatory and not a party to the agreement and therefore was not bound to its terms, and that the dispute resolution clauses were invalid because they violated the ULLCA.

ISSUE: May the parties contract to avoid the applicability of certain provisions of the Delaware Uniform Limited Liability Act?

HOLDING AND DECISION: (Veasey, C.J.) Yes. Because the policy of the ULLCA is to give maximum effect to the principle of freedom of contract and to the enforceability of LLC agreements, the parties may contract to avoid the applicability of certain provisions of the Act. The ULLCA is designed to permit members maximum flexibility in entering into an agreement to govern their relationship. The parties specifically agreed that no action could be brought, except in California, and then, only to enforce arbitration in California. There is no reason why the parties could not alter the default provisions of the statute and contract away their right to file suit in Delaware. Affirmed.

▶ ANALYSIS

The ULLCA was modeled on the popular Delaware Limited Partner Act. Many provisions of the Revised Uniform Limited Partners Act (RULPA) were also modeled on the Delaware Act. Almost all of the states have adopted some form of the RULPA.

■=■

Quicknotes

ARBITRATION An agreement to have a dispute heard and decided by a neutral third party, rather than through legal proceedings.

FIDUCIARY DUTY A legal obligation to act for the benefit of another, including subordinating one's personal interests to that of the other person.

JURISDICTION The authority of a court to hear and declare judgment in respect to a particular matter.

LIMITED LIABILITY COMPANY A business entity combining the features of both a corporation and a general partnership; the LLC provides its shareholders and officers with limited liability, but it is treated as a partnership for taxation purposes.

■=■

Kaycee Land and Livestock v. Flahive

Contaminated land owner (P) v. Limited liability company managing member (D)

46 P.3d 323, 2002 WY 73 (2002).

NATURE OF CASE: Certification of a legal question from a trial court to appellate court.

FACT SUMMARY: Trial court's certification to appellate court of question whether one may pierce the corporate veil of a limited liability company (LLC) in the same manner as of a corporation.

🏛 RULE OF LAW
In the absence of fraud, a claim to pierce the veil of an LLC is treated in the same manner as a court would pierce a corporate veil.

FACTS: Flahive Oil and Gas is a limited liability company with no present assets. Kaycee Land and Livestock (P) entered into a contract with Flahive Oil and Gas allowing Flahive Oil and Gas to use the surface of its real property. Roger Flahive (D) was the managing member of Flahive Oil and Gas. Flahive Oil and Gas caused environmental contamination to Kaycee's (P) real property. Seeking to pierce the LLC and disregard the LLC entity of Flahive Oil and Gas, Kaycee (P) brought suit directly against Roger Flahive (D) to hold him individually liable for the contamination. There was no allegation of fraud. The district court certified to the appellate court the question, in the abstract, whether, in the absence of fraud, a claim to pierce the veil of an LLC is treated in the same manner as a court would pierce a corporate veil.

ISSUE: In the absence of fraud, is a claim to pierce the veil of an LLC treated in the same manner as a court would pierce a corporate veil?

HOLDING AND DECISION: [Judge not stated in casebook excerpt.] Yes. In the absence of fraud, a claim to pierce the veil of an LLC is treated in the same manner as a court would pierce a corporate veil. Courts across the country typically utilize a fact driven inquiry to determine whether circumstances justify a decision to pierce a corporate veil. Piercing the corporate veil is an equitable doctrine developed through common law, and is absent from the statutes governing corporate organization. It is difficult to read any relevant legislation as intended to preclude courts from deciding to disregard the veil of an improperly used LLC. Because it is an equitable doctrine, the paucity of statutory authority for LLC piercing should not be considered a barrier to its application. The rules of common law are not to be changed by doubtful implication, nor overturned except by clear and unambiguous language. Applying the well established common law of piercing the corporate veil to LLCs does not run counter to what the legislature would have intended had it considered the issue.

There is no reason, in either law or policy, to treat LLCs differently than corporations are treated in this regard. If the members and officers fail to treat it as a separate entity as contemplated by statute, they should not enjoy immunity from individual liability for the LLC's acts that cause damage to third parties. Remanded.

▶ *ANALYSIS*

As noted in the *Kaycee* case, statutes which create corporations and LLCs have the same basic purpose: to limit the liability of individual investors with a corresponding benefit to economic development. Statutes created the legal fiction of the corporation being a completely separate entity which could act independently from individual persons. Certainly, the various factors which would justify piercing an LLC veil would not be identical to the corporate situation for the reason that many of the organizational formalities applicable to corporations do not apply to LLCs. The LLC's operation is intended to be much more flexible than a corporation's.

◼▭◼

Quicknotes

CERTIFIED QUESTION A question that is taken from federal court to the state supreme court so that the court may rule on the issue, or that is taken from a federal court of appeals to the United States Supreme Court.

COMMON LAW A body of law developed through the judicial decisions of the courts as opposed to the legislative process.

EQUITABLE Just; fair.

◼▭◼

McConnell v. Hunt Sports Enterprises

Community leader (P) v. Soccer team investor (D)

132 Ohio App. 3d 657, 725 N.E.2d 1193 (1999).

NATURE OF THE CASE: Appeal from declaratory judgment for plaintiff in action to determine the scope of a limited liability company (LLC) operating agreement.

FACT SUMMARY: Members of an LLC formed to explore the possibility of applying for a new NHL franchise sought a declaration for breach of contract against each other based on the exclusion of certain members' ownership interests in the franchise.

> **RULE OF LAW**
> A member of an LLC does not breach a fiduciary duty to the company by directly competing against it where the operating agreement expressly permits competition.

FACTS: Several community leaders in Columbus, Ohio, including McConnell (P), were contacted by the city mayor based on their involvement in professional sports to examine the possibility of applying for an NHL hockey franchise for Columbus. McConnell's (P) colleagues approached Hunt Sports Enterprises (HSE) (D) as a potential investor. Together, McConnell (P), HSE (D) and others formed Columbus Hockey Limited (CHL), a limited liability company whose general character was to invest in and operate a franchise in the NHL. Following an application for the franchise filed by CHL on behalf of the city of Columbus, difficulty arose when a planned tax to finance the construction of a required, appropriate arena failed to pass approval. When HSE (D) refused to accept an alternative lease proposal that would permit the required construction, McConnell (P) offered to lease the arena in HSE's (D) place. The offer was accepted and the NHL required that an ownership group be identified pursuant to its granting of a franchise. McConnell (P) signed the required documents in an individual capacity, in the place intended for CHL's participation as franchise owner, thus identifying him (P) as the majority owner. HSE (D), which continued to find the existing terms unacceptable, filed a complaint, and McConnell (P) requested a declaration permitting himself as a member of CHL to compete with CHL itself for the position of majority owner. The trial court proceedings included a jury trial and a directed verdict for McConnell (P). The trial court refused to allow introduction of extrinsic evidence of the meaning of the crucial language in the CHL operating agreement. The trial court also directed the jury that McConnell (P) had not violated any fiduciary duty by excluding HSE (D) from participating in the franchise and by preparing to compete with CHL. In addition, the trial court entered a directed verdict in favor of McConnell (P) on its claim that HSE (D) breached the

agreement by unilaterally rejecting the lease proposal, by failing to negotiate in good faith, by allowing the lease deadline to expire without response, by failing to advise or obtain the approval of the other members of CHL before unilaterally rejecting the lease offer, and by usurping control of CHL. The trial court's directed verdict rested on its finding that HSE (D) violated the operating agreement in failing to ask for and obtain the authorization of CHL members (other than McConnell (P)) before filing the answer and counterclaim in the action and before filing a separate action. The appellate court granted review.

ISSUE: Does a member of an LLC breach a fiduciary duty to the company by directly competing against it where the operating agreement expressly permits competition?

HOLDING AND DECISION: [Judge not stated in casebook excerpt.] No. A member of an LLC does not breach a fiduciary duty to the company by directly competing against it where the operating agreement expressly permits competition. Section 3.3 of the operating agreement stated that "members may compete." However, HSE (D) contends that members of CHL may only compete in any business venture that is different from the business of the company, which includes investing in and operating an NHL franchise. We believe this interpretation goes beyond the plain language of section 3.3, which permits "any other venture of any nature." Appellees may therefore engage in activities that are competitive with CHL. The injury complained of is the direct competition of McConnell (P) as a member of CHL, against CHL and HSE (D) as a co-member of the same limited liability company. The evidence does not show McConnell (P) interfered with HSE's (D) own dealings with the NHL. Thus, there was not sufficient evidence presented to suggest any breach of fiduciary duty on the part of appellees to interfere tortiously with the business relationships of their limited liability parent. A directed verdict in favor of appellees was therefore appropriate. HSE (D) incorrectly asserts that it could only be liable for willful misconduct and that it was the operating member of CHL and, therefore, had full authority to act on CHL's behalf. First, there was no evidence at trial that HSE (D) was the operating member of CHL. In fact, the operating agreement did not name any person or entity operating or managing member of CHL. Instead, all members of CHL had an equal number of units in the company. Under the terms of the operating agreement, no member could take action on behalf of the company, unless such action was approved by at least a majority of the allocated

Continued on next page.

units. Further, the approval of the members as to any action on behalf of CHL must have been evidenced by minutes of a meeting properly noticed and held or by an action in writing signed by the requisite number of members. Here, there was no evidence that HSE (D) obtained the approval of CHL members prior to filing the actions at issue. There was also no evidence that it even asked permission of any member to file the actions, let alone held a meeting or requested approval in writing. Because HSE (D) acted unilaterally, a directed verdict on the issue of breach of contract in favor of McConnell (P) was appropriate. Even if, as HSE (D) claims, McConnell (P) had to show willful misconduct, McConnell (P) would have made such a showing, because the evidence showed that HSE (D) engaged in willful misconduct in filing the actions at issue. Affirmed.

▶ *ANALYSIS*

Similar to a partnership, a limited liability company involves a fiduciary relationship that precludes direct competition between the members of the company. However, the court conceded that the operating agreement explicitly permitted competition, making that issue moot. The real dispute here rested in the ability of the operating agreement to define the scope of any individual member's fiduciary duties towards the company. In the present case, the court found that the operating agreement did in fact have the power to define these duties, and gave the applicable clause appropriate weight when ruling in favor of McConnell (P) and other appellees.

■━■

Quicknotes

DECLARATORY JUDGMENT A judgment of the court establishing the rights of the parties.

EXTRINSIC EVIDENCE Evidence that is not contained within the text of a document or contract, but which is derived from the parties' statements or the circumstances under which the agreement was made.

FIDUCIARY DUTY A legal obligation to act for the benefit of another, including subordinating one's personal interests to that of the other person.

FRANCHISE An agreement whereby one party (the franchisor) grants another (the franchisee) the right to market its product or service.

PARTNERSHIP A voluntary agreement entered into by two or more parties to engage in business and to share any attendant profits and losses.

■━■

New Horizons Supply Cooperative v. Haack

Creditor (P) v. Debtor (D)

224 Wis. 2d 644, 590 N.W.2d 282 (1999) (unpublished disposition).

NATURE OF CASE: Appeal of a creditor's judgment in its suit against a debtor.

FACT SUMMARY: When New Horizons Supply Cooperative (P) stopped receiving payments from Allison Haack (D) for fuel it had sold to her by use of a credit card she had taken out in her own name, New Horizons (P) sued Haack (D) for the remaining balance. Haack (D) defended on the grounds that she had charged the fuel as a member of a since-dissolved limited liability company (LLC), and, hence, had no personal liability for the remaining debt.

🏛 RULE OF LAW
A member or manager of an LLC is not personally liable for any debt, obligation, or liability of the company only if the member or manager follows statutorily prescribed formalities of LLC incorporation, dissolution, and creditor notice.

FACTS: New Horizons Supply Cooperative (P) sold fuel to Allison Haack (D) through the use of a credit card taken out by her. She had signed the credit card agreement as "Allison Haack" with no designation indicating whether her signature was given individually or in a representative capacity on behalf of Kickapoo Valley Freight LLC. She was a member/manager of Kickapoo Valley. Subsequently, payment on the card stopped, and negotiations began between New Horizons (P) and Haack (D) as to her making periodic payments on the account. Haack (D) at first began making the required payments and then stopped. New Horizons (P) sued Haack (D) for the $1,009.99 remaining due. Haack (D) argued that she was a member of Kickapoo Valley Freight, a limited liability company which had been dissolved, hence she could not be held individually liable on the debt. The trial court found for New Horizons (P), and Haack (D) appealed.

ISSUE: Is a member or manager of an LLC not personally liable for any debt, obligation, or liability of the company only if the member or manager follows statutorily prescribed formalities of LLC incorporation, dissolution, and creditor notice?

HOLDING AND DECISION: [Judge not stated in casebook excerpt.] Yes. A member or manager of an LLC is not personally liable for any debt, obligation, or liability of the company only if the member or manager follows statutorily prescribed formalities of LLC incorporation, dissolution, and creditor notice. New Horizons (P) incorrectly argues that the lower court properly applied the concept of "piercing the veil." The court's comments wrongfully deemed Kickapoo Valley's treatment as a partnership for tax purposes to be conclusive. Furthermore, there is little in the record to support a conclusion that Haack (D) organized, controlled, and conducted company affairs to the extent that it had no separate existence of its own and was Haacks's (D) mere instrumentality, which she used to evade an obligation, to gain an unjust advantage, or to commit an injustice. Rather, the entry of judgment against Haack (D) was proper because she failed to establish that she took appropriate steps to shield herself from liability for the company's debts following its dissolution and the distribution of its assets. The filing of articles with the state for the creation of a limited liability company constitutes conclusive proof that such a company is properly organized and formed. Here, however, Haack (D) testified that an attorney had drafted and filed the necessary paperwork, but no direct evidence of such was ever presented to the court. Furthermore, the record is devoid of any evidence showing that appropriate steps were taken upon the dissolution of the company to shield its members from liability for the entity's obligations. Haack (D) knew of New Horizons' (P) claim at the time Kickapoo Valley was dissolved, articles of dissolution for Kickapoo Valley were not filed, and New Horizons (P) was never formally notified of a claim filing procedure or deadline as required by statute. In short, Kickapoo Valley's affairs were never properly wound up following the dissolution. Hence, although Haack (D) correctly contends that the judgment cannot be sustained on the ground relied upon by the trial court the record in favor of New Horizons (P) is insurmountable. Judgment affirmed.

▶ ANALYSIS

The *New Horizons* court noted that, although the filing of articles of dissolution of a limited liability company is optional, the order for distributing the assets of an LLC following dissolution is fixed by statute, and the LLC's creditors enjoy first priority. A dissolved LLC may dispose of known claims against it by filing articles of dissolution, and then providing written notice to its known creditors containing information regarding the filing of claims.

■==■

Quicknotes

DISSOLUTION Annulment or termination of a formal or legal bond, tie or contract.

PERSONAL LIABILITY An obligation pursuant to which the personal assets of an individual may be required for payment.

■==■

The Duties of Officers, Directors, and Other Insiders

Quick Reference Rules of Law

Kamin v. American Express Company

Shareholder (P) v. Corporation (D)

86 Misc. 2d 809, 383 N.Y.S.2d 807, *aff'd*, 54 A.D.2d 654, 387 N.Y.S.2d 993 (1976).

NATURE OF CASE: Derivative action for damages for waste of corporate assets.

FACT SUMMARY: Kamin (P) brought a shareholders' derivative suit claiming American Express (D) had engaged in waste of corporate assets by declaring a certain dividend in kind.

🏛 RULE OF LAW
Whether or not a dividend is to be declared or a distribution made is exclusively a matter of business judgment for the board of directors, and the courts will not, therefore, interfere as long as the decision is made in good faith.

FACTS: American Express (D) had acquired for investment almost two million shares of common stock in Donaldson, Lufken and Jenrette (DLJ) at a cost of $29.9 million. Kamin (P), a minority stockholder in American Express (D), charged that the subsequent decision to declare a special dividend to all stockholders resulting in a distribution of the shares of DLJ in kind was a negligent violation of the directors' fiduciary duty. He argued that the market value of the DLJ shares was only $4 million and that American Express (D) should have sold the DLJ shares on the market so as to be able to offset the $25 million capital loss against taxable capital gains on other investments and thus obtain an $8 million tax saving that would be otherwise unavailable. In a shareholders' derivative action, Kamin (P) sought a declaration that the dividend in kind constituted a waste of corporate assets and sought damages therefor. American Express (D) moved to dismiss the complaint.

ISSUE: Should the courts interfere with a board of directors' good faith business judgment as to whether or not to declare a dividend or make a distribution?

HOLDING AND DECISION: [Judge not stated in casebook excerpt.] No. Whether or not to declare a dividend or make a distribution is exclusively a matter of business judgment for the board of directors, and thus the courts will not interfere with their decision as long as it is made in good faith. It is not enough to charge, as Kamin (P) has in this case, that the directors made an imprudent decision or that some other course of action would have been more advantageous. Such a charge cannot give rise to a cause of action. Thus, the motion for dismissal of the complaint is granted.

▶ ANALYSIS

The "business judgment rule" illustrated in this case expresses the traditional and still valid view of a director's duty of care. This common law standard is designed to allow the directors a wide berth in conducting the affairs of the corporation so that they can act effectively and efficiently in pursuing the corporation's best interests rather than being constantly influenced by the need to practice "defensive management" to prevent being held liable in this type of action.

■■■

Quicknotes

BUSINESS CORPORATION LAW, § 720 Permits an action against directors for failure to perform duties in managing corporate assets.

BUSINESS JUDGMENT RULE Doctrine relieving corporate directors and/or officers from liability for decisions honestly and rationally made in the corporation's best interests.

COMMON STOCK A class of stock representing the corporation's ownership, the holders of which are entitled to dividends only after the holders of preferred stock are paid.

DUTY OF CARE Duty that an officer or director owes to the corporation, by virtue of his fiduciary relationship, to act for the benefit of the corporation.

FIDUCIARY DUTY A legal obligation to act for the benefit of another, including subordinating one's personal interests to that of the other person.

SHAREHOLDER'S DERIVATIVE ACTION Action asserted by a shareholder in order to enforce a cause of action on behalf of the corporation.

■■■

Smith v. Van Gorkom

Shareholder (P) v. Chief executive officer (D)

488 A.2d 858 (Del. 1985).

NATURE OF CASE: Appeal from defense verdict in a class action suit brought by a corporation's shareholders against its board of directors.

FACT SUMMARY: The board of directors (D) of Trans Union Corporation (D) voted to approve a merger agreement based solely on the representations of Van Gorkom (D), one of its directors.

> ## 🏛 RULE OF LAW
> The business judgment rule shields directors or officers of a corporation from liability only if, in reaching a business decision, the directors or officers acted on an informed basis, availing themselves of all material information reasonably available.

FACTS: Van Gorkom (D), CEO and director of Trans Union Corporation (D), approached Pritzker, a corporate takeover specialist, to stage a leveraged buy-out at a proposed per share price of $55. Van Gorkom (D) consulted no other board members except Petersen, the company's controller, for help in calculating the feasibility of such a takeover. On September 18, 1980, Van Gorkom (D) met with Pritzker, who demanded that Trans Union (D) respond to his offer within three days. Van Gorkom (D) called a special meeting of the company's senior management and of the board (D) for the next day. Despite senior management's adverse reaction to the proposed merger, the board of directors (D) approved the agreement based on Van Gorkom's (D) twenty-minute oral presentation. The board (D) did not have sufficient time to study the merger documents, nor did Van Gorkom (D) substantiate the $55 per share price. Without reviewing its contents, Van Gorkom (D) executed the merger agreement on September 22. Smith (P) and other stockholders (P) subsequently filed a class action suit against Trans Union (D) and the board of directors (D). On February 10, 1981, however, the shareholders voted to approve the merger. The Court of Chancery found the board's (D) actions shielded by the business judgment rule.

ISSUE: Is a director or officer of a corporation shielded by the business judgment rule when he relies on the representations of other directors or officers?

HOLDING AND DECISION: (Horsey, J.) No. The business judgment rule shields directors or officers of a corporation from liability only, if in reaching a business decision, the directors or officers acted on an informed basis, availing themselves of all material information reasonably available. The director has a duty to the corporation's shareholders to make an informed business decision regarding a proposed merger before it is subjected to shareholder

approval. Subsequent shareholder ratification does not relieve the director from this duty, unless their approval is also based on an informed decision. In this case, the directors (D) breached their duty of care by failing to conduct further investigation as to the proposed merger, and by submitting the proposal for shareholder approval without providing them with the relevant facts necessary to make an educated decision. Reversed and remanded.

DISSENT: (McNeilly, J.) The board of directors (D) was capable of making prompt, informed business decisions regarding the corporation. The proxy materials provided to the shareholders contained sufficient information from which to ascertain that the value of their stock may be greater than its market value reflected.

▌ ANALYSIS

A director or officer may not passively rely on information provided by other directors or officers, outside advisers, or authorized committees. The director may only rely on credible information provided by competent individuals, after taking reasonable measures to substantiate it.

■━■

Quicknotes

BUSINESS JUDGMENT RULE Doctrine relieving corporate directors and/or officers from liability for decisions honestly and rationally made in the corporation's best interests.

CLASS ACTION A suit commenced by a representative on behalf of an ascertainable group that is too large to appear in court, who shares a commonality of interests and who will benefit from a successful result.

DUTY OF CARE Duty that an officer or director owes to the corporation, by virtue of his fiduciary relationship, to act for the benefit of the corporation.

■━■

Francis v. United Jersey Bank

Parties not identifed.

432 A.2d 814 (N.J. 1981).

NATURE OF CASE: Review of Appellate Division decision holding director of corporation liable for clients' losses.

FACT SUMMARY: Lillian Pritchard (D) ignored her duties as a director, allowing her sons to withdraw over $12 million from client trust accounts.

🏛 RULE OF LAW
Liability of a corporation's directors to its clients requires a demonstration that: (1) a duty existed; (2) the directors breached that duty; and (3) the breach was a proximate cause of the client's losses.

FACTS: Lillian Pritchard (D) inherited a 48% interest in Pritchard & Baird, a reinsurance broker, from her husband. She and her two sons, Charles, Jr. and William, served as directors of the corporation. Her sons withdrew over $12 million in the form of loans from client trust accounts. Mrs. Pritchard (D) was completely ignorant as to the fundamentals of the reinsurance business, and paid no attention to the affairs of the corporation. The trial court held her liable for the clients' losses, finding that although she was competent to act, she had made no effort to exercise her duties as a director.

ISSUE: Does individual liability of a corporation's directors to its clients require a duty, a breach, and proximate cause?

HOLDING AND DECISION: [Judge not stated in casebook excerpt.] Yes. Individual liability of a corporation's directors to its clients requires a demonstration that: (1) a duty existed; (2) the directors breached that duty; and (3) the breach was a proximate cause of the client's losses. This is a departure from the general rule that a director is immune from liability and is not an insurer of the corporation's success. The director of a corporation stands in a fiduciary relationship to both the corporation and its stockholders. Inherent in this role is a duty to acquire a basic understanding of the corporation's business and a continuing duty to keep informed of its activities. This entails an overall monitoring of the corporation's affairs, and a regular review of its financial statements. Such a review may present a duty of further inquiry. Here, Mrs. Pritchard (D) failed to exercise supervision over the corporation, including the examination of its financial statements, which would have revealed the misappropriation of funds by her sons. The cumulative effect of her negligence was a substantial factor contributing to the clients' losses. Affirmed.

▶ ANALYSIS

Directors do not ordinarily owe a duty of care to third parties unless the corporation is insolvent. Due to the nature of certain types of enterprises, the director stands in a fiduciary capacity to third parties. Because the reinsurance business relies on the entrustment of capital within the company, and on the transmission of funds to the appropriate parties, Mrs. Pritchard (D) owed a duty of care to third-party clients of Pritchard and Baird.

Quicknotes

FIDUCIARY DUTY A legal obligation to act for the benefit of another, including subordinating one's personal interests to that of the other person.

NEW JERSEY BUSINESS CORPORATION ACT § 14A Directors are obligated to discharge their duties in good faith and with skill of ordinary prudent person in similar position.

PROXIMATE CAUSE The natural sequence of events without which an injury would not have been sustained.

Bayer v. Beran

Parties not identifed.

49 N.Y.S.2d 2 (Sup. Ct. 1944).

NATURE OF CASE: Complaint alleging breach of fi-duciary duty.

FACT SUMMARY: Directors of the Celanese Corporation of America (D) were charged with negligence and self-interest in commencing a radio advertising program.

🏛 RULE OF LAW
Policies of business management are left solely to the discretion of the board of directors and may not be questioned absent a showing of fraud, improper motive, or self-interest.

FACTS: Prior to 1942, the Celanese Corporation of America (D) engaged in an advertising campaign aimed at developing brand awareness. Following a Federal Trade Commission ruling that it must label its products "rayon," Celanese (D) commenced a radio advertising program costing one million dollars per year. This decision was made following studies conducted by Celanese's (D) advertising department, and the employment of both a radio consultant and an advertising agency. Mrs. Dreyfus, wife of Celanese's (D) president, was selected to perform in the radio program. The board (D) was charged with commencing an illegal radio advertising program, negligence in its selection of the program and their decision to renew its contract, and self-interest in initiating the program and spending large sums of money in connection with it.

ISSUE: May the court question decisions of business management made by a corporation's board of directors?

HOLDING AND DECISION: [Judge not stated in casebook excerpt.] No. Policies of business management are left solely to the discretion of the board of directors and may not be questioned absent a showing of fraud, improper motive, or self-interest, even though the decision may later be judged unwise or unprofitable. However, the business judgment rule only protects directors from personal liability for their negligence if they have not violated their duty of loyalty to the corporation. In cases where directors enter into personal transactions with their companies, such transactions are rigorously scrutinized and, upon the showing of any unfair advantage, will be voided. The burden then shifts to the interested director to demonstrate the transaction's good faith and inherent fairness to the corporation. In this case, there is no evidence that the advertising program was inefficient, disproportionate in price, or conducted for the personal gain of Mrs. Dreyfus. Dismissed.

▶ ANALYSIS

When the court invokes the business judgment rule, the directors of the corporation are almost always shielded from liability. However, the court will only invoke the rule following a preliminary determination that the duties of care and loyalty have not been violated. The violation is not limited to direct action taken by the director. Where a relative of a director of a corporation is closely associated with the company's course of action, the motives supporting the transaction will be scrutinized.

Quicknotes

BUSINESS JUDGMENT RULE Doctrine relieving corporate directors and/or officers from liability for decisions honestly and rationally made in the corporation's best interests.

FIDUCIARY DUTY A legal obligation to act for the benefit of another, including subordinating one's personal interests to that of the other person.

Benihana of Tokyo v. Benihana, Inc.

Parent corporation (P) v. Subsidiary (D)

906 A.2d 114 (Del. 2006).

NATURE OF CASE: Appeal from judgment for defendants in breach of fiduciary action.

FACT SUMMARY: Benihana of Tokyo (BOT) (P) contended that the directors of its subsidiary, Benihana, Inc. (Benihana) (D), breached their fiduciary duties by authorizing the issuance of convertible preferred stock as part of a transaction to raise capital where one of the board members, Abdo (D), negotiated the deal on behalf of the buyer without the board's knowledge.

🏛 RULE OF LAW
(1) A statutory safe harbor for transactions involving interested directors is satisfied where the disinterested directors do not know that the interested director negotiated a financing transaction on behalf of a potential buyer, but know that the interested director is a principal of the buyer, and approached the company on behalf of the buyer about entering into the transaction.

(2) An interested director does not breach his fiduciary duty of loyalty where the director neither sets the terms of a transaction nor deceives, nor controls or dominates the disinterested directors' approval of the transaction.

(3) A board validly exercises business judgment where it subjectively believes a transaction it is approving is in the company's best interests and for a proper corporate purpose.

FACTS: Benihana (D), a subsidiary of Benihana of Tokyo (BOT) (P), which was owned by a family trust, had two classes of common stock. Benihana (D) needed to raise capital to renovate and upgrade its properties and retained Morgan Joseph as its financial advisor. One of several financing options that Morgan Joseph initially discussed with some executives and Abdo (D), a member of the board and executive committee, was the issuance of convertible preferred stock. The full Benihana (D) board met with Morgan Joseph's representative, who recommended using such financing. At the meeting, the board was given a book that detailed a possible transaction involving such financing. Not even a month later, the board met again to review the terms of the transaction and to clarify their preferences and negotiation strategy. Shortly after that meeting, Abdo (D) contacted Morgan Joseph and indicated that his firm, BFC Financial Corp. (BFC) was interested in purchasing the convertible stock. Abdo (D) negotiated with

Morgan Joseph for several weeks and came to agreement on the terms of a transaction. Afterwards, at its next meeting, the board was informed that BFC was the potential buyer. Although the board knew that Abdo (D) was a principal of BFC, it did not know that he had negotiated the deal on BFC's behalf. At the meeting, Abdo (D) made a presentation on BFC's behalf, and then left the meeting. A book distributed to the board by Morgan Joseph indicated that Abdo (D) had approached Morgan Joseph on behalf of BFC. After due deliberation, the board approved the transaction, subject to receipt of a favorable fairness opinion. After Morgan Joseph provided such an opinion, the stock issuance was publicly announced. The family trust (owning BOT) questioned the transaction and urged the board to consider other financing routes. The board considered this request at its next meeting, but general counsel advised that the trust's concerns had merit. Also, Morgan Joseph opined that the transaction was economically fair. The board then approved the transaction. During the next two weeks, the company received three alternative financing proposals, all of which were considered by a committee of outside directors, and rejected as inferior. After that, the Stock Purchase Agreement was executed and the stock issuance was authorized. BOT brought suit alleging all Benihana (D) directors (with the exception of one) had breached various fiduciary duties by approving the transaction and stock issuance. The Chancery Court ruled that the board was authorized to issue the preferred stock, and that the board's approval of the transaction was a valid exercise of its business judgment. The state's highest court granted review.

ISSUE:
(1) Is a statutory safe harbor for transactions involving interested directors satisfied where the disinterested directors do not know that the interested director negotiated a financing transaction on behalf of a potential buyer, but know that the interested director is a principal of the buyer and approached the company on behalf of the buyer about entering into the transaction?

(2) Does an interested director breach his fiduciary duty of loyalty where the director neither sets the terms of a transaction nor deceives, nor controls or dominates the disinterested directors' approval of the transaction?

(3) Does a board validly exercise business judgment where it subjectively believes a transaction it is approving is in the company's best interests and for a proper corporate purpose?

Continued on next page.

HOLDING AND DECISION: [Judge not stated in casebook excerpt.]

(1) Yes. A statutory safe harbor for transactions involving interested directors is satisfied when the disinterested directors do not know that the interested director negotiated a financing transaction on behalf of a potential buyer, but know that the interested director is a principal of the buyer and approached the company on behalf of the buyer about entering into the transaction. Here, a state statute (DGCL § 144(a)(1)) provides a safe harbor for interested transactions if "[t]he material facts as to the director's . . . relationship or interest and as to the contract or transaction are disclosed or are known to the board of directors . . . and the board . . . in good faith authorizes the contract or transaction by the affirmative votes of a majority of the disinterested directors. . . ." After approval by the disinterested directors, the interested transaction is reviewed under the business judgment rule. Here, the board should have been informed about Abdo's (D) involvement so it could make an informed decision, but the evidence shows that it had material information indicating such involvement when it approved the transaction. The board knew BFC was the potential buyer, and the board knew Abdo (D) was BFC's principal. Thus, the directors understood that he was BFC's representative in the transaction, and that the transaction could not proceed without his approval. Accordingly, the disinterested directors possessed all the material information about Abdo's (D) interest in the transaction, and their approval of it satisfied the safe harbor provision. Affirmed, as to this issue.

(2) No. An interested director does not breach his fiduciary duty of loyalty where the director neither sets the terms of a transaction nor deceives, nor controls or dominates the disinterested directors' approval of the transaction. Here, contrary to BOT's (P) assertions, Abdo (D) did not use any confidential company information to negotiate on behalf of BFC. The record shows that Abdo (D) knew the terms a buyer could expect in a transaction such as the one under negotiation. Moreover, the negotiations involved give and take and Benihana (D) prevailed on most of the key terms. Abdo (D) did not set the terms of the deal; he did not deceive the board; and he did not dominate or control the other directors' approval of the transaction. Therefore, Abdo did not breach his duty of loyalty. Affirmed, as to this issue.

(3) Yes. A board validly exercises business judgment where it subjectively believes a transaction it is approving is in the company's best interests and for a proper corporate purpose. The record here supports the Chancery Court's conclusion that the board's approval of the transaction was a valid exercise of its business judgment since the record shows that the primary purpose of the transaction was to provide the company with what the directors believed to be the best financing vehicle available for securing capital for renovating its properties. Conversely, the record does not support BOT's (P) assertion that the primary purpose was to dilute BOT's (P) voting control. Affirmed, as to this issue.

ANALYSIS

The court here rejected an entire fairness standard of review because it found that there had been no breach of the duty of loyalty. However, when a parent engages in a cash-out merger with a partially owned subsidiary, the entire fairness standard will be applied. Under the entire fairness standard—which is stricter than the business judgment standard—the corporation must show that the transaction satisfied both "fair dealing" and "fair price" to the cashed-out minority shareholders.

Quicknotes

BREACH OF FIDUCIARY DUTY The failure of a fiduciary to observe the standard of care exercised by professionals of similar education and experience.

BUSINESS JUDGMENT RULE Doctrine relieving corporate directors and/or officers from liability for decisions honestly and rationally made in the corporation's best interests.

CONVERTIBLE STOCK Stock that may be converted into common stock or some other type of security pursuant to its terms.

ENTIRE FAIRNESS A defense to a claim that a director engaged in an interested director transaction by showing the transaction's fairness to the corporation.

INTERESTED DIRECTOR A director of a corporation who has a personal interest in the subject matter of a transaction between the corporation and another party.

PREFERRED STOCK Shares of stock that are entitled to payment of dividends and other distributions before the holders of common stock.

SAFE HARBOR A tax code provision safeguarding the taxpayer from liability in respect to the payment of taxes, so long as he has made an effort to comply with the provisions of the code.

Broz v. Cellular Information Systems, Inc.

Corporate officer (D) v. Corporation (P)

673 A.2d 148 (Del. 1996).

NATURE OF CASE: Appeal from a judgment for Cellular Information Systems, Inc. (P) in an action alleging Broz (D) usurped a corporate opportunity.

FACT SUMMARY: Broz (D) utilized a business opportunity for his wholly owned corporation instead of Cellular Information Systems, Inc. (P) for which he served as a member of the board of directors.

🏛 RULE OF LAW

The corporate opportunity doctrine is implicated only in cases where the fiduciary's seizure of an opportunity results in a conflict between the fiduciary's duties to the corporation and the self-interest of the director as actualized by the exploitation of the opportunity.

FACTS: Broz (D) owned RFB Cellular, Inc. (RFBC), and he also served on the board of directors of Cellular Information Systems, Inc. (CIS) (P), which was a competitor of RFBC. RFBC owned and operated an FCC license area, known as Michigan-4, wherein RFBC provided cellular telephone service to a geographically defined area. Mackinac Cellular Corp. (Mackinac) owned Michigan-2, which was adjacent to Michigan-4. In an effort to divest itself of Michigan-2, Mackinac contacted Broz (D) in his personal capacity to see of RFBC would be interested in purchasing it. CIS (P), which had divested itself of numerous cellular licenses and which had emerged from bankruptcy, was not offered the opportunity to purchase Michigan-2. In addition, Broz (D) informed CIS's (P) CEO and two of its directors of RFBC's interest in purchasing Michigan-2, and none of them objected. In fact, they all indicated to Broz (D) that CIS (P) was not interested in Michigan-2. In the meantime, another corporation, PriCellular, was attempting to acquire CIS (P). While Broz (D) was submitting written offers to Mackinac, PriCellular began negotiations with Mackinac to arrange for an option to purchase Michigan-2. The option gave PriCellular the right to purchase at a certain price unless another potential buyer offered at least $500,000 more than that exercise price. CIS's (P) CEO was aware of PriCellular's interest in Michigan-2, but nonetheless maintained that CIS (P) was not interested in it. Broz (D) satisfied the option terms (by paying the additional amount) and purchased Michigan-2. Nine days later, PriCellular acquired CIS (P). Afterward, CIS (P) brought suit claiming that Broz (D) had breached his fiduciary duties by usurping for himself (through RFBC) a corporate opportunity that belonged to CIS (P) and that Broz (D) should have formally submitted to the CIS (P) board. The trial court agreed with CIS (P), and the state's highest court granted review.

ISSUE: Is the corporate opportunity doctrine implicated only in cases where the fiduciary's seizure of an opportunity results in a conflict between the fiduciary's duties to the corporation and the self-interest of the director as actualized by the exploitation of the opportunity?

HOLDING AND DECISION: [Judge not stated in casebook excerpt.] Yes. The corporate opportunity doctrine is implicated only in cases where the fiduciary's seizure of an opportunity results in a conflict between the fiduciary's duties to the corporation and the self-interest of the director as actualized by the exploitation of the opportunity. Here, the totality of the circumstances indicates that Broz (D) did not usurp an opportunity that properly belonged to CIS (P). Broz (D) was entitled to utilize a corporate opportunity for the benefit of RFBC, his wholly owned corporation, instead of for CIS (P), for which he served as an outside director because: (1) the opportunity became known to him in his individual and not corporate capacity; (2) the opportunity was related more closely to the business conducted by RFBC than to that engaged in by CIS (P); (3) CIS (P) did not have the financial capacity to exploit the opportunity; and (4) CIS (P) was aware of Broz's (D) potentially conflicting duties toward RFBC and did not object to his actions on RFBC's behalf. Reversed.

▶ ANALYSIS

In Klein and Ramseyer's hornbook on Business Associations, the authors note that a common argument made by executives accused of usurping corporate opportunities is that the corporation lacked the financial capacity to effectively exploit it. However, courts generally reject this defense unless the defendant has explicitly disclosed the corporate opportunity and the corporation rejects it. This case, however, represents the Delaware View that, if a corporation does not have the financial ability to utilize the opportunity, its financial incapacity will weigh against a court finding that the director was required to offer the opportunity to the corporation.

■▬■

Continued on next page.

Quicknotes

CORPORATE OPPORTUNITY   An opportunity that a fiduciary to a corporation has to take advantage of information acquired by virtue of his or her position for the individual's benefit.

FIDUCIARY DUTY   A legal obligation to act for the benefit of another, including subordinating one's personal interests to that of the other person.

TOTALITY OF THE CIRCUMSTANCES TEST   Standard which focuses on all the circumstances of a particular case, instead of individual factors.

■══■

In re eBay, Inc. Shareholders Litigation

Parties not identified.

2004 WL 253521 (Del. Ch. 2004) (Memorandum Opinion).

NATURE OF CASE: Motion to dismiss claims of breach of fiduciary duty, and aiding and abetting a breach of fiduciary duty.

FACT SUMMARY: Shareholders (P) of eBay, Inc. (eBay) brought derivative actions against certain eBay officers and directors (D) for usurping corporate opportunities by accepting from eBay's investment banker, Goldman Sachs Group (Goldman Sachs) (D), thousands of initial public offering (IPO) shares at the initial offering price. The shareholders also alleged that Goldman Sachs (D) had aided and abetted that breach of fiduciary duty.

RULE OF LAW
(1) Where a corporation regularly and consistently invests in marketable securities, a claim for usurpation of corporate opportunity is stated where it is alleged that the corporation's officers and directors accepted IPO share allocations at the initial offering price instead of having those allocations offered to the corporation.
(2) A claim of aiding and abetting a breach of fiduciary duty is stated where it is alleged that an investment banker has allocated lucrative IPO shares to a corporation's insiders knowing that the insiders owed a fiduciary duty to the corporation not to profit personally at the corporation's expense and that the corporation regularly invested in marketable securities.

FACTS: eBay retained Goldman Sachs (D) as its underwriting investment banker during a series of IPOs. eBay paid Goldman Sachs (D) millions of dollars for its underwriting services. During this time period, Goldman Sachs (D) "rewarded" individual eBay officers and directors (D) by allocating to them thousands of IPO shares, managed by Goldman Sachs (D), at the initial offering price. Because the IPO market during this particular period of time was extremely active, prices of initial stock offerings often doubled or tripled in a single day. Investors, who were well-connected, either to Goldman Sachs (D) or to similarly situated investment banks serving as IPO underwriters, were able to flip these investments into instant profit by selling the equities in a few days or even in a few hours after they were initially purchased. Shareholders (P) of eBay filed derivative actions against those eBay directors and officers (D) who had accepted the IPO shares from Goldman Sachs (D) on the grounds that such conduct usurped a corporate opportunity that rightfully belonged to eBay, which regularly invested in marketable securities,

and constituted a breach of fiduciary duty of loyalty. The shareholders also alleged that Goldman Sachs (D) aided and abetted this breach of fiduciary duty. The accused officers and directors (D), as well as Goldman Sachs (D), moved to dismiss for failure to state a claim.

ISSUE:
(1) Where a corporation regularly and consistently invests in marketable securities, is a claim for usurpation of corporate opportunity stated where it is alleged that the corporation's officers and directors accepted IPO share allocations at the initial offering price instead of having those allocations offered to the corporation?
(2) Is a claim of aiding and abetting a breach of fiduciary duty stated where it is alleged that an investment banker has allocated lucrative IPO shares to a corporation's insiders knowing that the insiders owed a fiduciary duty to the corporation not to profit personally at the corporation's expense and that the corporation regularly invested in marketable securities?

HOLDING AND DECISION: [Judge not stated in casebook excerpt.]
(1) Yes. Where a corporation regularly and consistently invests in marketable securities, a claim for usurpation of corporate opportunity is stated where it is alleged that the corporation's officers and directors accepted IPO share allocations at the initial offering price instead of having those allocations offered to the corporation. First, eBay financially was able to exploit the opportunities in question. Second, eBay was in the business of investing in securities, as it had hundreds of millions of dollars invested in such investments. Third, eBay was never given an opportunity to turn down the IPO allocations as too risky or to accept them. It is, therefore, unavailing to argue that the allocations were collateral investment opportunities that arose by virtue of the inside directors'/officers' (D) status as wealthy individuals. Here, the facts implied that the allocations were offered by Goldman Sachs (D) as financial inducements to maintain and secure corporate business. Because this case involved below-market-price investment opportunities, this was not an instance where a broker offered advice to a director about an investment in a marketable security. Instead, it would seem that the highly lucrative IPO allocations were made both to reward the insiders (D) for past business and to induce them to direct future business to Goldman Sachs (D). In addition, this conduct placed the insiders (D) in a position of conflict with

Continued on next page.

their duties to the corporation. Because the allocations can be viewed as a form of commercial discount or rebate for past or future investment banking services, steering such commercial rebates to certain insiders (D) placed those insiders (D) in an obvious conflict between their self-interest and the corporation's interest. Finally, even if one assumes that IPO allocations like those in question here do not constitute a corporate opportunity, a cognizable claim is nevertheless stated on the common law ground that an agent is under a duty to account for profits obtained personally in connection with transactions related to his or her company. In other words, the complaint gives rise to a reasonable inference that the insiders (D) accepted a commission or gratuity that rightfully belonged to eBay but that was improperly diverted to them. Thus, even if the complained-of conduct does not run afoul of the corporate opportunity doctrine, it may still constitute a breach of the fiduciary duty of loyalty.

(2) Yes. A claim of aiding and abetting a breach of fiduciary duty is stated where it is alleged that an investment banker has allocated lucrative initial public offering (IPO) shares to a corporation's insiders knowing that the insiders owed a fiduciary duty to the corporation not to profit personally at the corporation's expense and that the corporation regularly invested in marketable securities. Here, the shareholders (P) have adequately alleged the existence of a fiduciary relationship, that the insiders (D) breached their fiduciary duty, and that the corporation and shareholders (P) were damaged by such breach. It is also unavailing for Goldman Sachs (D) to dispute whether it knowingly participated in the breach of fiduciary duty. Goldman Sachs (D) had provided underwriting and investment advisory services to eBay for years, and knew, therefore, that each of the individual insiders (D) owed a fiduciary duty to eBay not to profit personally at eBay's expense and to devote their undivided loyalty to the interests of eBay. Goldman Sachs (D) also knew or should have known that eBay invested its excess cash in marketable securities and debt. Taken together, these allegations allege a claim for aiding and abetting sufficient to withstand a motion to dismiss. Motion to dismiss denied.

▶ *ANALYSIS*

The conduct engaged in by Goldman Sachs (D) in this case is commonly known as "spinning." Such conduct, under circumstances such as those alleged in this case, is widely regarded as unethical. Where there is a quid pro quo between the investment bank and the recipient of the share allocation, whereby the recipient directs business to the bank in return for the allocation, the transaction may be an illegal bribe. In fact, the court in this case noted that Goldman Sachs (D) should have been aware of earlier SEC interpretations that prohibited steering "hot issue" securities to persons in a position to direct future business to the broker-dealer.

■≡■

Quicknotes

AIDING AND ABETTING Assistance given in order to facilitate the commission of a criminal act.

CORPORATE OPPORTUNITY DOCTRINE Prohibits fiduciaries from usurping business opportunities that rightly belong to the corporation.

DUTY OF LOYALTY A director's duty to refrain from self-dealing or to take a position that is adverse to the corporation's best interests.

FIDUCIARY DUTY A legal obligation to act for the benefit of another, including subordinating one's personal interests to that of the other person.

INSIDER Any person within a corporation who has access to information not available to the public.

QUID PRO QUO What for what; in the contract context used synonymously with consideration to refer to the mutual promises between two parties rendering a contract enforceable.

SHAREHOLDER'S DERIVATIVE ACTION Action asserted by a shareholder in order to enforce a cause of action on behalf of the corporation.

■≡■

Sinclair Oil Corp. v. Levien

Corporation (D) v. Shareholder (P)

280 A.2d 717 (Del. 1971).

NATURE OF CASE: Appeal from an order requiring an accounting for damages.

FACT SUMMARY: Sinclair (D) contended that, although it controlled its subsidiary Sinven and owed it a fiduciary duty, its business transactions with Sinven should be governed by the business judgment rule, and not by the intrinsic fairness test.

RULE OF LAW
The intrinsic fairness test should not be applied to business transactions where a fiduciary duty exists but is unaccompanied by self-dealing.

FACTS: Sinclair (D), the majority shareholder of Sinven, nominated all members of Sinven's board of directors and effectively controlled that company and its board of directors. A derivative action was brought by Levien (P), a minority shareholder of Sinven, who alleged that over the course of several years, Sinclair (D) had caused Sinven to pay out excessive dividends, denied Sinven industrial development opportunities and, through its wholly owned subsidiary Sinclair International Oil, breached a contract with Sinven. Levien (P) sought an accounting for damages sustained as a result of the above actions. Because the relationship between the companies gave rise to a fiduciary duty on the part of Sinclair (D), the Court of Chancery applied the intrinsic fairness test to the complained-of transactions and found for Levien (P) on all three claims. Sinclair (D) appealed, contending that the proper standard by which its conduct should have been measured was the business judgment rule.

ISSUE: Should the intrinsic fairness test be applied to business transactions where a fiduciary duty exists but is not accompanied by self-dealing?

HOLDING AND DECISION: [Judge not stated in casebook excerpt.] No. The intrinsic fairness test should not be applied to business transactions where a fiduciary duty exists but is not accompanied by self-dealing, i.e., where the parent company receives some benefit to the detriment or exclusion of the minority shareholders of the subsidiary. Because Sinven's shareholders benefited from the payment of dividends and because Levien (P) could not show that Sinclair (D) took business opportunities away from Sinven that rightfully belonged to it, no self-dealing was demonstrated as to these claims. Accordingly, the business judgment rule applied to those transactions and Levien (P) did not demonstrate a violation of that rule. However, Sinclair (D) did engage in self-dealing when it forced Sinven to contract with Sinclair's (D) wholly owned subsidiary Sinclair International Oil and then failed to abide by the terms of that contract, thereby invoking the intrinsic fairness test. Because Sinclair (D) could not show that its actions under the contract were intrinsically fair to Sinven's minority shareholders, it was required to account for damages under that claim. Affirmed in part; reversed in part and remanded.

ANALYSIS

The use of the intrinsic fairness test to shift the burden to the defendant to demonstrate the fairness of a particular transaction may not be as great a victory as it sounds for the plaintiff. Note that in order to invoke the test and to shift the burden in the first place, the plaintiff must, in addition to demonstrating the existence of a fiduciary duty, show self-dealing on the part of the defendant. Hasn't the plaintiff in such an instance already gone a long way toward rebutting the presumption of good faith afforded the defendant under the business judgment rule? Self-dealing will rarely, if ever, pass muster under the business judgment rule either.

■=■

Quicknotes

BUSINESS JUDGMENT RULE Doctrine relieving corporate directors and/or officers from liability for decisions honestly and rationally made in the corporation's best interests.

FIDUCIARY DUTY A legal obligation to act for the benefit of another.

INTRINSIC FAIRNESS TEST A defense to a claim that a director engaged in an interested director transaction by showing the transaction's fairness to the corporation.

SELF-DEALING Transaction in which a fiduciary uses property of another, held by virtue of the confidential relationship, for personal gain.

SHAREHOLDER'S DERIVATIVE ACTION Action asserted by a shareholder in order to enforce a cause of action on behalf of the corporation.

■=■

Zahn v. Transamerica Corporation

Shareholder (P) v. Corporation (D)

162 F.2d 36 (3d Cir. 1947).

NATURE OF CASE: Action to recover payments to be made upon liquidation of corporation.

FACT SUMMARY: Transamerica (D), owning a majority of voting stock and thereby controlling the board of directors, had some of Axton-Fisher's stock redeemed so that Transamerica (D) would benefit from the liquidation.

🏛 RULE OF LAW
Majority shareholders owe a duty to minority shareholders that is similar to the duty owed by a director, and when a controlling stockholder is voting, he violates his duty if he votes for his own personal benefit at the expense of the stockholders.

FACTS: Axton-Fisher's stock was divided into three groups: preferred, class A, and class B. The charter provided that, upon liquidation of the corporation, a set amount was to be paid to the preferred shareholders, with the remainder of the assets to be divided between the class A and class B shareholders. The class A shareholders were to receive twice the amount per share as were the class B shareholders. The charter also provided that the board of directors could redeem the class A stock at its option by paying $60 per share and all unpaid dividends to the shareholders. Over a period of time, Transamerica (D) acquired 80% of the class B stock and two-thirds of the overall voting stock of Axton-Fisher and thereby controlled the board of directors. When the value of Axton-Fisher's assets increased greatly, the Transamerica (D) controlled board redeemed the class A stock and then sold the assets of the corporation, thereby liquidating it and benefiting Transamerica (D), who owned most of the remaining non-preferred stock.

ISSUE: Can a suit be maintained by minority shareholders against a majority shareholder where the majority shareholder uses his votes for personal benefit at the expense of the minority?

HOLDING AND DECISION: [Judge not stated in casebook excerpt.] Yes. There are two bases for the maintenance of such a suit. First, a dominant shareholder is held to the same duty as is a director, and when he benefits from dealings with the corporation, he has the burden of proving good faith of the transaction and also fairness to minority interests. Second, when a director votes for the benefit of an outside interest, rather than for the benefit of the shareholders as a whole, there has been a breach of duty. Here, the vote of the board of directors was to benefit Transamerica (D), the majority shareholder, rather than the total shareholders of Axton-Fisher, and, by exercising such power, Transamerica (D) breached its duty

as a majority shareholder and is thereby liable to the minority interests. Reversed.

▶ ANALYSIS

This case points up the general rule that a majority shareholder owes some fiduciary duty to the minority, even though he is only acting as a shareholder. (At common law no such duty was recognized.)

Quicknotes

DELAWARE C. § 144 Interested transactions are not voidable if approved in good faith by a majority of disinterested stockholders.

DUTY OF CARE Duty that an officer or director owes to the corporation, by virtue of his fiduciary relationship, to act for the benefit of the corporation.

DUTY OF LOYALTY A director's duty to refrain from self-dealing or to take a position that is adverse to the corporation's best interests.

FIDUCIARY DUTY A legal obligation to act for the benefit of another.

VOTING STOCK Stock that entitles its holders to vote for the corporation's directors and with respect to other matters.

Fliegler v. Lawrence

Shareholders (P) v. Officers and directors (D)

361 A.2d 218 (Del. 1976).

NATURE OF CASE: Shareholder derivative suit.

FACT SUMMARY: Shareholders (P) of Agau brought suit against its officers and directors (D) claiming the officers and directors (D) wrongfully usurped a corporate opportunity belonging to Agau and profited thereby.

🏛 RULE OF LAW
Ratification of an "interested transaction" by a majority of independent, fully informed shareholders shifts the burden of proof to the objecting shareholder to demonstrate that the terms of the transaction are so unequal as to amount to a gift or a waste of corporate assets.

FACTS: Lawrence (D), president of Agau, acquired certain properties in his individual capacity under a lease-option for $60,000. Lawrence (D) agreed to transfer the properties to Agau but, after consulting with Agau's board of directors, agreed that the corporation's legal and financial positions would not allow acquisition and development of the properties at that time. The directors (D) decided to transfer the properties to USAC, a closely held corporation formed for this purpose and a majority of whose stock was owned by Agau's directors, so that capital could be raised through the sale of stock, without risk to Agau. Agau was also granted a long-term option to acquire USAC if the properties later became commercially valuable. In 1970, Agau and USAC executed the option. Upon approval by the shareholders and the exercise of the option, Agau was to deliver 800,000 shares of its restricted investment stock for all authorized and issued shares of USAC. The board voted to exercise the option and a majority of the shareholders approved. Shareholders (P) brought a derivative suit on behalf of Agau to recover the 800,000 shares and for an accounting, claiming the officers and directors (D) wrongfully usurped a corporate opportunity and profited thereby.

ISSUE: Does ratification of an "interested transaction" by a majority of independent, fully informed shareholders shift the burden of proof to the objecting shareholder to demonstrate that the terms of the transaction are so unequal as to amount to a gift or a waste of corporate assets?

HOLDING AND DECISION: [Judge not stated in casebook excerpt.] Yes. Ratification of an "interested transaction" by a majority of independent, fully informed shareholders shifts the burden of proof to the objecting shareholder to demonstrate that the terms of the transaction are so unequal as to amount to a gift or a waste of corporate assets. The general rule in shareholder derivative suits involving interested director or officer transactions is that the burden of proof is on the defendant director/officer to prove the transaction was intrinsically fair. This court in *Gottlieb v. Hayden Chemical Corp.*, 91 A.2d 57 (1952), noted that when approval is granted by a majority of independent, fully informed shareholders the "entire atmosphere is freshened and a new set of rules invoked." Here that is not the case and the objective fairness test applies. On this basis, the court concluded that the directors (D) proved the intrinsic fairness of the transaction. Agau received properties of substantial value, a potentially self-financing and profit-generating enterprise, and the interest given to the USAC shareholders was at a fair price. Affirmed.

⏐ ANALYSIS

The court also rejected the directors' (D) contention that § 144 of the Delaware Code demonstrated the legislature's intent to eliminate the requirement that the ratifying shareholders be disinterested or independent. That section provided, in pertinent part, that a transaction between a corporation and one or more of its directors and officers is not void or voidable solely because of the officer or director's participation, if certain requirements are met. The court interprets this section as a safeguard against the invalidation of transactions merely because an officer or director of the corporation is involved.

■■■

Quicknotes

CORPORATE OPPORTUNITY An opportunity that a fiduciary to a corporation has to take advantage of information acquired by virtue of his or her position for the individual's benefit.

INTRINSIC FAIRNESS TEST A defense to a claim that a director engaged in an interested director transaction by showing the transaction's fairness to the corporation.

SHAREHOLDER'S DERIVATIVE ACTION Action asserted by a shareholder in order to enforce a cause of action on behalf of the corporation.

■■■

In re Wheelabrator Technologies, Inc. Shareholders Litigation

Shareholders (P) v. Corporation/board of directors (D)

663 A.2d 1194 (Del. Ch. 1995).

NATURE OF CASE: Shareholder class action suit challenging a corporate merger and alleging violations of directors' duty of care.

FACT SUMMARY: Shareholders (P) of Wheelabrator Technologies, Inc. (WTI) (D) filed a class action suit alleging that WTI (D) and its directors breached their fiduciary obligation to disclose material information concerning a corporate merger.

🏛 RULE OF LAW
Fully informed shareholder ratification does not extinguish a duty of loyalty claim, but it serves to make the business judgment rule the applicable review standard with the burden of proof resting on the plaintiff stockholder.

FACTS: WTI (D), a publicly held Delaware corporation engaged in the business of developing and providing refuse-to-energy services, entered into a transaction with Waste Management, Inc., a corporation that provided waste management services to commercial and industrial customers to take advantage of their complimentary business operations. The transaction gave Waste a 22% equity interest in WTI (D), as well as the right to nominate four of WTI's (D) eleven directors. Waste began to consider either acquiring a majority interest in WTI (D) or divesting all of its WTI (D) stock. Representatives from both Waste and WTI (D), as well as members of WTI's (D) investment banking firm, met and agreed that Waste would acquire an additional 33% of WTI (D). They further agreed that the transaction would be structured as a stock-for-stock merger conditioned upon the approval of a majority of WTI's (D) disinterested stockholders. The board members voted unanimously to approve the merger and recommend its approval to WTI (D) stockholders. At a special stockholders' meeting, the merger was approved by a majority of WTI (D) shareholders other than Waste. A group of shareholders (P) later filed a class action suit alleging that the directors breached their fiduciary obligation to disclose all material information concerning the merger and that they breached their fiduciary duties of loyalty and care. WTI (D) filed a motion for summary judgment arguing that because the merger was approved by a fully informed shareholder vote, the vote operated as a complete defense to the shareholders' (P) claims.

ISSUE: Does fully informed shareholder ratification serve to extinguish a duty of loyalty claim?

HOLDING AND DECISION: (Jacobs, V. Chan.) No. Fully informed shareholder ratification does not extinguish a duty of loyalty claim, but it serves to make the business judgment rule the applicable review standard with the burden of proof resting on the plaintiff stockholder. The business judgment standard requires proof that no person of ordinary sound business judgment would say that the consideration received for the shares was a fair exchange for what was received. Because the parties have not yet been heard on the question of how the business judgment standard would apply to the facts, summary judgment is denied and the issue is remanded for further proceedings. However, the fact that the merger was approved by a fully informed majority of WTI shareholders does provide a complete defense to the disclosure claim and the duty of care claim. Motion denied in part.

⯈ ANALYSIS

The court draws a pointed distinction between duty of care and duty of loyalty claims. The rationale is that even an informed shareholder vote may not afford the minority shareholders sufficient judicial protection in a duty of loyalty claim, while the duty of care claim is more of a procedural issue. Nonetheless, if the vote truly is fully informed, it would seem that the shareholders would already be protected.

■▬■

Quicknotes

BREACH OF FIDUCIARY DUTY The failure of a fiduciary to observe the standard of care exercised by professionals of similar education and experience.

BURDEN OF PROOF The duty of a party to introduce evidence to support a fact that is in dispute in an action.

BUSINESS JUDGMENT RULE Doctrine relieving corporate directors and/or officers from liability for decisions honestly and rationally made in the corporation's best interests.

DUTY OF LOYALTY A director's duty to refrain from self-dealing or to take a position that is adverse to the corporation's best interests.

■▬■

In re The Walt Disney Co. Derivative Litigation

Parties not identified.

906 A.2d 27 (Del. 2006).

NATURE OF CASE: Appeal from judgment for defendants in derivative action for breaches of fiduciary duties and contract, and for waste.

FACT SUMMARY: Shareholders (P) of The Walt Disney Company (Disney) contended that a $130 million severance package received by Ovitz (D) under his employment agreement (OEA) when he was terminated as Disney's president was the product of breaches of fiduciary duty and contract by Ovitz (D) and Disney's directors (D) and constituted a waste of assets.

🏛 **RULE OF LAW**

(1) An individual cannot be deemed to be a de facto corporate officer where that individual has not assumed or purported to assume the duties of a corporate office.

(2) Due care and bad faith may be treated as separate grounds for denying business judgment rule review.

(3) An entire board of directors does not have to consider and approve an officer's employment agreement.

(4) Members of a compensation committee do not breach their duty of due care where, although they do not follow best practices, they are sufficiently informed about all material facts regarding a decision they make.

(5) Directors do not breach their duty of care in electing an officer where they are informed of all material information reasonably available regarding their decision.

(6) "Intentional dereliction of duty, a conscious disregard for one's responsibilities" is an appropriate legal definition of bad faith.

(7) Where a corporation's governing instruments vest authority in the CEO/Chairman as well as in the entire board of directors to terminate an officer, the entire board of directors does not breach the fiduciary duties of due care and good faith by failing to terminate an officer and by permitting the CEO/Chairman to do so.

(8) A CEO/Chairman does not breach the duty of care or the duty to act in good faith by making a decision that is based in fact and that is made within his business judgment.

(9) Where directors rely on advice that is accurate, and their reliance is made in good faith, they do not breach any fiduciary duties.

(10) Where payment provisions of a corporate contract have a rational business purpose, directors do not commit waste of corporate assets by making payment under the contract.

FACTS: The Walt Disney Company (Disney) needed a president. Disney's Chairman and CEO, Eisner (D), knew Ovitz (D), who was a founder of, and partner in, Creative Artists Agency (CAA), a very successful Hollywood talent agency. Eisner (D) and Ovitz (D), who knew each other for more than 25 years, had previously discussed the possibility of working together, and Eisner (D) and Russell (D), who was a director and chairman of Disney's compensation committee, approached Ovitz (D) about joining Disney. Ovitz (D) was interested in joining as a co-CEO, and negotiations over his employment agreement (OEA) began. Ovitz (D) annually earned between $20 and $25 million from CAA, and insisted on downside protections to ensure similar income. The parties worked out a draft OEA that provided Ovitz (D) with a five-year contract and two tranches of options. The first tranche consisted of 3 million options vesting in equal parts in the third, fourth, and fifth years, and if the value of those options at the end of the five years had not appreciated to $50 million, Disney would make up the difference. The second tranche consisted of two million options that would vest immediately if Disney and Ovitz (D) opted to renew the contract. The draft OEA sought to protect both parties in the event that Ovitz's (D) employment ended prematurely, and provided that absent defined causes, neither party could terminate the agreement without penalty. If Ovitz (D) left Disney for any reason other than those permitted under the OEA, he would forfeit any benefits remaining under the OEA and could be enjoined from working for a competitor. Likewise, if Disney fired Ovitz (D) for any reason other than gross negligence or malfeasance, he would be entitled to a non-fault payment (NFT), which consisted of his remaining salary, $7.5 million a year for unaccrued bonuses, the immediate vesting of his first tranche of options, and $10 million cash out payment for the second tranche of options. Ovitz's (D) compensation was designed to induce him to work for Disney by compensating him for remuneration he would be forfeiting by leaving CAA. The parties understood that Ovitz's (D) salary would be at the top level for any corporate officer and significantly above that of even Eisner, the Disney CEO, and that the stock options granted under the OEA would exceed the standards applied within Disney and corporate America and would "raise very strong criticism." The financial terms of the draft OEA were reviewed by an executive compensation consultant and Watson (D), another member of Disney's compensation committee; it was determined that the OEA would approximate Ovitz's (D) annual compensation at CAA—around $24.1 million per year. Also under the OEA, Ovitz (D) would be president, and not a

Continued on next page.

co-CEO. Ovitz (D) agreed to the draft OEA terms, and these terms were memorialized in a letter agreement (OLA), which expressly provided that a formal contract was subject to approval by the Disney board (D) and compensation committee. Once the OLA was signed, a formal contract was drafted, and then reviewed for an hour by the Disney compensation committee. The committee unanimously recommended the employment agreement. Immediately after the compensation committee meeting, the Disney board (D) met in executive session. After being informed about Ovitz (D) and his proposed compensation package, the board (D) unanimously elected Ovitz (D) as president. Ovitz (D) remained with Disney for about 14 months. It became increasingly clear that he was not a good fit with his fellow executives, and the board (D) was informed of various problems with Ovitz (D). Eisner (D) eventually discussed these problems with Ovitz (D), making it clear that Ovitz (D) was no longer welcome at Disney. Eisner (D) also inquired of counsel, including Litvack (D), a board member, whether Ovitz (D) could be terminated for cause under the OEA, in which case Disney could avoid making the NFT payment, but counsel consistently informed Eisner that there was no cause for terminating Ovitz (D). Ovitz (D) was then terminated. His severance package under the OEA amounted to around $130 million. Disney shareholders (P) brought a derivative action, claiming that the severance payout was the product of fiduciary duty and contractual breaches by Ovitz (D), and breaches of fiduciary duty by the Disney directors (D) at the time of the events, and a waste of assets. The Chancery Court rejected these claims, and the state's highest court granted review.

ISSUE:

(1) Can an individual be deemed to be a de facto corporate officer where that individual has not assumed or purported to assume the duties of a corporate office?

(2) May due care and bad faith be treated as separate grounds for denying business judgment rule review?

(3) Does an entire board of directors have to consider and approve an officer's employment agreement?

(4) Do members of a compensation committee breach their duty of due care where, although they do not follow best practices, they are sufficiently informed about all material facts regarding a decision they make?

(5) Do directors breach their duty of care in electing an officer where they are informed of all material information reasonably available regarding their decision?

(6) Is "intentional dereliction of duty, a conscious disregard for one's responsibilities" an appropriate legal definition of bad faith?

(7) Where a corporation's governing instruments vest authority in the CEO/Chairman as well as in the entire board of directors to terminate an officer, does the entire board of directors breach the fiduciary duties of due

care and good faith by failing to terminate an officer and by permitting the CEO/Chairman to do so?

(8) Does a CEO/Chairman breach the duty of care or the duty to act in good faith by making a decision that is based in fact and that is made within his business judgment?

(9) Where directors rely on advice that is accurate, and their reliance is made in good faith, do they breach any fiduciary duties?

(10) Where payment provisions of a corporate contract have a rational business purpose, do directors commit waste of corporate assets by making payment under the contract?

HOLDING AND DECISION: [Judge not stated in casebook excerpt.]

(1) No. An individual cannot be deemed to be a de facto corporate officer where that individual has not assumed or purported to assume the duties of a corporate office. The shareholders (P) claim that it was error for the Chancery Court to summarily dismiss their claim that Ovitz (D) breached his fiduciary duties to Disney by negotiating and entering into the OEA. The Chancery Court found that Ovitz (D) was not an officer during this time, so that as a matter of law he could not have had any fiduciary duties to Disney. The shareholders (P) argue that Ovitz (D) was a de facto officer at that time by virtue of his contacts, receipt of confidential information, and request for reimbursement of certain expenses, which vested him with apparent authority. The shareholders' (D) argument lacks merit because a de facto officer is one who has assumed possession of an office under the claim and color of an election or appointment and who is actually discharging the duties of that office. Here, Ovitz's (D) conduct does not meet this definition, either factually or legally, because he did not assume, or purport to assume, the duties of Disney's President until after he signed the OEA. Therefore, the Chancery Court did not err as to this issue. Affirmed, as to this issue.

(2) Yes. Due care and bad faith may be treated as separate grounds for denying business judgment rule review. The shareholders (P) claim that the Chancery Court erred in treating as distinct questions whether they established by a preponderance of the evidence either gross negligence or a lack of good faith. Under the business judgment rule, director action is presumed to have been made on an informed basis, in good faith, and in the honest belief that the action taken is in the corporation's best interest. Those presumptions can be rebutted if the plaintiff shows that the directors breached their fiduciary duty of care or of loyalty or acted in bad faith. If that is

Continued on next page.

shown, the burden then shifts to the director defendants to demonstrate that the challenged act or transaction was entirely fair to the corporation and its shareholders. Here, however, there was no claim of the breach of the duty of loyalty. Therefore, the only way to rebut the business judgment rule presumption is to show that the directors (D) breached their duty of care or had not acted in good faith. The Chancery Court did not err in treating these grounds separately. Affirmed, as to this issue.

(3) No. An entire board of directors does not have to consider and approve an officer's employment agreement. The shareholders (P) argue that the Chancery Court erred in ruling that the entire Disney board (D) was not required to consider and approve the OEA. Where, as here, a corporation's governing instruments allocate that decision to a compensation committee, the entire board does not have to consider and approve that decision. There is nothing in the state's statutes that requires that an entire board of directors make decisions concerning executive compensation. Therefore, the Chancery Court did not err in ruling that only the compensation committee could consider and approve the OEA. Affirmed, as to this issue.

(4) No. Members of a compensation committee do not breach their duty of due care where, although they do not follow best practices, they are sufficiently informed about all material facts regarding a decision they make. The Chancery Court acknowledged that the compensation committee's decision-making process fell far short of corporate governance best practices, but nevertheless ruled that they were adequately informed about the OEA before approving it, so that they did not breach their duty of care. The shareholders (P) claim that the Chancery Court's decision was erroneous because the evidence showed that the compensation committee members did not properly inform themselves of the material facts, so that they were grossly negligent in approving the NFT provisions of the OEA. Under a best practices scenario, the committee members would have considered a matrix of alternative scenarios under the OEA. Instead, they considered a term sheet that summarized the material terms of the OEA. The term sheet disclosed what would happen in case of a non-fault termination. Thus, the compensation committee knew that in the event of an NFT, Ovitz's (D) severance payment alone could be in the range of $40 million cash, plus the value of the accelerated options. The question is whether they were informed that those options could reach a value of more than $90 million; the record shows they were. Although this knowledge was not imparted in one tidy source, such as a spreadsheet—which would have been desirable under a best practices scenario—the information was made available to the compensation committee in various spreadsheets that had been prepared for the committee's meetings. The compensation committee members derived their information about the potential magni-

tude of an NFT payout from two sources. The first was the value of the "benchmark" options previously granted to other officers, along with their valuations, and the second was the amount of downside protection Ovitz (D) was demanding. The committee members knew that by leaving CAA and coming to Disney, Ovitz (D) would be sacrificing "booked" CAA commissions of $150 to $200 million-an amount that Ovitz (D) demanded as protection against the risk that his employment relationship with Disney might not work out. Ovitz (D) wanted at least $50 million of that compensation to take the form of an "up-front" signing bonus. Because it was decided to not grant such a bonus, the committee members knew that the value of the options had to be greater. They also knew that under the NFT, the earlier in the contract that Ovitz (D) was terminated without cause, the greater the severance payment would be. For these reasons, the Chancery Court did not err in concluding that there was sufficient evidence that the compensation committee members were adequately (if, albeit, not ideally) informed about the potential magnitude of an early NFT severance payout. Affirmed, as to this issue.

(5) No. Directors do not breach their duty of care in electing an officer where they are informed of all material information reasonably available regarding their decision. The shareholders (P) contend that the directors (D) breached their duty of care in electing Ovitz (D) because they were not informed about their decision, and that the Chancery Court erred in ruling to the contrary. The record, however, does not support the shareholders' (P) stance. The directors (D) were well aware about the need for a new president. They knew from Eisner (D) about Ovitz (D) and his qualifications, and that Eisner (D) believed he would work well with Ovitz (D). They also knew that to accept a position at Disney, Ovitz (D) would have to leave CAA, an extremely successful and lucrative business. The directors (D) also knew that the public supported Ovitz's (D) hiring, as did Eisner (D) and other senior officers. The board (D) was also informed of the key terms of the OEA, and knew that the compensation committee approved and recommended the OEA. Based on these facts, the Chancery Court did not err in concluding that directors (D) were fully informed of all material facts, and, therefore, did not breach their duty of care. Affirmed, as to this issue.

(6) Yes. "Intentional dereliction of duty, a conscious disregard for one's responsibilities" is an appropriate legal definition of bad faith. This is the definition the Chancery Court used in assessing whether the directors (D) and compensation committee had not acted in good faith, and in holding that they had not acted in bad faith. The Chancery Court noted that this standard of bad faith is not the only one that can be used, but is an

Continued on next page.

appropriate definition. The shareholders (P) argue that this is not an appropriate standard. The Chancery Court did not err in using this definition, because there are at least three different categories of fiduciary conduct that can give rise to a bad faith claim. The first is "subjective bad faith," which is fiduciary conduct motivated by an actual intent to do harm. Such conduct is not claimed to have occurred here. The second category involves lack of due care, which does not involve malevolent intent, but sounds in gross negligence (here, the Chancery Court did not find gross negligence). In any event, gross negligence by itself cannot constitute bad faith, as these are clearly distinguished in common law and by statute. The third category falls between the first two, and this is the category intended to be captured by the Chancery Court's definition. The question is whether such misconduct is properly treated as a non-exculpable, non-indemnifiable violation of the fiduciary duty to act in good faith; the answer is "yes." That is because fiduciary misconduct is not limited to self-interested disloyalty or to gross negligence, but may lie somewhere in between these extremes. For example, the fiduciary may intentionally act with a purpose other than that of advancing the best interests of the corporation, may act with the intent to violate applicable positive law, or may intentionally fail to act in the face of a known duty to act, demonstrating a conscious disregard for his duties. Such an intermediate category of bad faith is also recognized statutorily. The Chancery Court's definition of bad faith encompasses this intermediate bad faith category, and, therefore, is appropriate. Affirmed, as to this issue.

(7) No. Where a corporation's governing instruments vest authority in the CEO/Chairman as well as in the entire board of directors to terminate an officer, the entire board of directors does not breach the fiduciary duties of due care and good faith by failing to terminate an officer and by permitting the CEO/Chairman to do so. The shareholders (P) assert that only the full board (D), but not Eisner (D) alone, could have terminated Ovitz (D). Although the board (D) had the authority to terminate Ovitz (D), it did not have the duty to do so, since Disney's governing instruments could be read to permit Eisner (D) to terminate Ovitz (D) and the board (D) understood this to be the case. Without a duty to act, the board (D) could not have breached any fiduciary duties. Because Eisner (D) had concurrent power with the board (D) to terminate lesser officers, such as Ovitz (D), board (D) approval was not necessary for Eisner (D) to terminate Ovitz (D). Affirmed, as to this issue.

(8) No. A CEO/Chairman does not breach the duty of care or the duty to act in good faith by making a decision that is based in fact and that is made within his business judgment. The shareholders (P) claim that Ovitz (D) could have been terminated for cause, and therefore Eisner (D) (as well as Litvack (D)) acted without due care and in bad faith in reaching the contrary conclusion. The factual

record does not support the shareholders' (P) assertions that Ovitz (D) intentionally failed to follow Eisner's (D) directives and was insubordinate, that Ovitz (D) was a habitual liar, and that Ovitz (D) violated policies relating to expenses and to reporting gifts he gave while at Disney. Therefore, Eisner (D) correctly concluded that Ovitz (D) could not be terminated for cause. Moreover, Eisner (D) also acted within his business judgment in pursuing termination of Ovitz (D) and triggering the NFT, since the other options were to keep Ovitz (D) as president or to offer him another position at Disney, which would have also triggered the NFT and a possible lawsuit, which would have potentially been very costly. Eisner (D) acted within his business judgment in choosing the course of action he did. Affirmed, as to this issue.

(9) No. Where directors rely on advice that is accurate, and their reliance is made in good faith, they do not breach any fiduciary duties. The shareholders (P) argue that the business judgment rule presumptions did not protect the Disney board's acquiescence in the NFT payout, because the board was not entitled to rely upon Eisner's (D) and Litvack's (D) advice that Ovitz (D) could not be terminated for cause. However, the advice given by Eisner (D) and Litvack (D) was accurate, and the directors (D) relied on this advice in good faith. For these reasons, the directors (D) did not breach any fiduciary duties, and their actions were protected by the business judgment rule. Affirmed, as to this issue.

(10) No. Where payment provisions of a corporate contract have a rational business purpose, directors do not commit waste of corporate assets by making payment under the contract. The shareholders (P) argue that the severance payment to Ovitz (D) constituted a waste of corporate assets. This claim is rooted in the doctrine that a plaintiff who fails to rebut the business judgment rule presumptions is not entitled to any remedy unless the transaction constitutes waste. To recover on a claim of corporate waste, a plaintiff must prove that the exchange was "so one sided that no business person of ordinary, sound judgment could conclude that the corporation has received adequate consideration." This very high standard for waste is a corollary of the proposition that where business judgment presumptions are applicable, the board's decision will be upheld unless it cannot be "attributed to any rational business purpose." The claim that the payment of the NFT amount to Ovitz (D) constituted waste is meritless on its face, because at the time the NFT amounts were paid, Disney was contractually obligated to pay them. Thus, the question becomes whether the OEA NFT severance provisions were wasteful to begin with. Although the shareholders (P) argue that those provisions gave Ovitz (D) every incentive to leave Disney as soon as possible, they ignore that those provisions had a rational business purpose—

Continued on next page.

to induce Ovitz (D) to leave CAA, at what would have been considerable cost to him. Because the provisions had a rational business purpose, the shareholders (P) cannot meet their burden of proving waste. Affirmed, as to this issue.

▶ *ANALYSIS*

This case demonstrates, among other things, how the duty of directors to act in good faith is an independent duty that is on the same footing as the duties of care and of loyalty, and how that duty interacts with the other independent duties. Although the duty to act in good faith has always been part of corporate governance jurisprudence, it has been only relatively recently that the duty has been viewed as an independent duty, rather than as a duty subsumed within the other fiduciary duties.

■══■

Quicknotes

BUSINESS JUDGMENT RULE Doctrine relieving corporate directors and/or officers from liability for decisions honestly and rationally made in the corporation's best interests.

BUSINESS PURPOSE RULE Doctrine relieving corporate directors and/or officers from liability for decisions honestly and rationally made in the corporation's best interests.

DUTY OF CARE Duty that an officer or director owes to the corporation, by virtue of his fiduciary relationship, to act for the benefit of the corporation.

DUTY OF LOYALTY A director's duty to refrain from self-dealing or to take a position that is adverse to the corporation's best interests.

FIDUCIARY DUTY A legal obligation to act for the benefit of another, including subordinating one's personal interests to that of the other person.

GOOD FAITH COMPLIANCE A sincere or unequivocal intention to fulfill an obligation or to comply with specifically requested conduct.

■══■

Jones v. Harris Associates L.P.

Mutual fund share owner (P) v. Investment advisor (D)

527 F.3d 627 (7th Cir. 2008).

NATURE OF CASE: Appeal from summary judgment for defendant in action for violation of the Investment Company Act of 1940, § 36(b).

FACT SUMMARY: Share owners (P) of Oakmark mutual funds contended that fees received by Harris Associates (D), the investment adviser for Oakmark, were too high and violated the Investment Company Act of 1940, § 36(b), which provides that investment advisers have a fiduciary duty regarding the receipt of compensation for services.

RULE OF LAW

An investment adviser does not violate its fiduciary duty under the Investment Company Act of 1940, § 36(b), where the fees it charges a related mutual fund are similar to those charged by other advisers under similar circumstances and are not so disproportionately large that they could not be the product of arm's-length negotiations.

FACTS: Share owners (P) of Oakmark mutual funds contended that advisory (management) fees received by Harris Associates (D), the investment adviser for Oakmark, were too high and violated the Investment Company Act of 1940 (Act), § 36(b), which provides that investment advisers have a fiduciary duty regarding the receipt of compensation for services. The Act requires that at least 40% of a mutual fund's trustees be disinterested in the adviser and the links between the trustees and the adviser must be disclosed. Compensation for the adviser is controlled by a majority of the disinterested trustees. Oakmark Fund paid Harris Associates (D) 1% per year of the first $2 billion of the fund's assets, 0.9% of the next $1 billion, 0.8% of the next $2 billion, and 0.75% of anything over $5 billion. These fees were about the same as those paid by other funds to their advisers. The district court found that Harris Associates' (D) fees were ordinary, in the sense that they were in the range of what would have been negotiated at arm's-length and were not so disproportionately large that they did not bear a reasonable relationship to the services rendered. Accordingly, the district court held that as a matter of law Harris Associates (D) had not violated the Act and granted it summary judgment. The Court of Appeals granted review.

ISSUE: Does an investment adviser violate its fiduciary duty under the Investment Company Act of 1940, § 36(b), where the fees it charges a related mutual fund are similar to those charged by other advisers under similar circumstances and are not so disproportionately large that they could not be the product of arm's-length negotiations?

HOLDING AND DECISION: [Judge not stated in casebook excerpt.] No. An investment adviser does not violate its fiduciary duty under the Investment Company Act of 1940, § 36(b), where the fees it charges a related mutual fund are similar to those charged by other advisers under similar circumstances and are not so disproportionately large that they could not be the product of arm's-length negotiations. The share owners (P) argue that market price should not be a benchmark of reasonable fees, because, they contend, such fees are not set by competition but by the advisers, which create the mutual funds, and because the market for advisers is not competitive. They also argue that since the advisers charge institutional clients less than they charge their controlled mutual fund clients, they may not charge the controlled clients more that they charge their independent clients without violating their fiduciary duties under the Act. These arguments are not persuasive. Mutual funds have a powerful incentive to keep costs down to attract investors. Because advisory fees are a large part of a fund's administrative costs, mutual funds have the incentive to keep these low unless higher fees can be associated with higher returns on investment. Merely because mutual funds are "captives" of investment advisers does not affect these competitive forces. If high costs drive investors away, the adviser cannot profit from its high fees. Also, a fiduciary duty is not tantamount to rate regulation. Fiduciaries are not subject to a cap on compensation, and they are in the best position to determine the value of their services. Section 36(b) does not require that the fees must be "reasonable" in relation to a judicially created standard, but says that the investment advisor is a fiduciary—which means the adviser must act honestly and with full disclosure. It also does not mean an advisor cannot negotiate in its own interests. This is equally true, for example for fiduciaries who run corporations, or who are lawyers. The only constraint on fiduciary compensation is market competition, which determines what clients are willing to pay. The reasonableness of fiduciary compensation should not be determined by judges; the only question for the judiciary is whether the fee was negotiated at arm's length. Instead, competition determines the fee. In the case of mutual funds, there are thousands of such funds that are competing for investors. Some of these do not even have investment advisers. Investors affect the advisory fees by leaving funds whose costs are excessive in relation to the results obtained as compared with alternative funds. Thus, the mutual fund market is more competitive than many others. Sophisticated investors who shop around protect unsophisticated

Continued on next page.

investors, and, in fact, the most sophisticated investors actually pay substantially more for investment advice than advisers subject to § 36(b) receive. When sophisticated investors who have the most to invest, and who act through professional advisers, place their assets in pools whose managers receive more than Harris Associates (D), it is hard to conclude that Harris Associates' (D) fees are excessive. In sum, regulating advisory fees through litigation is unlikely to do more good than harm. Affirmed.

▶ ANALYSIS

The federal securities laws, of which the Investment Company Act is one component, work largely by requiring disclosure, and then allowing price to be set by competition in which investors make their own choices. Here, in keeping with the Seventh Circuit's conclusion, Harris Associates (D) adhered to those standards and met its fiduciary obligations. There was no allegation that they pulled the wool over the eyes of the disinterested trustees or otherwise hindered their ability to negotiate a favorable price for advisory services. In addition, the fees were not hidden from investors. Thus, the fiduciary requirements of honesty and full disclosure were met.

Quicknotes

FIDUCIARY DUTY A legal obligation to act for the benefit of another, including subordinating one's personal interests to that of the other person.

INVESTMENT COMPANY ACT Federal law regulating investment companies.

Stone v. Ritter

Shareholder (P) v. Corporate directors (D)

911 A.2d 362 (Del. 2006).

NATURE OF CASE: Appeal from judgment dismissing derivative action.

FACT SUMMARY: Shareholders (P) bringing a derivative action against AmSouth Bancorporation (AmSouth) directors (D) contended that demand was excused because the directors (D) breached their oversight duty and utterly failed to act in good faith regarding compliance with various banking regulations, thus facing a likelihood of personal liability that would render them incapable of exercising independent and disinterested judgment in response to a demand request.

> ## 🏛 RULE OF LAW
> A derivative action will be dismissed for failure to make demand where alleged particularized facts do not create a reasonable doubt that the corporation's directors acted in good faith in exercising their oversight responsibilities.

FACTS: AmSouth Bancorporation (AmSouth) was a holding company whose wholly-owned subsidiary, AmSouth Bank, operated hundreds of banking branches. In 2004, AmSouth and AmSouth Bank paid $40 million in fines and $10 million in civil penalties to resolve government and regulatory investigations pertaining principally to the failure by bank employees to file "Suspicious Activity Reports" (SARs), as required by the federal Bank Secrecy Act (BSA) and various federal anti-money-laundering (AML) regulations. These violations were discovered after a "Ponzi" scheme, which was unwittingly aided by AmSouth branch employees, was uncovered. Although the corporation had in place an extensive information and reporting system, in its investigation, the government concluded that "AmSouth's compliance program lacked adequate board and management oversight." AmSouth shareholders (P) brought a derivative action against the corporation's present and former directors (D) based on these events, without first making demand on the board. AmSouth's Certificate of Incorporation contained a provision that would exculpate its directors for breaches of their duty of care, provided they acted in good faith. The directors (D) moved to dismiss for lack of demand, and the Chancery Court held that the shareholders (P) had failed to adequately plead that such a demand would have been futile, finding that the directors (D) had not been alerted by any "red flags" that violations of law were occurring. The state's highest court granted review.

ISSUE: Will a derivative action be dismissed for failure to make demand where alleged particularized facts do not create a reasonable doubt that the corporation's directors acted in good faith in exercising their oversight responsibilities?

HOLDING AND DECISION: [Judge not stated in casebook excerpt.] Yes. A derivative action will be dismissed for failure to make demand where alleged particularized facts do not create a reasonable doubt that the corporation's directors acted in good faith in exercising their oversight responsibilities. The allegations made by the shareholders (P) are a classic "*Caremark*" claim (named after *In re Caremark Int'l Deriv. Litig.* 698 A.2d 959 (Del. Ch. 1996)). Such a claim of directorial liability is premised on the directors' ignorance of liability-creating activities (such as criminal conduct or failure to follow regulations) within the corporation. In *Caremark*, the court ruled that directors will face personal liability only where there has been a sustained or systematic failure of the board to exercise oversight, as where there is an utter failure to even attempt to implement or monitor a reasonable information and reporting system. Here, the shareholders (P) assert that because it was likely the directors would face such personal liability, they could not be reasonably expected to exercise independent and disinterested judgment when faced with a pre-suit demand. However, AmSouth's Certificate of Incorporation's exculpatory provision will shield the directors (D) from liability as long as they acted in good faith—so if they acted in good faith, demand would not be excused. Thus, it must be determined whether the directors (D) acted in good faith. The standard for this determination has evolved. The standard in cases such as this is that the board must assure itself that information and reporting systems exist in the corporation that are reasonably designed to provide to senior management and to the board itself timely, accurate information to permit the board, as well as management, to reach informed decisions about the corporation's compliance with law and its business performance. As the *Caremark* court observed, "the duty to act in good faith cannot be thought to require directors to possess detailed information about all aspects of the operation of the enterprise." Thus, only where there is a sustained or systematic failure to ensure an adequate information and reporting system is in place, or, if such a system is in place, where the board consciously fails to monitor it or oversee its operations, will there be a showing of lack of good faith. Additionally, there must be a showing that the directors knew they were not discharging their fiduciary duties. In fact, recent decisions show that this formulation is consistent with examples of bad faith. The Chancery Court applied this standard and was, therefore, correct in doing so. When this standard is applied to the facts pleaded by the shareholders (P), it becomes clear that

Continued on next page.

the directors did not fail to act in good faith. The facts showed that the directors (D) had established a reasonable information and reporting system and had set up numerous departments and committees to oversee AmSouth's compliance with federal banking regulations. This system also permitted the board to periodically monitor such compliance. Here, while it is clear with hindsight, that the organization's internal controls were inadequate there were also no "red flags" to put the board on notice of any wrongdoing. The directors (D) took the steps they needed to ensure a reasonable information and reporting system existed. Therefore, although there ultimately may have been failures by employees to report deficiencies to the board, there is no basis for an oversight claim seeking to hold the directors personally liable for such failures by the employees; a bad (and very costly) outcome does not per se equate to bad faith. Affirmed.

▶ ANALYSIS

The court in this case makes a point of clarifying doctrinal issues related to the duty of good faith. First, the court emphasizes that the failure to act in good faith is a condition to finding a breach of the fiduciary duty of loyalty and imposing fiduciary liability. The court explains that "a failure to act in good faith is not conduct that results, ipso facto, in the direct imposition of fiduciary liability. The failure to act in good faith may result in liability because the requirement to act in good faith 'is a subsidiary element[,]' i.e., a condition, 'of the fundamental duty of loyalty.' It follows that because a showing of bad faith conduct ... is essential to establish director oversight liability, the fiduciary duty violated by that conduct is the duty of loyalty." Second, and as a corollary, the duty to act in good faith does not establish an independent fiduciary duty that stands on the same footing as the duty of care and loyalty. A failure to act in good faith gives rise to liability only indirectly. Also, as a corollary, the fiduciary duty of loyalty is not limited to financial or similar conflicts of interest, but also encompasses cases where a director has failed to act in good faith.

Quicknotes

DEMAND REQUIREMENT Requirement that a shareholder make a demand for corrective action by the board of directors before commencing a derivative suit.

DERIVATIVE SUIT Action asserted by a shareholder in order to enforce a cause of action on behalf of the corporation.

DUTY OF CARE Duty that an officer or director owes to the corporation, by virtue of his fiduciary relationship, to act for the benefit of the corporation.

DUTY OF LOYALTY A director's duty to refrain from self-dealing or to take a position that is adverse to the corporation's best interests.

FIDUCIARY DUTY A legal obligation to act for the benefit of another, including subordinating one's personal interests to that of the other person.

GOOD FAITH An honest intention to abstain from taking advantage of another.

Robinson v. Glynn

Purchaser of LLC interest (P) v. Seller of LLC interest (D)

349 F.3d 166 (4th Cir. 2003).

NATURE OF CASE: Appeal from dismissal of securities fraud claim.

FACT SUMMARY: Robinson (P) claimed that Glynn (D) committed securities fraud when Glynn (D) sold Robinson (P) a partial interest in GeoPhone Company, LLC (GeoPhone). Glynn (D) countered that the interest was not a security, given that Robinson (P) was a knowledgeable executive at GeoPhone.

🏛 RULE OF LAW
A membership in a limited liability company (LLC) is neither an "investment contract" nor "stock" under the federal Securities Acts where the purchaser is a sophisticated businessman who is a knowledgeable and active executive at the company.

FACTS: Glynn (D), the founder of GeoPhone Company, LLC (GeoPhone), contacted Robinson (P) in an effort to raise capital for the company. Eventually, Robinson (P) agreed to loan the company $1 million. Then, the parties executed a letter of intent in which Robinson (P) pledged to invest up to $25 million, contingent on successful testing of GeoPhone's "CAMA" technology. Robinson's (P) $25 million investment was to be comprised of his initial $1 million loan, an immediate $14 million investment upon successful completion of a field test, and a later $10 million investment. Engineers hired by Glynn (D) performed the field test, but, apparently with Glynn's (D) knowledge, they did not use CAMA in the test. Nevertheless, Glynn (D) allegedly told Robinson (P) that the field test had been a success. Accordingly, Robinson (P) and Glynn (D) executed an "Agreement to Purchase Membership Interests in GeoPhone" (APMIG). Under the APMIG, Robinson (P) agreed to convert his $1 million loan and his $14 million investment into equity and subsequently to invest the additional $10 million. Robinson (P) and Glynn (D) also entered into an "Amended and Restated GeoPhone Operating Agreement" (ARGOA), which detailed the capital contribution, share ownership, and management structure of GeoPhone. Pursuant to the ARGOA, Robinson (P) received 33,333 of GeoPhone's 133,333 shares. On the back of the share certificates, the restrictive legend referred to the certificates as "shares" and "securities." It also specified that the certificates were exempt from registration under the Securities Act of 1933, and stated that the certificates could not be transferred without proper registration under the federal and state securities laws. Robinson (P) became the company's treasurer and was appointed to the board of managers and executive committee. Robinson (P) was a very active member of the company who exercised his management rights and who had input on technology, marketing, and management.

Three years later, Robinson (P) allegedly learned for the first time that the CAMA technology had never been implemented. Robinson (P) then filed suit in federal court, claiming violation of the federal securities laws, specifically § 10(b) of the Securities Exchange Act of 1934 and Rule 10b-5. The district court granted summary judgment to Glynn (D) because it found that Robinson's (P) membership interest in GeoPhone did not constitute a security under the federal securities laws. The court of appeals granted review.

ISSUE: Is a membership in an LLC either an "investment contract" or "stock" under the federal Securities Acts where the purchaser is a sophisticated businessman who is a knowledgeable and active executive at the company?

HOLDING AND DECISION: [Judge not stated in casebook excerpt.] No. A membership in an LLC is neither an "investment contract" nor "stock" under the federal Securities Acts where the purchaser is a sophisticated businessman who is a knowledgeable and active executive at the company. An "investment contract" is "a contract, transaction or scheme whereby a person invests his money in a common enterprise and is led to expect profits solely from the efforts of the promoter or a third party." The issue under this test is whether Robinson (P) expected profits solely from the efforts of others, i.e., Glynn (D). However, this test had been relaxed so that an investor like Robinson (P) need not expect profits "solely" from others' efforts. Requiring investors to rely wholly on the efforts of others would exclude from the protection of the securities laws any agreement that involved even slight efforts from investors themselves. However, what matters more than the form of an investment scheme is the "economic reality" that it represents. The issue thus becomes whether the investor, as a result of the investment agreement itself or the factual circumstances that surround it, is left unable to exercise meaningful control over his investment. Elevating substance over form in this way ensures that the term "investment contract" embodies a flexible principle that is capable of adaptation to meet the many and variable schemes devised by those who seek the use of the money of others on the promise of profits. Here, the facts reveal that Robinson (P) was not a passive investor who was heavily dependent on others' efforts. Given that he was an active member of the board and executive committee, who exercised his management rights despite an alleged lack of technical expertise, Robinson (P) cannot be said to have been powerless to exercise control over his investment. Even if Robinson (P)

Continued on next page.

lacked technical expertise, that alone would not be grounds for protecting his investment under the securities laws. To do so would work a fundamental and unjustifiable expansion in the securities laws by bringing innumerable commercial ventures within their purview. Business ventures often find their genesis in the different contributions of diverse individuals—for instance, as here, where one contributes technical expertise and another capital and business acumen. Yet the securities laws do not extend to every person who lacks the specialized knowledge of his partners or colleagues, without a showing that this lack of knowledge prevents him from meaningfully controlling his investment. Further, notwithstanding that the certificates issued to Robinson (P) indicated they were securities, it is the economic reality of a particular instrument, rather than the label attached to it that ultimately determines whether it falls within the reach of the securities laws. Here, the "economic reality" was that Robinson (P) was not a passive investor relying on the efforts of others, but a knowledgeable executive actively protecting his interest and position in the company. Therefore, his interest was not an investment contract. His investment also was not, as he claims, "stock." The term "stock" refers to a narrower set of instruments with a common name and characteristics, and the securities laws apply to such instruments when they are both called "stock" and bear stock's usual characteristics. The characteristics typically associated with common stock are (i) the right to receive dividends contingent upon an apportionment of profits; (ii) negotiability; (iii) the ability to be pledged or hypothecated; (iv) a conference of voting rights in proportion to the number of shares owned; and (v) the capacity to appreciate in value. Robinson's (P) membership interest in GeoPhone, however, lacked several of these characteristics. GeoPhone's members did not share in the profits in proportion to the number of their shares; the membership interests were not freely negotiable; acquirers of his interest would not acquire any management or control rights, but only distribution rights, and even Robinson (P) and Glynn (D) viewed the investment as a membership interest and not stock. Therefore, his interest cannot be said to be "stock" under the federal Securities Acts. Affirmed.

▶ ANALYSIS

The court in this case declined to rule broadly—either to generally classify all LLC membership interests as investment contracts or as non-securities. Instead, the court adopted a fact-based, flexible approach regarding LLCs. As the court noted, LLCs are particularly difficult to characterize under the securities laws because they are hybrid business entities that combine features of corporations, general partnerships, and limited partnerships. LLC members can be either passive investors or active company participants. The court said, "Precisely because LLCs lack standardized membership rights or organizational structures, they can assume an almost unlimited variety of forms. It becomes, then,

exceedingly difficult to declare that LLCs, whatever their form, either possess or lack the economic characteristics associated with investment contracts."

Quicknotes

CAPITAL In tax, is often used synonymously with basis; in accounting, refers to an account that represents the equity (ownership) interests of the owners, i.e., the amounts they would obtain if the business were liquidated.

CONTINGENT Based on the uncertain happening of another event.

LETTER OF INTENT A written draft embodying the proposed intent of the parties and which is not enforceable or binding.

LIMITED LIABILITY COMPANY A business entity combining the features of both a corporation and a general partnership; the LLC provides its shareholders and officers with limited liability, but it is treated as a partnership for taxation purposes.

Doran v. Petroleum Management Corp.

Investor (P) v. Limited partnership (D)

545 F.2d 893 (5th Cir. 1977).

NATURE OF CASE: Appeal from judgment denying rescission of contract, damages, and declaratory relief under the Securities Act of 1933.

FACT SUMMARY: A limited partnership in an oil drilling venture was offered, in an informal manner, to a handful of sophisticated investors, including Doran (P), and the venture subsequently faired poorly.

🏛 RULE OF LAW
Even where an offering of securities is relatively small and is made informally to just a few sophisticated investors, it will not be deemed a "private offering" exempt from the registration requirements of the 1933 Act absent proof that each offeree had been furnished, or had access to, such information about the issuer that a registration statement would have disclosed.

FACTS: Petroleum Management Corp. (D) organized a limited partnership for the purpose of drilling and operating four oil wells in Wyoming. Petroleum (D) contacted a total of five persons, including Doran (P), regarding possible participation in the partnership. Doran (P) was contacted by telephone by a broker he knew. Thereafter Doran (P) agreed to purchase a limited partnership interest in the drilling program for $125,000, paying $25,000 down and assuming the payments on a $113,643 note Petroleum (D) owed to Mid-Continent Supply Co. Doran's (P) share of the earnings payments from the wells was to be used to make the payments on the Mid-Continent note. During 1970 and 1971, the wells were deliberately overproduced in violation of the production allowances established by the Wyoming Oil and Gas Conservation Commission, and in November 1971, the Commission ordered the wells sealed for 338 days. After the 338-day period, the wells yielded a production income below that obtained prior to the Commission's order. Doran (P) defaulted in his payments on the Mid-Continent note. Mid-Continent obtained a state-court judgment against Doran (P). Doran (P) then filed suit in federal court, seeking damages for breach of contract, rescission of the contract based on violations of the Securities Acts of 1933 and 1934, and a judgment declaring Petroleum (D) liable for payment of Mid-Continent's state-court judgment. The trial court denied all relief requested by Doran (P), finding, among other things, that the offer and sale of the limited partnership was a private offering because Doran (P) was a sophisticated investor who did not need the protection of the Securities Act. Doran (P) appealed.

ISSUE: Where an offering of securities is relatively small, consists of a small number of shares and is made informally to just a few sophisticated investors, can it be deemed a "private offering" exempt from the registration requirements of the 1933 Act absent proof that each offeree had been furnished, or had access to, such information about the issuer that a registration statement would have disclosed?

HOLDING AND DECISION: [Judge not stated in casebook excerpt.] No. The term "private offering" is not defined in the 1933 Act. This court has previously identified four factors relevant to determining whether a securities offering will be deemed a private offering: (1) the number of offerees and their relationship to each other and the issuer; (2) the number of units offered; (3) the size of the offering; and (4) the manner of the offering. Congress intended to exempt from the Act's registration requirements any offerings to those who are shown not to need the protection of the Act. Where, as in this case, an offering is relatively small, consists of a small number of units, and is made informally (such as by telephone call) to just a few sophisticated investors, the offering should be deemed a "private offering" if, and only if, it can be shown that each offeree had been furnished, or had access to, such information that a registration statement would have disclosed. If investors do not possess such information, they cannot bring their sophisticated knowledge of business affairs to bear in deciding whether to invest. Thus the relationship between the company and the investors, and the access to the kind of information that registration would disclose, become highly relevant factors, but the record in this case does not sufficiently address them. Reversed in part and remanded for proceedings on this issue.

▶ ANALYSIS

The 1933 Act provides two types of exemptions: (1) it exempts certain securities completely; (2) it exempts certain transactions in securities not falling into Category 1 (e.g., the "private offering" exemption). Note that the private offering exemption applies only to the initial sale, and not to a resale of the same security.

■═■

Quicknotes

LIMITED PARTNERSHIP A voluntary agreement entered into by two or more parties whereby one or more general partners are responsible for the enterprise's liabilities and management and the other partners are only liable to the extent of their investment.

Continued on next page.

PRIVATE OFFERING   An offering of securities in a corporation for sale to a limited number of investors and which is not subject to the requirements of the Securities Act of 1933.

RESCISSION   The canceling of an agreement and the return of the parties to their positions prior to the formation of the contract.

Escott v. BarChris Construction Corp.

Debenture purchaser (P) v. Corporation (D)

283 F. Supp. 643 (S.D.N.Y. 1968).

NATURE OF CASE: Motion to dismiss an action for damages for material false statement of facts and material omissions to shareholders.

FACT SUMMARY: Escott (P) and other purchasers of debentures (P) sued BarChris (D) for material false statements and material omissions on the registration statement of the debentures.

RULE OF LAW
Due diligence is a defense under § 11 of the Securities Act of 1933 when the defendant believes after a reasonable investigation, and there are reasonable grounds to believe, that alleged misstatements are correct and that there are no material omissions.

FACTS: BarChris (D) was engaged in the construction of bowling alleys. As BarChris's (D) business increased from 1956 to 1960, it was in constant need of capital. Debentures were sold in early 1961 to fulfill this need. The registration statement for the debentures became effective on May 16, 1961. The capital infusion, however, did not end BarChris's (D) problems, and BarChris (D) filed for bankruptcy on October 29, 1962. Escott (P) claimed that the registration statement of the debentures had material false statements and material omissions. Defendants were BarChris (D), persons signing the registration statement (D), the underwriters (D), and BarChris's auditors, Peat, Marwick, Mitchell, and Co. (D). All defendants argued that there were no material false statements or material omissions. Due diligence was pled by Vitolo (D), Pugliese (D), Kircher (D), Birnbaum (D), Auslander (D), and Grant (D), who all signed the registration statement and by Peat, Marwick (D), who certified the 1960 figures, but not the 1961 figures.

ISSUE: Is due diligence a defense under § 11 of the Securities Act of 1933 when the defendant believes after a reasonable investigation, and there are reasonable grounds to believe, that the alleged misstatements are correct and that there are no material omissions?

HOLDING AND DECISION: [Judge not stated in casebook excerpt.] Yes. Due diligence is a defense under § 11 of the Securities Act of 1933 when the defendant believes after a reasonable investigation, and there are reasonable grounds to believe, that the alleged misstatements are correct and that there are no material omissions. Section 11(c) defines reasonable investigation as that "required of a prudent man in the management of his business." In this case, the certified section of the registration statement

contained an abundance of material misstatements pertaining to 1961 affairs. Vitolo (D) and Pugliese (D), who were officers of BarChris (D), did not exert due diligence with regards to the registration statements, since they personally knew the financial problems BarChris (D) was having and could not have believed the registration statement to be completely true or that there were no material omissions. The same holds true for Kircher (D), who was BarChris's (D) treasurer and chief financial officer (D), and knew that the registration statement contained incorrect figures. Birnbaum (D), as a director for BarChris (D), had no personal knowledge of the inaccuracies of the registration statement, but was under an obligation to investigate uncertified portions of the registration statement to see if there were reasonable grounds to believe it was true. Birnbaum (D) does not qualify for the due diligence defense, except for the certified 1960 figures. Auslander (D), as an outside director, has failed to prove his due diligence defense for the certified sections of the registration statement, because he relied solely on others and on general information provided to him. Grant (D), who drafted the registration statement, has proved his due diligence defense for the certified figures but not for the uncertified figures, because Grant (D) made no reasonable investigation into the certified portions. Lastly, Peat, Marwick (D), BarChris's (D) auditors, were given answers by BarChris (D) but did nothing to verify the answers. As such, Peat, Marwick (D) has not proven the defense of due diligence as to the 1960 figures only, which they certified. Motion to dismiss denied.

▶ ANALYSIS

To successfully assert the due diligence defense under § 11, newly elected directors and outside counsel cannot rely on corporate officers and directors as to the accuracy of statements. They must conduct a reasonable investigation of the accuracy of these statements. These may include reviewing corporate documents and speaking with employees.

■━■

Quicknotes

DEBENTURES Long-term unsecured debt securities issued by a corporation.

DUE DILIGENCE The standard of care as would be taken by a reasonable person in accordance with the attendant facts and circumstances.

Continued on next page.

MATERIAL FALSE REPRESENTATIONS A statement or conduct by one party to another that constitutes a false representation of a material fact.

MATERIALITY Importance; the degree of relevance or necessity to the particular matter.

SECURITIES ACT § 11 Makes it unlawful to make untrue statements in registration statements.

■═■

Basic Inc. v. Levinson

Corporation (D) v. Former shareholders (P)

485 U.S. 224 (1988).

NATURE OF CASE: Review of grant of class certification and reversal of summary judgment for the defense.

FACT SUMMARY: Levinson (P) alleged that Basic's (D) repeated denials regarding its participation in merger discussions and negotiations were material misrepresentations as to which Basic (D) shareholders should be entitled to a presumption of reliance for purposes of class certification.

🏛 RULE OF LAW
(1) Whether a company statement is material, in the context of merger discussions, requires a case-by-case analysis of the probability that the transaction will be consummated and the significance of the transaction to the issuer of the securities.
(2) An investor's reliance on material, public misrepresentations may be presumed under a fraud-on-the-market theory for purposes of a Rule 10b-5 action.

FACTS: Despite participating in merger discussions and subsequent negotiations with Combustion, Basic (D) three times publicly denied that it was engaged in any merger negotiations. After a merger was announced, Levinson (P) and other former shareholders (P) of Basic (D) stock brought a class action asserting that the three public statements were materially misleading and therefore actionable under § 10(b) of the Securities Exchange Act and Rule 10b-5. Levinson (P) and the other shareholders (P) sought class certification, alleging that each had sold Basic (D) stock in reliance on a market price artificially depressed as a result of the misleading statements. The district court certified the class, adopting a presumption of reliance, and then granted summary judgment for Basic (D). The court of appeals affirmed the class certification, reversed the grant of summary judgment, and remanded the case to the district court. The U.S. Supreme Court granted certiorari.

ISSUE:
(1) Does an inquiry into materiality in the merger context require a case-by-case analysis of the probability that the transaction will be consummated and its significance to the issuer of the securities?
(2) May an investor's reliance on material public misrepresentations be presumed under a fraud-on-the-market theory for purposes of a Rule 10b-5 action?

HOLDING AND DECISION: [Judge not stated in casebook excerpt.]

(1) Yes. A company statement is material if a reasonable investor would consider it important in deciding how to invest. In the context of merger discussions, this determination requires a case-by-case analysis of the probability that the transaction will be consummated and the significance of the transaction to the issuer of the securities. Where an event is contingent or speculative, it is difficult to ascertain whether a reasonable investor would consider omitted information significant. However, this is by no means an insurmountable problem given the many factors available to weigh the probability and magnitude of success in each individual case. Because this standard of materiality differs from that used by the courts below, the case is remanded.

(2) Yes. An investor's reliance on material public misrepresentations may be presumed under a fraud-on-the-market theory for purposes of a Rule 10b-5 action. Requiring plaintiffs in these types of actions to prove actual reliance would place an unrealistic evidentiary burden on them. Common sense and probability support the notion that the market price of a company's stock is a reflection of all information available in the marketplace. Thus, an investor who buys or sells stock at the price set by the market can be presumed to have relied on any material misrepresentations affecting that price. Vacated and remanded.

DISSENT AND CONCURRENCE: (White, J.) The Court should not engage in economic theorization. The majority assumes that the market price truly reflects the value of a stock and that investors believe that valuation to be accurate when, in fact, many investors invest in a stock because they believe the market price does not accurately reflect the value of the stock. Moreover, based on its facts, this case is a poor candidate for the application of the fraud-on-the-market theory.

▶ ANALYSIS

This case applied the fraud-on-the-market presumption of reliance in the context of affirmative misrepresentations as to material facts. However, the same rationale applies to cases in which there is an omission to state material facts. Note again, however, that the party failing to make disclosure of material facts must be under a duty to disclose because of a fiduciary or other relationship of trust or confidence.

■=■

Quicknotes

FRAUD ON THE MARKET THEORY A theory of liability of securities fraud cases in which a defendant's material

Continued on next page.

misrepresentation regarding a security traded in the open market affects the price of the security so that a plaintiff who purchased the security and suffered a loss is presumed to have relied on the misrepresentation.

MATERIALITY Importance; the degree of relevance or necessity to the particular matter.

MISREPRESENTATION A statement or conduct by one party to another that constitutes a false representation of fact.

RULE 10B-5 Unlawful to defend or make untrue statements in connection with purchase or sale of securities.

■══■

West v. Prudential Securities, Inc.

Members of a class (P) v. Stock brokerage firm (D)

282 F.3d 935 (7th Cir. 2002).

NATURE OF CASE: Appeal from a class certification in a securities fraud suit.

FACT SUMMARY: James Hofman, a Prudential Securities (D) stockbroker, gave material non-public information (apparently false) to his clients about a forthcoming company merger. A class action was certified on behalf of everyone who bought the touted stock during the period the misinformation was being given.

RULE OF LAW
A class action may not be brought on behalf of everyone who purchased stock during a period when a broker was violating securities laws by providing material non-public information.

FACTS: James Hofman, a stockbroker working for Prudential Securities (D), told eleven of his customers that Jefferson Savings Bancorp was "certain" to be acquired, at a big premium, in the near future. Hofman continued making this statement for seven months. The statement was a lie since no acquisition was pending. And, if the statement had been the truth, then Hofman was inviting unlawful trading on the basis of material non-public information. A class action was brought against Prudential (D) not on behalf on those who received Hofman's "news" in person, but on behalf of everyone who bought Jefferson stock during the months when Hofman was misbehaving. The district judge certified such a class, invoking the fraud-on-the-market doctrine. Prudential (D) appealed the class certification.

ISSUE: May a class action be brought on behalf of everyone who purchased stock during a period when a broker was violating securities laws by providing material non-public information?

HOLDING AND DECISION: (Easterbrook, J.) No. A class action may not be brought on behalf of everyone who purchased stock during a period when a broker was violating securities laws by providing material non-public information. The district court's order, certifying everyone who purchased stock during this period as a class, would mark a substantial extension of the fraud-on-the-market approach whose rationale is that public information reaches professional investors whose evaluations of that information and trades quickly influence securities prices. Here, however, Hofman did not release information to the public, and his clients thought that they were receiving and acting on non-public information; its value, if any, lay precisely in the fact that other traders did not know the news. No newspaper or other organ of general circulation reported that Jefferson was soon to be acquired. Extending the fraud-on-the-market doctrine in this way would require a departure not only from existing law, but also a novelty in fraud cases as a class. Oral frauds have not been allowed to proceed as class actions since the details of the deceit differ from victim to victim, and the nature of the loss also may be statement-specific. Furthermore, very few securities class actions are litigated to conclusion, thus review of this novel and important legal issue may be possible only through other devices. Here, causation is the shortcoming in this class certification. With many professional investors alert to news, markets are efficient in the sense that they rapidly adjust to all public information. If some of this information is false, the price will reach an incorrect level, staying there until the truth emerges. Few propositions in economics are better established than the quick adjustment of securities prices to public information. However, no similar mechanism explains how prices would respond to non-public information, such as the statements made by Hofman to a handful of his clients. These do not come to the attention of professional investors or money managers, so the price-adjustment mechanism just described does not operate. Thus, it is hard to see how Hofman's non-public statements could have caused changes in the price of Jefferson's Savings stock. The class certification is reversed.

ANALYSIS

As noted in the *West* decision, sometimes full-time market watchers can infer important news from the identity of a trader (when the corporation's CEO goes on a buying spree, this implies good news) or from the sheer volume of trades (an unprecedented buying volume may suggest that a bidder is accumulating stock in anticipation of a tender offer), but here neither the identity of Hofman's customers nor the volume of their trades would have conveyed information to the market in this fashion.

Quicknotes

CLASS CERTIFICATION Certification by a court's granting of a motion to allow individual litigants to join as one plaintiff in a class action against the defendant.

FRAUD ON THE MARKET THEORY A theory of liability of securities fraud cases in which a defendant's material misrepresentation regarding a security traded in the open market affects the price of the security so that a plaintiff who purchased the security and suffered a loss is presumed to have relied on the misrepresentation.

Santa Fe Industries, Inc. v. Green

Corporation (D) v. Shareholder (P)

430 U.S. 462 (1977).

NATURE OF CASE: Action for violation of § 10(b) of the Securities Exchange Act of 1934 and Rule 10b-5.

FACT SUMMARY: Santa Fe Industries (D) merged with Kirby Lumber for the sole purpose of eliminating minority shareholders.

🏛 RULE OF LAW
Before a claim of fraud or breach of fiduciary duty may be maintained under § 10(b) of the Securities Exchange Act of 1934 or Rule 10b-5, there must first be a showing of manipulation or deception.

FACTS: Santa Fe Industries (D) owned 90% of Kirby Lumber's stock. Under Delaware law, a parent could merge with a subsidiary without prior notice to minority shareholders and could pay them the fair market value of the stock. Solely to eliminate these minority shareholders, Santa Fe (D) merged with Kirby. A complete audit was run of the business and shareholders were sent an offer of $150 a share plus the asset appraisal report and an opinion letter that the shares were worth $125. Green (P) and other shareholders did not appeal the price offered them as provided by state law. Instead, they initiated suit under § 10(b) of the Securities Exchange Act of 1934 and Rule 10b-5. Green (P) alleged that the merger had not been made for a business purpose and no prior notice was given shareholders. Green (P) further alleged that the value of the stock as disclosed in the appraisal should have been $722 per share based on the assets of Kirby divided by the number of shares. The court held that the merger was valid under state law which did not require a business purpose or prior notice for such mergers. The court held there was no misrepresentation, manipulation, or deception as to the value of the shares since all relevant information appeared in the appraisal report. The court of appeals reversed, finding a breach of fiduciary duty to the minority shareholders and no business purpose or notice.

ISSUE: Is breach of duty alone without a showing of deception or manipulation grounds for a § 10(b) or Rule 10b-5 action?

HOLDING AND DECISION: [Judge not stated in casebook excerpt.] No. Before any action may be brought under § 10(b) or Rule 10b-5, there must be a showing of manipulation or deception. The Act and Rule speak plainly in these terms. Not every act by a corporation or its officers was intended to be actionable under § 10(b) or Rule 10b-5. Here, there was full disclosure. If the minority shareholders were dissatisfied they could seek a court appraisal under the state statute. Neither notice nor a business purpose is required under state law. If minority shareholders feel aggrieved they must pursue state remedies since no private right of action has even been granted under § 10(b) or Rule 10b-5 in cases such as this one. Ample state remedies exist for breach of fiduciary duty actions and for appraisals. Reversed and remanded.

▶ *ANALYSIS*

In *Blue Chip Stamps v. Manor Drug Stores*, the Court also held that mere negligence is not grounds for an action under § 10(b) and Rule 10b-5. In *Ernst & Ernst v. Hochfelder*, 425 U.S. 185 (1976), the Court held that the SEC could not enact rules which conflicted with plain expressions of Congressional intent. Hence, Rule 10b-5 could not be more restrictive in nature than could actions under § 10(b) of the Securities Act of 1934.

▬▬▬

Quicknotes

FAIR MARKET VALUE The price of particular property or goods that a buyer would offer and a seller accept in the open market, following full disclosure.

FIDUCIARY DUTY A legal obligation to act for the benefit of another.

MINORITY SHAREHOLDER A stockholder in a corporation controlling such a small portion of those shares which are outstanding that its votes have no influence in the management of the corporation.

SECURITIES EXCHANGE ACT § 10(B) Makes it unlawful for any person to use manipulation or deception in the buying or selling of securities.

▬▬▬

Deutschman v. Beneficial Corp.

Stock option buyer (P) v. Corporation (D)

841 F.2d 502 (3d Cir. 1988), *cert. denied*, 490 U.S. 1114 (1989).

NATURE OF CASE: Appeal from judgment dismissing class action for damages for securities violation.

FACT SUMMARY: Deutschman (P) claimed that Beneficial Corp. (D) and its officers, Caspersen (D) and Halvorsen (D), violated § 10(b) of the Securities Exchange Act when they made knowingly false statements causing artificial inflation in the market price of options to buy Beneficial stock.

🏛 RULE OF LAW
A purchaser of options to buy stock in a corporation may state a § 10(b) claim against that corporation and its officers for affirmative misrepresentations affecting the market price of the options whether or not there is any fiduciary relationship between the purchaser and the corporation or its officers.

FACTS: Deutschman (P) alleged that Caspersen (D) and Halvorsen (D), officers of Beneficial Corp. (D), issued knowingly false and misleading statements about Beneficial (D) in an effort to prevent further decline in the market price of Beneficial (D) stock; that the statements placed an artificial floor under the market price of Beneficial stock; that he and other members of the public purchased "call options" (the right to buy the stock at a fixed price by a given date) on Beneficial (D) stock at the artificially inflated market price; and that when the true facts regarding Beneficial's problems were disclosed, the call options Deutschman (P) had purchased became worthless. But because Deutschman (P) did not claim that Beneficial (D), Caspersen (D), or Halvorson (D) traded Beneficial stock or stock options during the time period in question, or that Deutschman (P) had purchased Beneficial (D) stock, the district court dismissed for lack of standing. Deutschman (P) appealed.

ISSUE: May a purchaser of options to buy stock in a corporation state a § 10(b) claim against that corporation and its officers for affirmative misrepresentations affecting the market price of the stock when there is no fiduciary relationship between the purchaser and the corporation or its officers?

HOLDING AND DECISION: [Judge not stated in casebook excerpt.] Yes. A purchaser of options to buy stock in a corporation may state a § 10(b) claim against that corporation and its officers for affirmative misrepresentations affecting the market price of the options whether or not there is any fiduciary relationship between the purchaser and the corporation or its officers. Section 10(b) prohibits the use "in connection with the purchase or sale of any security. . . [of] any manipulative or deceptive device or contrivance in contravention of such rules and regulations as the [SEC] may prescribe." The affirmative misrepresentations pleaded by Deutschman (P) would, if proved, amount to untrue statements of material fact that would operate to deceive a purchaser of Beneficial (D) stock. The complaint alleges that the misrepresentations were made intentionally or with reckless disregard of the truth. Thus, if the allegations are true, Beneficial (D), Caspersen (D), and Halvorson (D) could be held liable to a purchaser of Beneficial (D) stock. Congress extended the same protection to purchasers of options when it amended the Securities Exchange Act of 1934 and other federal statutes. The district court erroneously relied on cases dealing with the problem of trading on undisclosed information, as opposed to injuries caused by affirmative misrepresentations, in finding the existence of a fiduciary relationship to be essential to stating a cause of action. Reversed.

▶ ANALYSIS

In addition to erroneously treating affirmative misrepresentations the same as trading on undisclosed information, it seems unusual that the trial court characterized the issue as one of "standing." The standing requirement generally deals with the question of whether a plaintiff has a concrete stake in the outcome of the litigation. The only standing limitation recognized by the Supreme Court with respect to § 10(b) damage actions is the requirement that the plaintiff be a purchaser or seller of a security, and Congress amended the 1934 Act to explicitly include option contracts within the concept of "security."

■═■

Quicknotes

FIDUCIARY DUTY A legal obligation to act for the benefit of another.

MISREPRESENTATION A statement or conduct by one party to another that constitutes a false representation of fact.

SECURITIES EXCHANGE ACT § 10(B) Makes it unlawful for any person to use manipulation or deception in the buying or selling of securities.

■═■

Goodwin v. Agassiz

Former shareholder (P) v. Corporate director (D)

283 Mass. 358, 186 N.E. 659 (1933).

NATURE OF CASE: Action for rescission of sale of stock.

FACT SUMMARY: Agassiz (D) and another, president and directors of the corporation, purchased stock of Goodwin (P) in the corporation (through a stock exchange) without disclosing inside information which turned out to be important.

RULE OF LAW
A director of a corporation may not personally seek out a stockholder for the purpose of buying his shares without disclosing material facts within his peculiar knowledge as a director and not within reach of the stockholder; but, the fiduciary obligations of directors are not so onerous as to preclude all dealing in the corporation's stock where there is no evidence of fraud.

FACTS: Agassiz (D) and another, president and directors of the Cliff Mining Co., purchased Goodwin's (P) stock in that corporation through a broker on the Boston Stock Exchange. Prior to the sale, certain corporate property had been explored for mineral deposits, unsuccessfully. The director and president, however, had knowledge of a geological theory by which they expected to discover minerals on that land. They decided not to disclose it publicly, however, so that another mining company, in which they were also stockholders, could acquire options on adjacent land. Goodwin (P) sued to force a rescission of the stock sale on the grounds that the director and president had breached their fiduciary duties by failing to disclose the geological theory, their belief in it, and its subsequent successful testing. From a dismissal of the complaint, Goodwin (P) appealed.

ISSUE: May a director of a corporation deal in the corporation's shares where his action is based upon inside knowledge?

HOLDING AND DECISION: [Judge not stated in casebook excerpt.] Yes. A director of a corporation may not personally seek out a stockholder for the purpose of buying his shares without disclosing material facts within his peculiar knowledge as a director and not within reach of the stockholder, but the fiduciary obligations of directors are not so onerous as to preclude all dealing in the corporation's stock where there is no evidence of fraud. Business must be governed by practical rules. An honest director would be in a difficult situation if he could neither buy nor sell stock in his own corporation without seeking out the other actual ultimate party to such transaction. Absent fraud, he must be permitted to deal. Here, there is no evidence of any fraud: (1) Agassiz (D) did not personally solicit Goodwin (P) to sell his stock; (2) Agassiz (D) was an experienced stock dealer who made a voluntary decision to sell; (3) at the time of sale, the undisclosed theory had not yet been proven; and, (4) had the director and president disclosed it prematurely, they would have exposed themselves to litigation if it proved to be false. The judgment below must be affirmed.

ANALYSIS

Prior to the Securities Exchange Act of 1934, this case pointed up the general standard for "insider" liability: fraud. The use of inside information by corporate officers to gain personal profit could be proscribed only if some showing of fraud could be made. Note that this is consistent with the general common law caveat emptor approach to the relationship between shareholders and management. At common law, it was held that no fiduciary relationship existed between management and shareholders, so, by caveat emptor, any trading done by either was legal unless provably fraudulent. Note, finally, that even where a common law duty was found to exist, it was always limited to direct dealings between directors and shareholders. Shareholders selling to or buying from third parties were never protected.

Quicknotes

FIDUCIARY DUTY A legal obligation to act for the benefit of another.

MATERIALITY Importance; the degree of relevance or necessity to the particular matter.

RESCISSION The canceling of an agreement and the return of the parties to their positions prior to the formation of the contract.

Securities and Exchange Commission v. Texas Gulf Sulphur Co.

Government regulatory agency (P) v. Corporation (D)

401 F.2d 833 (2d Cir.), *cert. denied sub nom. Coates v. S.E.C*, 394 U.S. 976 (1969).

NATURE OF CASE: Appeal from dismissal of Securities and Exchange Commission (SEC) enforcement action for violations of federal securities laws.

FACT SUMMARY: Texas Gulf Sulphur (TGS) (D) maintained that, because its employees were ordered not to disclose material information to the public, those employees were entitled to trade on that information prior to its dissemination to the public. TGS (D) further maintained that, because its press release was not issued in order to affect the market price of TGS's (D) stock, it could not form the basis for a violation of the federal securities laws.

> 🏛 **RULE OF LAW**
> (1) It is unlawful to trade on material inside information until such information has been disclosed to the public and has had time to become equally available to all investors.
> (2) A company press release is considered to have been issued in connection with the purchase or sale of a security for purposes of imposing liability under the federal securities laws, and liability will flow if a reasonable investor, in the exercise of due care, would have been misled by it.

FACTS: Gulf TGS (D) discovered a potentially promising ore site. TGS (D) employees were ordered to keep information regarding the site secret so that TGS (D) could continue testing and could purchase surrounding land at a price beneficial to TGS (D). While not disclosing the information to the public, numerous TGS (D) employees bought TGS (D) stock and call options, anticipating an increase in the price of TGS's (D) stock. After rumors of the strike hit the press, TGS (D) issued a press release denying any significant discoveries. Several days later, TGS (D) confirmed the discovery of a vast mineral strike, sending TGS's (D) stock soaring. The SEC (P) brought an action against several of TGS's employees (D) for insider trading and against TGS (D) for dissemination of a misleading press release. The trial court ruled in favor of TGS (D) and its employees (D). The SEC (P) appealed.

ISSUE:
(1) Is it unlawful to trade on material inside information until such information has been disclosed to the public and has had time to become equally available to all investors?
(2) Is a company press release considered to have been issued in connection with the purchase or sale of a security for purposes of imposing liability under the federal securities laws and will liability flow therefrom

if a reasonable investor, in the exercise of due care, would have been misled by it?

HOLDING AND DECISION: [Judge not stated in casebook excerpt.]
(1) Yes. It is unlawful to trade on material inside information until such information has been disclosed to the public and has had time to become equally available to all investors. Rule 10b-5 is based on the justifiable expectation of the securities marketplace that all investors have equal access to material information. Anyone in possession of material nonpublic information cannot properly trade on that information, even if he is forbidden by the company from disclosing it to the public, until it has been publicly disseminated. In this case, all transactions in TGS (D) stock or calls by those employees (D) apprised of the exploratory drilling results were made in violation of Rule 10b-5. Reversed.
(2) Yes. A company press release is considered to have been issued in connection with the purchase or sale of a security for purposes of imposing liability under the federal securities laws, and liability will flow therefrom if a reasonable investor, in the exercise of due care, would have been misled by it. The purchase or sale requirement under § 10(b) of the Securities Exchange Act requires merely that the deceptive device employed be likely to cause a reasonable investor, exercising due care, to have been misled. TGS's (D) press release could satisfy this test, although the lower court did not properly apply this standard to the facts before it. Reversed in part. Remanded.

▶ **ANALYSIS**

The purchase or sale requirement of § 10(b) operates to limit those who can recover under that section to actual purchasers or sellers of a company's securities. However, consider the case of persons who choose not to purchase or sell a company's stock because of misrepresentations or omissions of material information. These persons are no less injured as a result of the offending conduct. They will not, however, have private cause of action against the corporation under § 10(b) and Rule 10b-5. See *Blue Chip Stamps v. Manor Drug Stores*, 421 U.S. 723 (1975).

■■■

Quicknotes

RULE 10B-5 Unlawful to defend or make untrue statements in connection with purchase or sale of securities.

■■■

Dirks v. Securities and Exchange Commission

Broker (D) v. Government regulatory agency (P)

463 U.S. 646 (1983).

NATURE OF CASE: SEC action for violation of § 10(b).

FACT SUMMARY: Dirks (D), based on some non-public information he received and a subsequent investigation, aided the Securities and Exchange Commission (SEC) (P) in convicting Equity Funding of America for corporate fraud and was then sued by the SEC (P) for violating § 10(b) because he openly disclosed the nonpublic information to investors.

RULE OF LAW
A tippee will be held liable for openly disclosing nonpublic information received from an insider, if the tippee knows or should know that the insider will benefit in some fashion from disclosing the information to the tippee.

FACTS: Dirks (D), officer of a brokerage firm, was told by Secrist, the insider, Equity Funding of America (EFA) was engaging in corporate fraud. Dirks (D) then investigated EFA to verify Secrist's information. Neither Dirks (D) nor his firm owned or traded EFA stock. However, during Dirks' (D) investigation, he openly revealed the information to investors and caused many of them to sell their EFA stock. Consequently, the price of EFA stock dropped from $26 to $15. However, largely due to Dirks' (D) investigation, the SEC (P) was able to convict the officers of EFA for corporate fraud. Still, the SEC (P) sued and reprimanded Dirks (D) for his disclosure of the nonpublic information to the investors. The court of appeals affirmed. Dirks (D) next requested and subsequently granted certiorari by the U.S. Supreme Court.

ISSUE: Will a tippee automatically be liable for openly disclosing nonpublic information received from an insider?

HOLDING AND DECISION: (Powell, J.) No. A tippee will be held liable for openly disclosing nonpublic information received from an insider if the tippee knows or should know that the insider will benefit in some fashion for disclosing the information to the tippee. Mere receipt for nonpublic information by a tippee from an insider does not automatically carry with it the fiduciary duty of an insider. In this case, Secrist, the insider, did not receive a benefit for his disclosure. He disclosed the information to Dirks (D), the tippee, solely to help expose the fraud being perpetrated by the officers of EFA. Therefore, since Secrist, the insider, did not receive a benefit for his disclosure of nonpublic information to Dirks (D), the tippee, Secrist did not breach his fiduciary duty to the shareholders. Consequently, since Secrist, the insider, did not breach his duty to the shareholders, there was no derivative breach by Dirks (D) when he passed on the nonpublic information to investors. Reversed.

ANALYSIS

This case is consistent with the Court's decision in *Chiarella v. United States* (445 U.S. 222 [1980]), where the Court found that there is no general duty to disclose before trading on material nonpublic information and held that a duty to disclose under § 10(b) does not arise from mere possession of nonpublic market information. Rather, such a duty, the Court found, arises from the existence of a fiduciary relationship.

Quicknotes

FIDUCIARY DUTY A legal obligation to act for the benefit of another.

FRAUD A false representation of facts with the intent that another will rely on the misrepresentation to his detriment.

RULE 10B-5 It is unlawful to defend or make untrue statements in connection with purchase or sale of securities.

SECURITIES EXCHANGE ACT § 10(B) Makes it unlawful for any person to use manipulation or deception in the buying or selling of securities.

United States v. O'Hagan

Federal government (P) v. Lawyer (D)

521 U.S. 642 (1997).

NATURE OF CASE: Writ of certiori reviewing reversal of convictions for mail and securities fraud, fraudulent trading, and money laundering.

FACT SUMMARY: O'Hagan (D), an attorney, was indicted for trading securities in Pillsbury based on confidential information he obtained by virtue of his association with the corporation's law firm.

RULE OF LAW
(1) When a person misappropriates confidential information in violation of a fiduciary duty, and trades on that information for his own personal benefit, he is in violation of § 10(b) of the Securities Exchange Act of 1934 and Rule 10b-5.
(2) The Securities and Exchange Commission (SEC) did not exceed its rulemaking authority by promulgating Rule 14e-3(a), which prohibits trading on undisclosed information in a tender offer situation, even where the person has no fiduciary duty to disclose the information.

FACTS: Dorsey & Whitney, a law firm, was retained by Grand Metropolitan PLC (Grand Met) as counsel in a proposed tender offer for the stock of Pillsbury. O'Hagan (D), a partner in Dorsey & Whitney, was not assigned to the case. However, during the course of the representation, O'Hagan (D) purchased a total of 2,500 Pillsbury call options and 5,000 shares of common stock. Following the announcement of the tender offer, he sold his interests, at a profit of more than $4.3 million. The SEC (P) commenced an investigation of O'Hagan (D), and indicted him on fifty-seven counts of mail and securities fraud, fraudulent trading, and money laundering. He was convicted on all fifty-seven counts and sentenced to forty-one months of imprisonment. The Eighth Circuit Court of Appeals reversed all of the convictions on the basis that Rule 10b-5 liability may not be based on a misappropriation theory. Furthermore, the court held that SEC Rule 14e-3(a) was beyond the scope of the SEC's (P) rulemaking power. As a result, none of the convictions could stand since they were based on the underlying securities fraud violations. The Supreme Court granted certiori to determine the propriety of the misappropriation theory, and the authority of the SEC (P) to promulgate Rule 14e-3(a).

ISSUE:
(1) When a person misappropriates confidential information in violation of a fiduciary duty, and trades on that information for his own personal benefit, is he in violation

of § 10(b) of the Securities Exchange Act of 1934 and Rule 10b-5?
(2) Did the SEC exceed its rulemaking authority by promulgating Rule 14e-3(a), which prohibits trading on nondisclosed information in a tender offer situation, even where the person has no fiduciary duty to disclose the information?

HOLDING AND DECISION: [Judge not stated in casebook excerpt.]

(1) Yes. When a person misappropriates confidential information in violation of a fiduciary duty, and trades on that information for his own personal benefit, he is in violation of § 10(b) of the Securities Exchange Act of 1934 and Rule 10b-5. Section 10(b) prohibits the use of any deceptive device in conjunction with the purchase or sale of securities. The "traditional" theory holds an insider liable for trading in securities of his corporation based on relevant, nonpublic information. Such trading satisfies the requirement of deception due to the relationship of trust and confidence reposed in the insider by virtue of his position. Such entrustment requires the insider to disclose or abstain from trading in the securities of the corporation in order to protect unsuspecting shareholders. This duty applies to officers and directors, as well as to anyone else who acts in a fiduciary capacity towards the corporation, including attorneys, accountants, and consultants. In contrast, the "misappropriation" theory holds a person liable for the misappropriation of material, nonpublic information for the purpose of trading thereon, in breach of a fiduciary duty due to the provider of the information. The misappropriation theory extends liability to include corporate outsiders who owe no duty to the shareholders of the corporation, but who nonetheless have access to the confidential information by virtue of their fiduciary position. Here, O'Hagan (D) did not owe a duty to the shareholders of Pillsbury since he was not an attorney involved in the case. However, O'Hagan (D) owed a fiduciary duty to his law firm, Dorsey & Whitney, to refrain from trading on the basis of material, nonpublic information he may have acquired by virtue of his position in the firm.
(2) No. The SEC (P) did not exceed its rulemaking authority in promulgating Rule 14e-3(a), which prohibits trading on undisclosed information in a tender offer situation, even where the person has no fiduciary

Continued on next page.

duty to disclose the information. Under § 14(e) of the Securities Exchange Act, the SEC (P) is granted the authority to pass such rules and regulations as are necessary to prevent the commission of fraud or deception in connection with the sale of securities. The rationale supporting the rule is the protection of uninformed shareholders involved in a potential tender offer situation. The rule imposes a duty on the trader to disclose the confidential information, or abstain from trading on it. This rule is consistent with the legislative goal of proscribing fraudulent or deceptive acts in the purchase or sale of securities. In reviewing the propriety of SEC (P) regulations, the Court must give great deference to the SEC's (P) judgment absent a patently contrary intent. Reversed.

▶ *ANALYSIS*

The validity of the misappropriation theory turned on whether it satisfied the requirement of a "deceptive device" under § 10(b). The Court holds that a misappropriator of confidential information necessarily effectuates a deception on the source of that information through his non-disclosure of his intent to trade on it. Such deception involves illusory loyalty to the company that has the exclusive right to use of the information, and is equivalent to an act of embezzlement.

■▬■

Quicknotes

EMBEZZLEMENT The fraudulent appropriation of property lawfully in one's possession.

FIDUCIARY DUTY A legal obligation to act for the benefit of another, including subordinating one's personal interests to that of the other person.

MISAPPROPRIATION The unlawful use of another's property or funds.

RULE 10B-5 It is unlawful to defend or make untrue statements in connection with purchase or sale of securities.

RULE 14E-3(A) Makes it unlawful to make false statements in connection with tender offers.

TENDER OFFER An offer made by one corporation to the shareholders of a target corporation to purchase their shares subject to number, time, and price specifications.

■▬■

Reliance Electric Co. v. Emerson Electric Co.

Corporation (D) v. Corporate shareholder (P)

404 U.S. 418, *rehearing denied*, 405 U.S. 969 (1972).

NATURE OF CASE: Discretionary review of reversal of declaratory judgment finding liability for damages under § 16(b) of the Securities Exchange Act of 1934.

FACT SUMMARY: Reliance Electric Co. (D) argued that since Emerson Electric Co. (P) intentionally disposed of its stock in two separate sales in an effort to avoid liability under § 16(b) as to the bulk of its short-swing profits, the two sales should be treated as one.

> 🏛 **RULE OF LAW**
> When a holder of more than 10% of the stock in a corporation sells enough shares to reduce its holdings to less than 10%, and then sells the balance of its shares to another buyer within six months of its original purchase, it is not liable to the corporation for the profit it made on the second sale.

FACTS: On June 16, 1967, Emerson (P) acquired 13.2% of the outstanding common stock of Dodge Manufacturing Co. pursuant to a tender offer it made in an unsuccessful attempt to take over Dodge. Shortly thereafter, Dodge merged with Reliance (D). Emerson (P), desiring to dispose of its Dodge stock, decided to first sell enough shares to bring its holdings below 10%, thereby immunizing the sale of the remainder of its shares from liability under § 16(b). On August 28, Emerson (P) sold to a brokerage house enough of its stock in Dodge to reduce its holdings to 9.96%. The remaining shares were then sold to Dodge on September 11. Reliance (D) then demanded from Emerson (P) all the profits Emerson (P) made on both sales. Emerson (P) then filed an action for a declaratory judgment as to its liability under § 16(b). The trial court held Emerson (P) was liable for the profits from both sales. The court of appeals reversed as to the profits from the second sale. The Supreme Court granted certiorari.

ISSUE: If a holder of more than 10% of the stock in a corporation sells enough shares to reduce its holdings to less than 10%, and then sells the balance to another buyer within six months after its acquisition of the stock, is it liable to the corporation for the profit it made on the second sale?

HOLDING AND DECISION: [Judge not stated in casebook excerpt.] No. When a holder of more than 10% of the stock in a corporation sells enough shares to reduce its holdings to less than 10%, and then sells the balance of its shares to another buyer within six months of its original purchase, it is not liable to the corporation for the profit it made on the second sale. In enacting § 16(b), Congress chose a relatively arbitrary rule, capable of easy administration, in an effort to take the profits out of a class of transactions in which the possibility of abuse was believed to be intolerably great. Section 16(b) imposes strict liability, regardless of the intent of the insider; and yet Congress did not reach every transaction in which an investor actually relies on inside information. A person avoids liability if he does not meet the statute's definition of "insider," or if he sells more than six months after purchase. Section 16(b) clearly states that a 10% owner must be such "both at the time of the purchase and sale . . . of the security involved." This language clearly contemplates that a person might sell enough shares to bring his holdings below 10%, and later, but still within six months, sell additional shares free from liability under the statute. In fact, commentators on the securities laws have recommended this exact procedure for a 10% owner who wishes to dispose of his holdings within six months of purchase. Affirmed.

▶ *ANALYSIS*

Note that under *Foremost-McKesson, Inc. v. Provident Securities Co.*, 423 U.S. 232 (1976), a purchaser who becomes a 10% owner only by virtue of the purchase is not subject to § 16(b). Thus Emerson (P) would not have been liable for the profit on either sale had its purchase of the stock taken place after the decision in *Foremost-McKesson*.

■=■

Quicknotes

COMMON STOCK A class of stock representing the corporation's ownership, the holders of which are entitled to dividends only after the holders of preferred stock are paid.

DECLARATORY JUDGMENT An adjudication by the courts which grants not relief but is binding over the legal status of the parties involved in the dispute.

SECURITIES EXCHANGE ACT § 16(B) Provides that corporations may recover profits realized by an owner of more than 10% of shares when that owner buys and sells stock within a 6-month period.

STRICT LIABILITY Liability for all injuries proximately caused by a party's conducting of certain inherently dangerous activities without regard to negligence or fault.

■=■

Foremost-McKesson, Inc. v. Provident Securities Company

Acquiring company (D) v. Purchased company (P)

423 U.S. 232 (1976).

NATURE OF CASE: Appeal from suit for a declaration of liability under Section 16 of the Securities and Exchange Act of 1934.

FACT SUMMARY: Provident (P) brought suit seeking a declaration that it was not liable to Foremost (D) under Section 16(b) of the Securities and Exchange Act of 1934 for any profits it realized on the sale of a $25 million debenture to underwriters.

🏛 RULE OF LAW
In a purchase-sale sequence, a beneficial owner must account for profits only if he was a beneficial owner before the purchase.

FACTS: Provident (P), a personal holding company, decided to liquidate and dissolve. Foremost (D) was a potential purchaser, but the parties disagreed as to the form of consideration to be paid. The parties reached a compromise and executed a purchase agreement, providing that Foremost (D) would buy two-thirds of Provident's (P) assets for $4.25 million in cash and $49.75 million in convertible subordinated debentures. The agreement also provided Foremost (D) would register $25 million and participate in an underwriting agreement by which the debentures would be sold to the public. Provident (P), Foremost (D) and a group of underwriters executed an underwriting agreement on October 28, after which Provident (P) distributed the cash proceeds to its stockholders and dissolved. Provident's (P) holdings in Foremost (D) debentures on October 20 were large enough to make it a beneficial owner of Foremost (D) within the meaning of section 16. Thus, Foremost (D) could potentially sue Provident (P) to recover any profits realized on the sale of the $25 million debenture to the underwriters under the statute. Provident (P) sued for a declaration that it would not be liable to Foremost (D) under Section 16(b). The district court granted summary judgment for Provident (P) and the court of appeals affirmed. Foremost (D) appealed.

ISSUE: In a purchase-sale sequence, must a beneficial owner account for profits only if he was a beneficial owner before the purchase?

HOLDING AND DECISION: [Judge not stated in casebook excerpt.] Yes. In a purchase-sale sequence, a beneficial owner must account for profits only if he was a beneficial owner before the purchase. Section 16(b) of the Securities and Exchange Act of 1934 does not require that a person purchasing securities placing his holdings above the 10% level is a beneficial owner at the time of the purchase so that he must account for his profits realized on the same of those securities within six months. Section 16(b) was intended to prevent corporate officers and directors or the beneficial owner of more than 10% of a corporation from profiteering through short-swing securities transactions due to inside information. The section allows a corporation to retain profits realized on a purchase and sale, or sale and purchase, of its securities within six months of a director, officer or beneficial owner. The last sentence, however, provides that the provision should "not be construed to cover any transaction where such beneficial owner was not such, both at the time of the purchase and sale, or the sale and purchase, of the security involved." Jurisdictions are divided as to whether the "time of sale" means before or immediately after the purchase. The legislative record indicates that this provision was intended to preserve the requirement of beneficial ownership before the purchase. Affirmed.

▶ ANALYSIS

The Court noted that its holding was also confirmed by the legislature's differentiation between short-term trading by shareholders and trading by corporate officers and directors. In the latter case, such trading has greater potential for abuse due to the officers' and directors' extensive involvement in the corporation. Such abuse by shareholders was only in issue when the extent of their holdings permitted them access to insider information. This was not a risk in a situation in which the purchase was made prior to achieving insider status.

■=■

Quicknotes

DEBENTURES Long-term unsecured debt securities issued by a corporation.

SECURITIES EXCHANGE ACT § 16(B) Provides that corporations may recover profits realized by an owner of more than 10% of shares when that owner buys and sells stock within a 6-month period.

■=■

Waltuch v. Conticommodity Services, Inc.

Officer (P) v. Corporation (D)

88 F.3d 87 (2d Cir. 1996).

NATURE OF CASE: Appeal from denial of indemnity claims.

FACT SUMMARY: Waltuch (P) sought indemnification of his legal expenses from his former employer, Conticommodity Services, Inc. (D) (Conti), after lawsuits against him were dismissed.

🏛 RULE OF LAW
A corporate director or officer, who has been successful on the merits or otherwise vindicated from the claims asserted against him, is entitled to indemnification from the corporation against reasonably incurred legal expenses.

FACTS: Waltuch (P), chief metals trader and vice president of Conti (D), traded silver for the firm's clients, as well as for his own account. When the silver market collapsed, he became the subject of numerous lawsuits alleging fraud, market manipulation, and antitrust violations. All of the lawsuits were eventually settled, and Waltuch (P) was dismissed from the suits with no settlement contribution imposed. His unreimbursed legal expenses in these actions totaled approximately $1.2 million. Waltuch (P) sued Conti (D), claiming that Article Ninth of Conti's (D) Articles of Incorporation requires Conti (D) to indemnify him in both the private and Commodity Futures Trading Commission actions. Conti (D) alleged that this claim was barred by § 145(a) of Delaware's General Corporation Law, which permits indemnification only if the corporate officer acted in good faith. The district court ruled that Waltuch (P) could recover only if he met the good faith requirement of the Delaware statute. The parties stipulated that they would forego trial on the issue of Waltuch's (P) good faith and allow Waltuch (P) to take an immediate appeal of the judgment to this court. Waltuch's (P) second claim required Conti (D) to indemnify him under Delaware's General Corporation Law because he was successful on the merits or otherwise in the private lawsuits. The district court ruled for Conti (D) on this issue as well, reasoning that Waltuch (P) was not successful on the merits or otherwise because Conti's (D) settlement payments to the plaintiffs were partially on Waltuch's (P) behalf. Waltuch (P) appealed.

ISSUE: Is a corporate director or officer who has been successful on the merits or otherwise vindicated from the claims assessed against him and may he be entitled to indemnification from the corporation against expenses reasonably incurred?

HOLDING AND DECISION: [Judge not stated in casebook excerpt.] Yes. A corporate director or officer who has been successful on the merits or otherwise vindicated from the claims asserted against him is entitled to indemnification from the corporation against expenses reasonably incurred. Success is vindication. Going behind the result is not consistent with the statute or with the presumption of innocence. If a suit has been dismissed, a party has been successful, whether or not the victory was deserved in terms of merits. A technical defense is deemed vindication under Delaware law. Waltuch (P) emerged unscathed, and such success is vindication enough. Waltuch (P) was therefore successful on the merits or otherwise in the private lawsuits because they were dismissed against him with prejudice without any payment or assumption of liability by him. The district court's holding that there was no vindication here is reversed, and Conti (D) must indemnify Waltuch (P) for the $1.2 million in unreimbursed legal fees he spent. In contrast, Conti's Article Ninth assertion, which would require indemnification of Waltuch (P) even if he acted in bad faith, is inconsistent with Delaware's General Corporation Law. Since Waltuch (P) has agreed to forego his opportunity to prove at trial that he acted in good faith, he is not entitled to indemnification under that provision. The district court's decision on that issue is affirmed.

▶ ANALYSIS

Indemnification rights provided by contract cannot exceed the scope of a corporation's indemnification powers as set out by statute. Although indemnification rights may be broader than those set out in the statute, they cannot be inconsistent with the scope of the statute. Delaware case law suggests a consistency rule which was reinforced by the court's reading of the state statute as well.

■=■

Quicknotes

GOOD FAITH An honest intention to abstain from any unconscientious advantage of another.

INDEMNIFICATION Reimbursement for losses sustained or security against anticipated loss or damages.

■=■

Citadel Holding Corporation v. Roven

Corporation (D) v. Former director (P)

603 A.2d 818 (Del. 1992).

NATURE OF CASE: Appeal from award of damages for reimbursement of litigation expenses.

FACT SUMMARY: Roven (P) sought to have Citadel (D) reimburse him for legal expenses he incurred defending a securities action filed against him by Citadel (D).

🏛 RULE OF LAW
A corporation may advance reasonable costs in defending a suit to a director even when the suit is brought by the corporation.

FACTS: Roven (P) was a director of Citadel (D) from July, 1985, to July, 1988. Roven (P) owned over 9% of Citadel's (D) common stock for most of that time. Roven (P) and Citadel (D) entered into an indemnity agreement in May, 1987. In an effort to keep Roven (P) as a director, Citadel (D) agreed to provide Roven (P) with more protection than was provided by Citadel's (D) Certificate of Incorporation, Bylaws, and Insurance. The resulting indemnification agreement promised to indemnify Roven (P) for expenses and liabilities incurred while serving Citadel (D). There was, however, an exception for expenses or liabilities incurred due to profits made by Roven (P) from the purchase or sale of Citadel (D) securities falling under § 16(b) of the Securities Exchange Act of 1934. The indemnification agreement also promised to advance Roven (P) costs in defending lawsuits or investigations. Roven (P) subsequently sought to have costs advanced when Citadel (D) brought suit against Roven (P) in federal court for violations of § 16(b) after Roven (P) purchased options to buy Citadel (D) stock while still a director. Citadel (D) argued that the advancement provision was not intended to cover the federal action brought by Citadel (D) against Roven (P). Citadel (D) also argued that the suit brought against Roven (P) was exempted under the § 16(b) exception to the indemnity agreement. The superior court disagreed and found in favor of Roven (P). Citadel (D) appealed.

ISSUE: May a corporation advance reasonable costs of defending a suit to a director even when the suit is brought by the corporation?

HOLDING AND DECISION: [Judge not stated in casebook excerpt.] Yes. A corporation may advance reasonable costs of defending a suit to a director even when the suit is brought by the corporation. Reasonable expenses are expenses related to the corporation's business. In this case, the intent of the indemnification agreement was to provide Roven (P) with more protection than before. Under the General Corporation Law of Delaware, a corporation may advance such costs to a director. Moreover, the indemnification agreement between Roven (P) and Citadel (D) made this advancement mandatory. Since these proceedings are related to proceedings that deal with Citadel's (D) business, they are reasonable. Affirmed with prejudgment and post-judgment-interest awarded to Roven (P).

▶ ANALYSIS

Corporations often enter into indemnification agreements in an effort to recruit key employees or retain them as in the case of Roven (P). These agreements, however, are criticized by some as leading to irresponsible actions by the employees. This is because the employee would not really be personally liable for anything except intentional misconduct.

Quicknotes

8 DEL. C. § 145(E) Expressly allows corporations to advance the costs of defending a suit to a director.

COMMON STOCK A class of stock representing the corporation's ownership, the holders of which are entitled to dividends only after the holders of preferred stock are paid.

INDEMNIFICATION The payment by a corporation of expenses incurred by its officers or directors as a result of litigation involving the corporation.

Problems of Control

Quick Reference Rules of Law

Levin v. Metro-Goldwyn-Mayer, Inc.

Stockholders (P) v. Movie company (D)

264 F. Supp. 797 (S.D.N.Y. 1967).

NATURE OF CASE: Motion for temporary and permanent injunctive relief and derivative suit for damages for illegal solicitation of proxies.

FACT SUMMARY: Levin (P) and stockholders (P) owning 11% of common stock of Metro-Goldwyn-Mayer, Inc. (D) brought suit against MGM (D) and five of its board of directors (D) for using corporate funds to pay for special attorneys, a public relations firm, and a proxy solicitation organization in a proxy solicitation contest between the Levin group (P) and the O'Brien group (D).

> 🏛 **RULE OF LAW**
> Incumbent directors may use corporate funds and resources in a proxy solicitation contest if the sums are not excessive and the shareholders are fully informed.

FACTS: An annual stockholder meeting of MGM (D) was to take place on February 23, 1967. At this meeting both the O'Brien group (D)—five members of present management—and the Levin group (P)—stockholders owning 11% of the common stock of MGM (D)—sought to nominate a set of directors. The Levin Group (P) charged that MGM (D) and the O'Brien group (D) had wrongfully used corporate funds to pay for special attorneys, a public relations firm, and a proxy solicitation organization in this proxy solicitation contest. The Levin group (P) also charged that the O'Brien group (D) and MGM (D) had improperly used offices and employees in this fight. The Levin group (P) sued for temporary and permanent injunctive relief to stop the O'Brien group's (D) method of soliciting proxies and to prevent the O'Brien group (D) from voting these proxies. The Levin group (P) also sought, on behalf of MGM (D), $2.5 million from the individual defendants.

ISSUE: May incumbent directors use corporate funds and resources in a proxy solicitation contest if the sums are not excessive and the shareholders are fully informed?

HOLDING AND DECISION: [Judge not stated in casebook excerpt.] Yes. Incumbent directors may use corporate funds and resources in a proxy solicitation contest if the sums are not excessive and the shareholders are fully informed. The proxy statement filed by MGM (D) on January 6, 1967, stated that MGM (D) would bear all of the costs incurred in the solicitation of the proxies. The statement also disclosed that Georgeson and Co. was retained for $15,000 and Kissel-Blake Organization, Inc. was retained for $5,000. It also disclosed that an estimated $125,000 would be spent, excluding amounts that would normally be spent on solicitation of proxies and costs for salaries and wages of employees and officers. The proxy statement fully disclosed this situation to stockholders. The sums were not found excessive under the circumstances. Motion for injunction denied.

▶ **ANALYSIS**

This decision reflects the concerns of the court in *Rosenfeld v. Fairchild Engine & Airplane Corp.*, 128 N.E.2d 291 (1955). In *Rosenfeld*, the court was concerned about a corporation being left at the mercy of insurgent groups with enough money to take on a proxy fight. By allowing incumbent directors to reasonably use corporate funds and resources, the incumbent directors are better able to defend corporate positions and policies.

■=■

Quicknotes

INJUNCTIVE RELIEF A court order issued as a remedy, requiring a person to do, or prohibiting that person from doing, a specific act.

PROXY A person authorized to act for another.

■=■

Rosenfeld v. Fairchild Engine & Airplane Corp.

Shareholder (P) v. Corporation (D)

309 N.Y. 168, 128 N.E.2d 291 (1955).

NATURE OF CASE: Appeal from dismissal of a shareholder's derivative suit.

FACT SUMMARY: Rosenfeld (P) brought a derivative suit to have the $261,522 that had been paid to both sides of a proxy contest returned to the corporation (D).

🏛 RULE OF LAW
In a contest over policy, corporate directors have the right to make reasonable and proper expenditures from the corporate treasury for the purpose of persuading the stockholders of the correctness of their position and soliciting their support for policies that the directors believe, in all good faith, are in the best interests of the corporation.

FACTS: $261,522 was paid out of Fairchild Engine & Airplane Corp.'s (D) corporate treasury to reimburse both sides in a proxy contest. Of the $261,522 at issue, $106,000 of corporate funds was spent by the old board of directors in defense of their positions in the proxy contest. The new board paid $28,000 to the old board for the remaining expenses incurred after the proxy contest was over. The new board found this to be fair and reasonable. The new board was paid expenses in the proxy contest. This was ratified by stockholders. Stockholder Rosenfeld (P) admitted the sums were reasonable. Rosenfeld (P), however, argued that they were not legal charges that could be reimbursed and sued to compel the return of the $261,522. The appellate division affirmed the judgment of an official referee, who had dismissed Rosenfeld's (P) complaint, having concluded that this was a contest over corporate policy. Rosenfeld (P) appealed.

ISSUE: In a contest over policy, do directors have a right to make reasonable and proper expenditures from the corporate treasury for the purpose of persuading the stockholders of the correctness of their position and soliciting their support for policies that the directors believe, in all good faith, are in the best interests of the corporation?

HOLDING AND DECISION: (Froessel, J.) Yes. In a contest over policy, directors have a right to make reasonable and proper expenditures from the corporate treasury for the purpose of persuading the stockholders of the correctness of their position and soliciting their support for policies that the directors believe, in all good faith, are in the best interests of the corporation. If not, incumbent directors would be unable to defend their positions and corporate policies. As such, the old board was reimbursed for reasonable and proper expenditures in defending their positions. Stockholders also have the right to reimburse successful contestants for their reasonable expenses. As such, the new board was also reimbursed for its expenditures by the stockholders. Dismissal affirmed.

DISSENT: (Van Voorhis, J.) Incumbent directors have the burden of going forward with evidence explaining and justifying their expenditures. Only those reasonably related to fully informing stockholders of corporate affairs should have been allowed, however, personal expenses were also allowed.

▶ ANALYSIS

This case represents the popularity of proxy contests in the 1950's. One of the advantages of proxy contests is that they are considered to be cheaper than tender offers where a bidder offers to buy voting shares at a particular price. Another advantage is that insurgent groups may be reimbursed for their expenses, as in this case. Lastly, proxy contests are often considered successful in contests alleging incompetence.

■═■

Quicknotes

PROXY A person authorized to act for another.

SHAREHOLDER'S DERIVATIVE ACTION Action asserted by a shareholder in order to enforce a cause of action on behalf of the corporation.

■═■

J.I. Case Co. v. Borak

Corporation (D) v. Shareholder (P)

377 U.S. 426 (1964).

NATURE OF CASE: Civil action brought by a shareholder against the corporation for violation of prohibitions against false and misleading proxy statements.

FACT SUMMARY: Borak (P) was a shareholder of J.I. Case Co. (D). The shareholders approved a merger with another corporation, and Borak (P) contended the proxy statements violated federal securities laws and sought private relief.

🏛 RULE OF LAW
Where a federal securities act has been violated, but no private right of action is specifically authorized or prohibited, a private civil action will lie and the court is free to fashion an appropriate remedy.

FACTS: The management of J.I. Case Co. (D) submitted a proposal of merger to the shareholders for their approval. In connection with this proposal, management solicited shareholder proxies in support of the merger. Borak (P) contended that the proxy solicitations were false and misleading in violation of § 14(a) of the Securities Exchange Act, and he sought rescission of the consummated merger plus damages for himself and all other shareholders similarly situated and any other appropriate equitable relief. The trial court held that the federal statute authorized only declaratory relief, and any other remedies would have to be sought under state law. The applicable Wisconsin statute required the posting of security for expenses which was set at $75,000 by the court. Borak (P) refused to post security, and all counts of the complaint were dismissed save the portion which would result in a judgment of declaratory relief. Borak (P) appealed, contending that the Securities Exchange Act authorized a private right of action by implication and that he was not limited to the state courts for other than declaratory relief.

ISSUE: May a shareholder seek rescission of a merger or damages for a violation of a federal regulation relating to proxy statements where no private right of action is specifically authorized nor private remedies specified?

HOLDING AND DECISION: [Judge not stated in casebook excerpt.] Yes. The purpose of § 14(a) is to prevent management or others from obtaining authorization for corporate action through the use of false or misleading proxy solicitations. The Act under which the rule was promulgated authorized the Securities and Exchange Commission (SEC) to enact whatever rules and regulations are deemed necessary to protect both the public interest and interests of shareholders. The congressional mandate to protect the interests of the investors requires an available judicial remedy to enforce that protection. The

SEC states that it is not equipped to probe the accuracy of all proxy statements submitted for registration. If the investors' interests are to be protected in the spirit of the congressional mandate, a private right of action for shareholders who believe they have been wronged must be afforded. Since the statute does not provide for specific types of relief, the court must determine for itself what remedies are appropriate to redress the alleged wrong. In this regard, any remedy which is available to a federal court can be utilized to provide relief for the plaintiff. To hold that the plaintiff is restricted to declaratory relief in federal courts, with any other relief to be pursued in a state court, could conceivably leave the plaintiff without an effective remedy. Once having obtained the federal declaration of his rights, the plaintiff might find that the state does not recognize the defendant's actions as unlawful. This would leave the plaintiff without a means to enforce his judicially declared rights. The case is remanded to the trial court for a hearing on the merits with relief to be granted abiding the outcome. Affirmed.

▶ ANALYSIS

By completely removing state law from consideration in cases alleging violations of federal securities laws, the court relieved plaintiffs of a tremendous burden in many instances. A large number of jurisdictions have a requirement that the plaintiff post a security for expenses on behalf of the defendant. The posting of such security can be an onerous burden, particularly if the case involves complex issues that would result in prolonged litigation. Had Borak (P) been required to proceed under state law, he would have had to post $75,000. This type of burden might very well stop the plaintiff from proceeding with his case, no matter how meritorious. Further, the court's ruling greatly expands the remedies available to a plaintiff shareholder. Most state statutes limit a shareholder who dissents from a merger to a right of appraisal for his shares. The federal court could conceivably rescind the merger completely if that action was warranted. This decision greatly expanded the effectiveness of the federal securities regulations by providing a broad range of enforcement techniques.

■═■

Quicknotes

SECURITIES EXCHANGE ACT, § 14 (a) Prevents management from obtaining illegal proxies.

■═■

Mills v. Electric Auto-Lite Co.

Shareholder (P) v. Corporation (D)

396 U.S. 375 (1970).

NATURE OF CASE: Derivative suit and class action to set aside a merger.

FACT SUMMARY: Mills (P) brought a derivative suit and class action against the management of Auto-Lite (D) and other companies to set aside a merger obtained through allegedly misleading proxy solicitations.

RULE OF LAW

Where a trial court makes a finding that a proxy solicitation contains a materially false or misleading statement under § 14(a) of the Securities Exchange Act of 1934, a stockholder seeking to establish a cause of action under such finding does not have to further prove that his reliance on the contents of the defects in the proxy solicitation caused him to vote for proposed transactions that later proved unfair to his interests in the corporation.

FACTS: In 1963, Electric Auto-Lite Co. (D) sought merger with Mergenthaler Linotype Co. The day before shareholders were to vote on the merger, Mills (P) and other shareholders (P) of Auto-Lite (D) sought an injunction against Auto-Lite's (D) management to stop them from voting proxies obtained by means of an allegedly misleading proxy solicitation. The suit also named American Manufacturing Co., which owned about one-third of Mergenthaler's shares and had voting control of Mergenthaler. Mergenthaler owned about 50% of Auto-Lite's (D) common stock and had control of that company. But, since Mills (P) failed to seek a temporary restraining order, the voting on the merger proceeded and the merger was approved. Subsequently, Mills (P) amended his complaint, seeking to set aside the merger and to obtain other relief. The district court found that a two-thirds vote of Auto-Lite's (D) shares was required to approve the merger. Since Mergenthaler and American Manufacturing controlled about 54% of Auto-Lite's (D) shares, it was necessary to gain the approval of a substantial minority shareholder vote. At the stockholder's meeting, about 950,000 of 1,160,000 shares were voted in favor of the merger; 317,000 of these votes were obtained by the allegedly misleading proxy solicitation from minority shareholders. The district court found these votes necessary and indispensable to the approval of the merger, and granted an interlocutory judgment in favor of Mills (P) on grounds that a causal relationship had been shown between the solicitation and the injury. An interlocutory appeal was taken to the court of appeals. The court of appeals affirmed the district court's conclusion that the proxy statement was materially misleading, but reversed on the causation issue, holding that Mills (P) must further show that there was a causal

connection between the injury suffered by Auto-Lite (D) stockholders (P) and the misleading proxy solicitations. They held that the causation issue should be determined on the fairness of the terms of the merger. Mills (P) appealed from this reversal.

ISSUE: Where a trial court finds that a proxy solicitation contains materially false or misleading statements in violation of § 14(a), does a shareholder, in seeking to establish a cause of action for injury from such act, have to further prove that he relied on the contents of the defects in the proxy solicitation and such reliance caused him to vote for the proposed transaction?

HOLDING AND DECISION: [Judge not stated in casebook excerpt.] No. Where the misstatement or omission in a proxy statement is shown to be material, as is the case here, that determination alone embodies the conclusion that the defective statement was such that it might have been considered important enough by a shareholder to use it as a basis for deciding how to vote. Section 14(a) contains the express requirement that the defect have a significant propensity to affect the voting process. There is no need to add to this requirement, as the court of appeals attempted to do, the further requirement of proof as to whether the defect did in fact have a decisive effect on voting. Where there has been a finding of materiality, a shareholder has made a sufficient showing of causal relationship between the violation of § 14(a) and the resulting injury, but only if there is proof by the plaintiff that the proxy solicitation and not the defect was the deciding link in causing such injury. The court of appeals "fairness test" as a defense to a violation of § 14(a) would confront small shareholders with an added obstacle to establishing a cause of action to a defective proxy statement. Whether or not the merger was fair has no bearing on establishing a cause of action under that section. As held in the *Borak* case, the purpose of § 14(a) was stated to be the promotion of the free exercise of stockholder voting rights by requiring proxy solicitations contain explanations of the real nature of the questions for which authority to cast the proxies is sought. In the present case, once the causal relationship of the proxy material and the merger were established at trial— essentially questions of fact—the Supreme Court's only issue was whether the facts on which that conclusion was reached were sufficient at law to establish Mills's (P) cause of action under 14(a). The Court concluded they were. (III): This Court held in *Borak* that on finding a violation of § 14(a), remedies must effect the Congressional purpose

Continued on next page.

behind the act. Such remedies are not limited to prospective relief, but may include retrospective relief based on
factors governing relief in similar fraud cases. Possible
terms of relief could be the setting aside of the merger or
granting other equitable relief with fairness of the merger a
contributing factor. But the courts are not required to
unscramble a corporate transaction. A merger can't be set
aside merely because the merger agreement is a void contract, compelling a conclusion that no enforceable rights
are created even when a party is innocent of the violation.
But the guilty party is precluded from enforcing the contract against the unwilling innocent party. Thus, the
contract becomes voidable at the option of the innocent
party. As to monetary relief, if the defect in the proxy
solicitations relates to specific terms of the merger, an
accounting may be ordered; but if the misleading aspect
does not relate to the merger terms, monetary relief is
available to shareholders to the extent they can be shown.
(IV): Concerning the awarding of the attorney fees and
litigation expenses, although the general American rule
does not allow for such recovery, one primary judge-
made exception is to award such expenses where a plaintiff
has successfully maintained a class action suit benefitting a
group of others as he is benefitted. Mills (P) has rendered
a substantial service to Auto-Lite (D) shareholders. The
benefit furnished all the shareholders here, is enforcement
of the proxy statute. Vacated and remanded.

▶ *ANALYSIS*

The rationale behind § 14(a) is to create an informed elec-
torate of shareholders and, thus, further the ideal of
corporate democracy. The Court in the present case realized, however, that the purpose of the rule would be
destroyed if oppressive burdens of proof of misuse of
proxy statements were placed on shareholders in attempting to establish a cause of action against management. If
stockholders in the present case were required to prove
that they had actually relied on the false proxy statements,
the burden of proof would be so heavy that many potentially valid causes of actions would be dropped before they
were even started. This would give management an effective shield against shareholder action and prosecution for
misuse of corporate proxy solicitations. The Court in this
case refused to encourage such wrongdoing.

Quicknotes

MATERIALITY Importance; the degree of relevance or
necessity to the particular matter.

PROXY STATEMENT A statement, containing specified information by the Securities and Exchange Commission, in
order to provide shareholders with adequate information
upon which to make an informed decision regarding the
solicitation of their proxies.

SECURITIES EXCHANGE ACT, § 14 (a) Prevents management
from obtaining illegal proxies.

SECURITIES EXCHANGE ACT, § 29(B) Contracts made in
violation of the Act are void.

Seinfeld v. Bartz

Shareholders (P) v. Corporation (D)

2002 WL 243597 (N.D. Cal. 2002).

NATURE OF CASE: Derivative suit for the corporate mailing of a solicitation to obtain proxy votes which violated the Securities Exchange Act.

FACT SUMMARY: When Cisco Systems, Inc. (D) and its directors (D) mailed shareholders a solicitation for proxy votes, they did not include the value of option grants based on a commonly used theoretical so-called Black-Scholes pricing model, whereupon Seinfeld (P) sued Cisco (D) and its directors (D) for the violation of SEC rules relating to proxy solicitations.

🏛 RULE OF LAW
Valuations of option grants to outside directors are not material information which must be included in a corporation's shareholder statement to solicit proxy votes.

FACTS: At the 1999 annual meeting of Cisco Systems, Inc. (D), the shareholders approved an amendment that raised the number of stock options granted to outside directors upon joining the board of directors from 20,000 shares to 30,000 shares. Additionally, the amendment raised the number of options granted annually to each continuing outside director from 10,000 shares to 15,000 shares. Seinfeld (P) brought a derivative action against Cisco (D) and its ten directors (D), alleging that, when mailing the shareholder solicitation for the proxy votes, they had violated SEC proxy rules by failing to include the value of the option grants based on a commonly used theoretical so-called Black-Scholes pricing model.

ISSUE: Are valuations of option grants to outside directors material information which must be included in a corporation's shareholder statement to solicit proxy votes?

HOLDING AND DECISION: [Judge not stated in casebook excerpt.] No. Valuations of option grants to outside directors are not material information which must be included in a corporation's shareholder statement to solicit proxy votes. Here, Seinfeld (P) wrongfully asserts that the valuations of the option grants set forth in the proxy mailings are omitted material facts. Such valuations are not material as a matter of law. The pricing model utilized to value the option grants (referred to as the Black-Scholes valuations) causes an option to depend, among other things, on the value of the underlying asset at the time the option is exercised. Although the formula is complex, and its derivation bewilderingly mathematical, it has become the most widely accepted method for valuing options. While tax regulations in some cases require that options be valued at the time of their grant, here, by contrast, nothing requires that Cisco (D)

calculate the value of the options at the time of grant. Further-more, although Seinfeld (P) argues that the SEC regulations require the Black-Scholes valuations calculations, Seinfeld (P) points to no specific regulation which requires them. Seinfeld (P) has not shown a substantial likelihood that, under all of the circumstances, any omitted fact would have assumed actual significance in the deliberations of a reasonable shareholder. In other words, here there was no substantial likelihood that the disclosure of omitted facts would have been viewed by the reasonable investor as having significantly altered the "total mix" of information made available. Judgment for Cisco (D).

▶ ANALYSIS

As noted in *Seinfeld*, § 14(a) of the Securities Exchange Act and Rule 14a-9 of the Securities and Exchange Commission make it unlawful to solicit proxies in violation of SEC rules. 15 U.S.C. § 78n(a) (2002). SEC Rule 14a-9 prohibits solicitation of a proxy by a statement containing either (1) a false or misleading declaration of material fact or (2) an omission of material fact that makes any portion of the statement false or misleading. An omitted fact is "material" if there is a substantial likelihood that a reasonable shareholder would consider it important in deciding how to vote.

Quicknotes

MATERIALITY Importance; the degree of relevance or necessity to the particular matter.

PROXY STATEMENT A statement, containing specified information by the Securities and Exchange Commission, in order to provide shareholders with adequate information upon which to make an informed decision regarding the solicitation of their proxies.

Lovenheim v. Iroquois Brands, Ltd.

Shareholder (P) v. Corporation (D)

618 F. Supp. 554 (D.D.C. 1985).

NATURE OF CASE: Motion for preliminary injunction.

FACT SUMMARY: Lovenheim (P) sought an injunction barring Iroquois Brands (D) from excluding from its proxy statements a proposed resolution he intended to offer at the upcoming shareholders meeting.

🏛 RULE OF LAW
A shareholder proposal can be significantly related to the business of a securities issuer for non-economic reasons, including social and ethical issues, and therefore may not be omitted from the issuer's proxy statement even if it relates to operations which account for less that 5% of the issuer's total assets.

FACTS: Iroquois (D) was engaged in the business of importing foie gras, and Lovenheim (P), a shareholder, intended to offer a resolution at the next shareholders meeting relating to the procedure used to force-feed geese for production of the pâté de foie gras in France. A rule promulgated by the Securities and Exchange Commission under § 14(a) of the Securities Exchange Act of 1934 required that Iroquois (D) allow information regarding the proposal to be included in proxy materials sent to all shareholders. Iroquois (D) refused to allow information concerning Lovenheim's (P) proposal to be included in the proxy materials being sent in connection with the annual shareholders meeting because its foie gras sales implicated less than .05 per cent of its assets, and an exception to the rule thus precluded application of the shareholders proposal rule. Lovenheim (P) asserted that the rule and statute on which it was based did not permit omission simply because a proposal is not economically significant where a proposal has either ethical or social significance, and sought an injunction in federal court.

ISSUE: Can a shareholder proposal be significantly related to the business of a securities issuer for noneconomic reasons, including social and ethical issues, and may it therefore not be omitted from the issuer's proxy statement even if it relates to operations which account for less than 5% of the issuer's total assets?

HOLDING AND DECISION: [Judge not stated in casebook excerpt.] Yes. A shareholder proposal can be significantly related to the business of a securities issuer for noneconomic reasons, including social and ethical issues, and therefore may not be omitted from the issuer's proxy statement even if it relates to operations which account for less than 5% of the issuer's total assets. In light of the ethical and social significance of Lovenheim's (P) proposal and the fact that it implicates significant levels of sales, Lovenheim

(P) has shown a likelihood of prevailing on the merits with regard to the issue of whether his proposal is otherwise significantly related to Iroquois's (D) business. Lovenheim (P) will suffer irreparable injury without such relief, Iroquois (D) will not suffer any undue harm, and the public interest is served by granting the injunction. Motion granted.

▶ ANALYSIS

The court in this case discussed the requirements for an injunction to issue. First, the proponent must demonstrate a likelihood he will prevail on the merits. Then a determination must be made as to whether plaintiff will suffer irreparable injury without such relief, whether issuance of the requested relief will substantially harm other parties, and the public interest.

■═■

Quicknotes

INJUNCTION A court order requiring a person to do or prohibiting that person from doing, a specific act.

IRREPARABLE INJURY Such harm that because it is either too great, too small or of a continuing character that it cannot be properly compensated in damages, and the remedy for which is typically injunctive relief.

SECURITIES EXCHANGE ACT OF 1934 Regulates the conduct of shareholder meetings.

■═■

AFSCME v. AIG, Inc.

Shareholder (P) v. Corporation (D)

462 F.3d 121 (2d Cir. 2006).

NATURE OF CASE: Appeal from denial of injunctive and declaratory relief in action to compel inclusion of a shareholder proposal in a proxy statement.

FACT SUMMARY: The American Federation of State, County & Municipal Employees (AFSCME) (P) contended that its shareholder proposal—to require American International Group (AIG) (D) to amend its bylaws to require AIG (D), under certain circumstances, to publish the names of shareholder-nominated candidates for director positions together with any candidates nominated by AIG's (D) board of directors—could not be excluded from AIG's (D) proxy statement under SEC Rule 14a-8(i)(8) as relating to an election.

🏛 RULE OF LAW
Under SEC Rule 14a-8(i)(8), a shareholder proposal does not relate "to an election," and is therefore not excludable from a proxy statement, if it seeks to amend the corporate bylaws to establish a procedure by which certain shareholders are entitled to include in the corporate proxy materials their nominees for the board of directors.

FACTS: The American Federation of State, County & Municipal Employees (AFSCME) (P), a large shareholder of American International Group (AIG) (D), submitted a shareholder proposal for inclusion in AIG's (D) proxy statement for the company's annual meeting that if passed would require AIG (D) to amend its bylaws to require AIG (D), under certain circumstances, to publish the names of shareholder-nominated candidates for director positions together with any candidates nominated by AIG's (D) board of directors. AIG (D) received a no-action letter from the SEC's Division of Corporate Finance (Division) indicating that it would not take action against AIG (D) if it excluded the proposal from its proxy statement, on the basis that under SEC Rule 14a-8(i)(8), the proposal could be excluded as relating "to an election." For nearly 16 years, the SEC's interpretation of Rule 14a-8(i)(8) had been that it related only to shareholder proposals used to oppose solicitations dealing with an identified board seat in an upcoming election and rejected the somewhat broader interpretation that the Rule's election exclusion applied to shareholder proposals that would institute procedures making such election contests more likely. The SEC then changed course and, as indicated by its no-action letter to AIG (D), interpreted the Rule to apply to proxy access bylaw proposals. Based on the no-action letter, AIG (D) excluded the proposal from its proxy statement, and AFSCME (P) brought suit seeking a court order compelling AIG (D) to include the proposal in its next proxy statement. The district court denied

AFSCME's (P) request for declaratory and injunctive relief and dismissed the action. The court of appeals granted review.

ISSUE: Under SEC Rule 14a-8(i)(8), does a shareholder proposal relate "to an election," and is therefore excludable from a proxy statement, if it seeks to amend the corporate bylaws to establish a procedure by which certain shareholders are entitled to include in the corporate proxy materials their nominees for the board of directors?

HOLDING AND DECISION: [Judge not stated in casebook excerpt.] No. Under SEC Rule 14a-8(i)(8), a shareholder proposal does not relate "to an election," and is therefore not excludable from a proxy statement, if it seeks to amend the corporate bylaws to establish a procedure by which certain shareholders are entitled to include in the corporate proxy materials their nominees for the board of directors. Rule 14a-8(i)(8) is ambiguous. It permits a corporation to exclude a shareholder proposal—a recommendation(s) or requirement(s) that the company and/or its board of directors take some action, which the submitting shareholder(s) intend to present at a meeting of the company's shareholders—if the proposal "relates to an election" for membership on the board. The relevant language, "relates to an election," could be read as creating a distinction between proposals addressing a particular seat in a particular election, and those (such as AFSCME's (P)), that simply set the background rules governing elections generally. It is a plausible reading of the language, which uses the article "an" preceding "election," that the Rule was intended to cover only particular elections, rather than elections generally. It is, however, also plausible that the phrase was intended to create a comparatively broader exclusion, one covering "a particular election or elections generally" since any proposal that relates to elections in general will necessarily relate to an election in particular. Because the Rule itself provides no reason to adopt one interpretation over the other, the Rule is ambiguous on its face. When the language of a regulation is ambiguous, courts typically look for guidance in any interpretation made by the agency that promulgated the regulation in question, and usually defers to that agency's interpretation. Here, however, the SEC has over time rendered two distinctly different and conflicting interpretations of the Rule. The earlier interpretation took a narrower view of the Rule's exclusion, whereas the later interpretation took a significantly broader view of the exclusion. Because the SEC has taken these conflicting views, it does not merit

Continued on next page.

the usual deference reserved for an agency's interpretation of its own regulations. Moreover, the SEC has not provided reasons for its changed position, despite a "duty to explain its departure from prior norms." Therefore, it is appropriate to defer to the SEC's earlier interpretation, which deems proxy access bylaw proposal non-excludable. If the SEC wants to change its earlier position, it should do so by explaining its shift in position, or amending the Rule. Reversed.

▶ ANALYSIS

Rule 14a-8(i)(8), also known as "the town meeting rule," is one of the 13 substantive bases upon which a company may rely to exclude a shareholder proposal from its proxy materials. In response to the AIG decision, the SEC in 2007 adopted an amendment to Rule 14a-8(i)(8) that codified the agency's more recent interpretation of the rule. The language of the rule, as amended, specifies that a company may exclude a proposal "If the proposal relates to a nomination or an election for membership on the company's board of directors or analogous governing body or a procedure for such nomination or election." In addition, the adopting release for this rule clarifies that the amended rule text relates only to procedures that would result in a contested election, either in the year in which the proposal is submitted or in subsequent years, and does not affect or address any other aspect of the agency's prior interpretation of the exclusion.

■═■

Quicknotes

NO-ACTION LETTER A letter issued by an attorney of a governmental agency stating that if the facts are as stated, he or she would not advise the agency to prosecute.

■═■

Crane Co. v. Anaconda Co.

Shareholder (P) v. Company (D)

39 N.Y.2d 14, 382 N.Y.S.2d 707, 346 N.E.2d 507 (1976).

NATURE OF CASE: Appeal from judgment reinstating petition to compel inspection of a corporation's shareholder list.

FACT SUMMARY: Crane Company (P), a stockholder, demanded access to Anaconda's (D) shareholder list for the purpose of informing other shareholders of a pending tender offer.

RULE OF LAW
A shareholder wishing to inform others regarding a pending tender offer should be permitted access to the company's shareholder list unless it is sought for an objective adverse to the company or its stockholders.

FACTS: Crane Company (P) proposed a tender offer of Anaconda's (D) stock. Crane (P) requested a copy of Anaconda's (D) shareholder list for the purposes of informing other shareholders of the tender offer, and to rebut misleading statements disseminated by Anaconda (D). Crane (P) had acquired over 11% of Anaconda's (D) common stock, making Crane (P) Anaconda's (D) single largest shareholder. Anaconda (D) refused to furnish the shareholder list, claiming that Crane's (P) motives were not for a purpose relating to the business of the corporation. Special Term dismissed, but the appellate division reversed. Anaconda (D) appealed.

ISSUE: May a qualified stockholder inspect the corporation's shareholder list for the purpose of soliciting a tender offer?

HOLDING AND DECISION: [Judge not stated in casebook excerpt.] Yes. A shareholder wishing to make a tender offer should be permitted access to the company's shareholder list unless it is sought for an objective adverse to the company or its stockholders. The New York state statute permits access to qualified shareholders on written demand accompanied by an affidavit stating the inspection is not unrelated to the business of the company and that the shareholder has not sold stock lists within the previous five years. The pendency of a tender offer necessarily relates to the business of the corporation and to the safeguarding of the shareholders' investment. Anaconda's (D) shareholders should be afforded the opportunity to make an informed judgment regarding the sale. Affirmed.

▶ ANALYSIS

Note that the shareholders' right to examine the corporation's shareholder list is derived from both state statute and the common law right of inspection. Federal proxy rules do not provide for stockholder access to a corporation's shareholder list; however, they do not preclude the right either. Most states require that the shareholder meet minimum percentage or period of ownership prerequisites, and that the inspection further a "proper purpose."

■═■

Quicknotes

BUSINESS CORPORATION LAW, § 1315 Provides that access to shareholder lists must be permitted to qualified stockholdings.

■═■

State ex rel. Pillsbury v. Honeywell, Inc.

Stockholder (P) v. Company (D)

291 Minn. 322, 191 N.W.2d 406 (1971).

NATURE OF CASE: Appeal from district court judgment denying writ of mandamus.

FACT SUMMARY: Stockholder Pillsbury (P) purchased shares in Honeywell (D) for the sole purpose of persuading Honeywell (D) to cease its production of munitions for use in the Vietnam War.

🏛 RULE OF LAW
In order for a stockholder to inspect shareholder lists and corporate records, the stockholder must demonstrate a proper purpose relating to an economic interest.

FACTS: After learning of Honeywell's (D) involvement in the production of munitions for use in the Vietnam War, Pillsbury (P) bought a sufficient number of shares to give him a voice in Honeywell's (D) affairs for the purpose of altering its policies. Pillsbury (P) submitted two formal requests for the inspection of Honeywell's (D) shareholder list and corporate records. Honeywell (D) refused, and Pillsbury (P) initiated suit. The trial court dismissed the petition on the basis that the demand to inspect Honeywell's (D) records was not in furtherance of a proper purpose related to Pillsbury's (P) interest as a shareholder. Pillsbury (P) appealed.

ISSUE: Must a stockholder demonstrate that he is motivated by a proper purpose related to his economic interest in the corporation in order to inspect shareholder lists and records?

HOLDING AND DECISION: [Judge not stated in casebook excerpt.] Yes. In order for a stockholder to inspect shareholder lists and corporate records, the stockholder must demonstrate a proper purpose relating to an economic interest. This standard is derived from both Delaware statute and the common law. The requisite of a proper purpose is also necessary to compel shareholder inspection of corporate records other than the shareholder list. A proper purpose constitutes those relating to a shareholder's economic interest in the corporation. In this case, Pillsbury's (P) sole purpose in obtaining access to Honeywell's (D) shareholder list and corporate records was for the furtherance of his personal political views, regardless of any economic implications to himself or the corporation. Affirmed.

▶ ANALYSIS

Note that Pillsbury (P) could have accomplished his goal had his motivation been different. A shareholder with legitimate concerns for the economic implications of Honeywell's (D) armament production on his investment would have a purpose germane to his investment. Likewise, a shareholder concerned with the negative effects of ceasing such production could also request review of Honeywell's (D) records.

Quicknotes

WRIT OF MANDAMUS A court order issued commanding a public or private entity, or an official thereof, to perform a duty required by law.

Sadler v. NCR Corporation

Shareholders (P) v. Telephone company (D)

928 F.2d 48 (2d Cir. 1991).

NATURE OF CASE: Appeal from order to disclose shareholder list.

FACT SUMMARY: Mr. and Mrs. Sadler (P) and AT&T (P) attempted to obtain shareholder lists from NCR (D) in an effort to execute a tender offer.

🏛 RULE OF LAW
A state may require a foreign corporation with substantial ties to its forum to provide resident shareholders access to its shareholder list and to compile a non-objecting beneficial owners (NOBO) list, in a situation where the shareholder could not obtain such documents in the company's own state of incorporation.

FACTS: AT&T (P), a New York corporation with its principal place of business in New York, commenced a tender offer for the stock of NCR (D), a Maryland corporation with its principal place of business in Ohio and substantial ties to New York. NCR (D) attempted to block the tender offer, and AT&T (P) sought to call a special meeting in order to replace the board of directors. AT&T (P) enlisted the Sadlers (P), residents of New York and owners of 6,000 shares of NCR (D) stock, to assist it in attempting to acquire a list of non-objecting beneficial owners (a NOBO list) and other related documents. Neither AT&T (P) nor the Sadlers (P) met the State of Maryland's criteria for production of stockholder records. When NCR (D) refused to assemble a NOBO list, the Sadlers (P) and AT&T (P) initiated suit. The district court ordered NCR (D) to comply with the request. NCR (D) appealed.

ISSUE: May a state require a foreign corporation with substantial ties to its forum to provide resident shareholders access to its shareholder list and to compile a NOBO list, in a situation where the shareholder could not obtain such documents in the company's state of incorporation?

HOLDING AND DECISION: [Judge not stated in casebook excerpt.] Yes. A state may require a foreign corporation, with substantial ties to its forum, to provide resident shareholders access to its shareholder list and to compile a NOBO list, in a situation where the shareholder could not obtain such documents in the company's own state of incorporation. Such a result is authorized under New York law, and is not in violation with the Commerce Clause of the Constitution. The state statute permits a qualified shareholder to compel a defendant corporation to compile and produce a NOBO list. Such a determination is consistent with the legislative intent to facilitate shareholder access to information regarding his investment. Though compilation may not be required in every case, here shareholder access was particularly crucial due to NCR's (D) policy of treating nonvoting shares as voting in favor of management. NCR (D) claims the application of N.Y. Bus. Corp. Law § 1315 compelling it to furnish the NOBO list violates the dormant Commerce Clause by imposing inconsistent regulations on interstate commerce. However, states have traditionally required foreign corporations with significant ties to their forum to produce shareholder lists. Moreover, the application of the statute does not discriminate between foreign and domestic corporations. It applies equally to both. Affirmed.

▶ ANALYSIS

Note that the dormant Commerce Clause power is derived from Congress's enumerated but unexercised power to regulate interstate commerce. The dormant Commerce Clause prohibits state regulations that impose burdens on interstate commerce through discriminatory or inconsistent regulations. The requirement that a foreign corporation, transacting substantial business in the forum state, disclose its shareholder lists does not rise to the level of irreconcilable conflict that the Commerce Clause circumscribes.

■═■

Quicknotes

DORMANT COMMERCE CLAUSE The regulatory effect of the commerce clause on state activity affecting interstate commerce, where Congress itself has not acted to control the activity; a provision inferred from, but not expressly present in, the language of the Commerce Clause.

NOBO LIST List of beneficial owners of shares who do not object to disclosure of their name.

N.Y. BUS. CORP. LAW § 1315 Permits New York residents who have owned stock in a foreign corporation for six months to require the corporation to produce a shareholder list.

TENDER OFFER An offer made by one corporation to the shareholders of a target corporation to purchase their shares subject to number, time, and price specifications.

■═■

Stroh v. Blackhawk Holding Corp.

Shareholder (P) v. Corporation (D)

48 Ill. 2d 471, 272 N.E.2d 1 (1971).

NATURE OF CASE: Shareholder derivative suit seeking to declare shares of stock invalid.

FACT SUMMARY: Shareholders (P) of Class B stock in Blackhawk Holding Corporation (D) claimed that a limitation on their rights at dissolution rendered their shares invalid.

> ## 🏛 RULE OF LAW
> A corporation may prescribe whatever restrictions or limitations it deems necessary in regard to the issuance of stock, provided that it not limit or negate the voting power of any share.

FACTS: Blackhawk's (D) articles of incorporation provided for the issuance of three million shares of Class A stock and 500,000 shares of Class B stock. Each share was entitled to one vote. The articles also provided that in the case of liquidation, shares of Class B stock were not entitled to dividends. The shareholders (P) sued claiming this limitation on their economic interest in the shares rendered the shares invalid.

ISSUE: May a corporation prescribe, whatever restrictions or limitations it deems necessary, in regard to the issuance of stock?

HOLDING AND DECISION: [Judge not stated in casebook excerpt.] Yes. A corporation may prescribe whatever restrictions or limitations it deems necessary in regard to the issuance of stock, provided that it not limit or negate the voting power of any share. Under the applicable statute, § 14 of the Illinois Business Corporation Act, a corporation may proscribe the relative rights of its classes of shares in its articles of incorporation, subject to their absolute right to vote. A corporation is expressly afforded the right to establish classes of stock in regards to preferential distribution of the corporation's assets. However, the shareholder's right to vote is guaranteed, and must be in proportion to the number of shares possessed. Here the Class B stock possessed equal voting rights, though it did not possess the right to share in the dividends or assets of the company. Thus the stock is valid. Affirmed.

DISSENT: (Schaefer, J.) Prescription of a shareholder's financial interest in his stock effectively invalidates that interest.

▶ *ANALYSIS*

The shareholders (P) and Blackhawk Holding Corp. (D) differed on the definition of the term "proprietary" in respect to the statutory definition of shares. Shareholders (P) defined this as a property right, necessarily encompassing

a correlating economic interest in the corporation. However, the court adopted Blackhawk's (D) definition as the right to management or control.

Quicknotes

DISSOLUTION Annulment or termination of a formal or legal bond, tie or contract.

ILL. BUS. CORP. ACT, § 14 Allows the stock in Illinois corporations to be divided into classes.

VOTING RIGHTS A shareholder's right to vote his shares with respect to corporate matters.

Ringling Bros.-Barnum & Bailey Combined Shows v. Ringling

Corporation (D) v. Shareholder (P)

29 Del. Ch. 610, 53 A.2d 441 (1947).

NATURE OF CASE: Review of directors' election.

FACT SUMMARY: Edith Ringling (P) and Aubrey Haley (D) entered into a written agreement to act jointly in regard to all matters pertaining to ownership of their stock.

🏛 RULE OF LAW
A group of shareholders may lawfully contract to vote in any manner they determine.

FACTS: Edith Ringling (P) and Aubrey Haley (D) entered into a voting trust agreement binding them to act jointly in all matters relating to their stock and ownership interests in Ringling Bros.-Barnum & Bailey Combined Shows (D). The contract further provided in the event that the parties failed to reach a joint conclusion in respect to the exercise of their voting rights, the issue would be submitted to an arbitrator. Prior to the 1946 annual shareholders meeting, Ringling (P) and Haley (D) failed to agree on the selection of a fifth director. Haley (D) was absent from the shareholder's meeting, and her stock was voted in accordance with the arbitrator's direction. Edith Ringling (P) sued to review the election. The Court of Chancery held that the agreement to vote in accordance with the determination of the arbitrator was valid, and a new election was ordered.

ISSUE: Is a shareholder agreement to vote jointly illegal and revocable?

HOLDING AND DECISION: [Judge not stated in casebook excerpt.] No. A group of shareholders may lawfully contract to vote in any manner they determine. Both the common law and statutes recognize the right of a shareholder to contract away his voting rights while still retaining other rights incident to stock ownership. Similarly, agreements between shareholders purporting to bind the exercise of their voting rights have also been upheld as a valid means of obtaining the advantages of concerted action. The provision submitting the decision to the arbitrator in the case of a deadlock is consistent with this goal of joint action. Haley's (D) failure to vote consistent with the arbitrator's decision was a breach of this contract. Order modified.

▶ ANALYSIS

Although the agreement provided for concerted action, there was no express grant of authority to either the other shareholders or to the arbitrator authorizing them to vote the dissenting stockholders' shares in accordance

with the majority. The arbitrator was not vested with the power to enforce his decision. Though such agreements to transfer one's voting rights are upheld as valid, this was not what the parties in this case bargained for.

■═■

Quicknotes

ARBITRATION An agreement to have a dispute heard and decided by a neutral third party, rather than through legal proceedings.

FIDUCIARY STOCKHOLDER A stockholder that owes a legal obligation to deal fairly with, and not to exploit or oppress, minority shareholders.

VOTING RIGHTS A shareholder's right to vote his shares with respect to corporate matters.

VOTING TRUST An agreement establishing a trust, whereby shareholders transfer their title to shares to a trustee who is authorized to exercise their voting powers.

■═■

McQuade v. Stoneham

Minority shareholder (P) v. Majority shareholder (D)

263 N.Y. 323, 189 N.E. 234 (1934).

NATURE OF CASE: Appeal from award of damages in action to compel specific performance.

FACT SUMMARY: McQuade (P), officer and director of National Exhibition Company, was voted out of office in violation of a shareholder agreement he entered into with Stoneham (D) for the purchase of stock in National Exhibition.

🏛 RULE OF LAW
A shareholder agreement prohibiting the board of directors from changing officers, salaries, or policies, or retaining individuals in office, is illegal and void absent express contractual consent.

FACTS: Stoneham (D) owned a majority of shares in the National Exhibition Company, also known as the New York Giants. McQuade (P) and McGraw (D) each purchased seventy shares of Stoneham's (D) stock, and entered into a shareholder agreement to preserve themselves as directors and officers of the corporation. The agreement further prohibited the amendment of salaries, shares, or bylaws of the corporation except with unanimous consent of the three aforementioned parties. The board of directors consisted of seven men including Stoneham (D), McGraw (D), and McQuade (P). McQuade (P) was named treasurer, until he was discharged from the corporation in his capacities both as officer and director. In contravention of the agreement with McQuade (P), Stoneham (D) and McGraw (D) both abstained from voting. The lower court refused specific performance of McQuade's (P) reinstatement, but gave him damages for wrongful discharge and a cause of action for future damages.

ISSUE: Is a shareholder agreement precluding the board of directors from changing officers, salaries, or retaining individuals in office void and illegal?

HOLDING AND DECISION: (Pound, C.J.) Yes. A shareholder agreement prohibiting the board of directors from changing officers, salaries, or policies or retaining individuals is illegal and void absent express contractual consent of the parties. Shareholders of a corporation possess an inalienable right to elect directors, and may combine to achieve this purpose. Stockholders may form a voting trust and thereby elect directors who they believe will manage consistent with the stockholders' views. However, shareholders may not enter agreements interfering with the directors' powers to exercise their independent judgment in the management of the corporation's affairs. There is no evidence in this case that Stoneham (D) and McGraw (D) did not act consistent with their business judgment. A second reason the contract is unenforceable is because

McQuade (P) was a city magistrate at the time the contract was entered into. The law governing magistrates prohibits them from engaging in any business while they are magistrates. Therefore, the performance of the contract constituted a violation of this law. Reversed.

CONCURRENCE AND DISSENT: (Lehman, J.) The majority's second ground for reversal is correct insofar as the contract is unenforceable because it resulted in an employment that was illegal. However, the majority's first ground is incorrect. Shareholders owning a majority of the stock may combine to obtain and exercise any control that a single majority owner could exercise, because what may be done lawfully by one may be done lawfully by a combination of individuals. Here, the contract did not restrict the powers of the board of directors, except regarding the election and remuneration of officers and the adhesion by the corporation to established policies. The directors retain the power to exercise their business judgment, subject to the majority shareholder(s) removal. Thus, in reality, the majority stockholders have effective control of the board of directors, except to the extent that the board may check the stockholders when their will is arbitrary. A contract that destroys this check is illegal, but a contract that provides that the stockholders shall use their power to achieve a legitimate purpose is not illegal. The directors may not disregard the best interests of the corporation, but within that limitation, they may be swayed by the wishes of the majority. The contract here is within that limitation, and is, therefore, valid, because it provides for the election of fit officers and adhesion to a particular policy determined in advance; it is designed to protect legitimate interests without prejudicing the corporation.

▶ ANALYSIS

Courts are suspicious of contracts purporting to limit directors' discretion. Such contracts violate a foundation of corporate law that management of a corporation shall be centralized in a board of directors. Courts will decline to validate agreements not approved by all the shareholders in an effort to protect the interests of the minority.

■═■

Quicknotes

BUSINESS JUDGMENT RULE Doctrine relieving corporate directors and/or officers from liability for decisions honestly and rationally made in the corporation's best interests.

Continued on next page.

SPECIFIC PERFORMANCE An equitable remedy whereby the court requires the parties to perform their obligations pursuant to a contract.

VOTING TRUST An agreement establishing a trust, whereby shareholders transfer their title to shares to a trustee who is authorized to exercise their voting powers.

■■■

Clark v. Dodge

Minority shareholder (P) v. Majority shareholder (D)

269 N.Y. 410, 199 N.E. 641 (1936).

NATURE OF CASE: Suit for specific performance of a shareholder agreement.

FACT SUMMARY: Clark (P) and Dodge (D), sole shareholders in two pharmaceutical companies, entered into a shareholders' agreement regarding Clark's (P) continuation as manager and director.

🏛 RULE OF LAW
Where the directors are also the sole stockholders of a corporation, a contract between them to vote for specified persons to serve as directors is legal, and not in contravention of public policy.

FACTS: Clark (P) and Dodge (D) owned 25% and 75%, respectively, of the stock of two pharmaceutical corporations in the business of manufacturing medicinal compounds from secret formulas. Though he was a director, Dodge (D) did not take an active role in the management of the companies. Clark (P) served as director, treasurer, and manager of Bell & Co. and also managed most of the business of Hollings-Smith Company. Clark (P) possessed sole knowledge of the formulas. Both entered a written contract that Dodge (D) should vote so that Clark (P) would continue as director of Bell, he would receive one-fourth net income from the corporations, and that no unreasonable salaries would be paid to other officers of the corporations. Clark in turn (P) agreed to disclose the formula to one of Dodge's (D) sons, and to bequeath his interest in the companies to Dodge's (D) wife and sons should he have no heirs of his own. Clark (P) claimed Dodge (D) breached the contract by failing to continue Clark (P) as a director, preventing Clark's (P) receipt of his income, and paying excessive salaries. Clark (P) sought reinstatement, an accounting, and an injunction against future violations. The appellate division dismissed, and he appealed.

ISSUE: Where the directors are the sole stockholders of a corporation, is a contract between them to vote for specified persons as officers illegal?

HOLDING AND DECISION: [Judge not stated in casebook excerpt.] No. Where the directors are also the sole stockholders of a corporation, a contract between them to vote for specified persons to serve as directors is legal, and not in contravention of public policy. The general rule is the board of directors has the unfettered responsibility of managing the daily operation of the corporation's business. Courts have held that any departure from this standard is illegal as against public policy. However, in a case such as this, where the directors are also the sole shareholders of the corporation, policy concerns of shareholder interference with management decisions are no longer applicable. Reversed.

▶ ANALYSIS

The *Clark* court distinguished its decision from the decision rendered in *McQuade v. Stoneham*, 189 N.E. 234 (1934). The court read that decision as allowing for no variation from the statutory norm that the corporation be governed exclusively by its board of directors, but chose to confine its broad statements to its facts. The court then determined that if a contract presents no harm of injury to anyone, there is no reason for holding it invalid, even though it departs from the general rule.

■═■

Quicknotes

INJUNCTION A court order requiring a person to do or prohibiting that person from doing a specific act.

SPECIFIC PERFORMANCE An equitable remedy whereby the court requires the parties to perform their obligations pursuant to a contract.

■═■

Galler v. Galler

Shareholder (P) v. Shareholder (D)

32 Ill. 2d 16, 203 N.E.2d 577 (1964).

NATURE OF CASE: Suit for specific enforcement of a shareholder agreement.

FACT SUMMARY: Benjamin and Isadore (D) Galler entered into a shareholder agreement for the purpose of maintaining themselves and their spouses as officers of the company, and for the continued support and maintenance of their families.

🏛 RULE OF LAW
Shareholders in a closely held corporation are free to contract regarding the management of the corporation absent the presence of an objecting minority, and threat of public injury.

FACTS: Benjamin and Isadore (D) Galler, partners who each owned an equal share of stock in Galler Drug Company, entered into a shareholder agreement providing for the support and maintenance of both their families. The agreement further bound the shareholders to elect as directors Isadore, Benjamin, and each of their spouses. Benjamin transferred his shares into his wife, Emma's (P), possession as trustee. Isadore (D) sought to have Emma (P) modify the shareholder agreement, and remove herself as a director. She refused and initiated suit. The appellate court held the shareholder agreement void due to indefinite duration, election of officers, salary continuation, and mandatory declaration of dividends.

ISSUE: May shareholders in a closely held corporation contract in regards to the company's management?

HOLDING AND DECISION: [Judge not stated in casebook excerpt.] Yes. Shareholders in a closely held corporation are free to contract regarding the management of the corporation absent the presence of an objecting minority, and threat of public injury. The general rule is that majority shareholders in a corporation have the right to select its managers. Shareholders' interests in publicly held corporations must be distinguished from those in closely held corporations. The shareholder in the closely held corporation is in greater need of methods of protecting his investment, as he does not have the option of selling his shares on the open market. Moreover, shareholders in a closely held corporation often also serve as its directors and officers. Consequently, such shareholder agreements are the result of informed decisions, and the safeguards afforded shareholders in a publicly held corporation do not apply. There is no reason to extend the durational limits imposed on voting trusts to a straight voting control agreement in the absence of fraud or disadvantage to minority interests. Likewise, the provision for the election of ascertained persons as officers for a definite period should be upheld. The purpose of the contract to provide for maintenance and support of the two families is a valid purpose, and the provisions for minimum earned surplus requirement and salary continuation are valid means of protecting the corporations' interests. Reversed.

▶ ANALYSIS

Some jurisdictions differentiate in their treatment of closely held corporations from other corporate entities. The purpose of the distinction is to alleviate the potentially adverse consequences of the close corporation's failure to comply with statutory regulations, and to promote fair dealing among the parties. Jurisdictions recognizing the distinction hold shareholders in the closely held corporation to the standard of care of partners, and impart to them the correlating fiduciary duties of good faith and fair dealing.

■■■■

Quicknotes

CLOSELY HELD CORPORATION A corporation whose shares (or at least voting shares) are held by a closely knit group of shareholders or a single person.

FAIR DEALING An implied warranty that the parties will deal honestly in the satisfaction of their obligations and without intent to defraud.

■■■■

Ramos v. Estrada

Shareholder (P) v. Director (D)

8 Cal. App. 4th 1070, 10 Cal. Rptr. 2d 833 (1992).

NATURE OF CASE: Breach of contract action seeking specific performance.

FACT SUMMARY: Tila Estrada (D) violated a shareholder voting agreement by voting her shares in opposition to the majority.

> 🏛 **RULE OF LAW**
> Voting agreements binding individual shareholders to vote in concurrence with the majority constitute valid contracts.

FACTS: Broadcast Group and Ventura 41 combined to form Television, Inc., for the purpose of establishing a Spanish language television station. Broadcast Group was owned 50% by the Ramoses (P), and the Estradas (D) and four other couples each owned 10%. The shareholders of Broadcast Group entered an agreement to vote their shares in Television, Inc., in accordance with the majority view. In addition, the contract placed restrictions on transfer, and treated a shareholder's noncompliance with the voting provision as an election to sell his shares. Tila Estrada (D) voted in opposition to Broadcast Group's majority, and declared the agreement void. Ramos (P) sued Estrada (D) for breach of contract. The trial court held the Estradas (D) in breach of contract, ordered their shares in Television, Inc., sold, and restrained them from further voting their shares in violation of the shareholders' agreement. The Estradas (D) appealed.

ISSUE: Is a shareholder agreement to vote shares in accordance with the will of the majority a valid contract?

HOLDING AND DECISION: [Judge not stated in casebook excerpt.] Yes. Voting agreements binding individual shareholders to vote in concurrence with the majority constitute valid contracts. Although Broadcast Group did not qualify as a closely held corporation, the court upheld the contract, recognizing that voting agreements are valid in various other corporate forms. The agreement purports to limit transferability of shares consistent with the theme of effectuating the majority's interests. It expressly provides that in the event of a member's failure to vote in accordance with the majority, the member effectively elects to sell his shares to the other members. The agreement further provides for the remedy of specific performance in the event of a breach. The Estradas' (D) departure from the majority constituted a breach of the agreement, and an election to sell their interest in Television, Inc. Affirmed.

▶ **ANALYSIS**

Closely held corporations present an unusual situation requiring departure from the corporate norm. Shareholders in large, publicly held corporations necessarily relinquish their control over mundane, daily activities to the board of directors, and only function to elect the board and decide on fundamental transactions. Shareholders who disagree with corporate management may elect a new board, or sell their shares. In a closely held corporation, however, shareholders often serve also as directors and officers of the corporation, and do not have available the alternative of selling their shares on the open market. Thus, shareholder agreements regarding the transfer of shares, voting rights, and election of directors are necessary for investors in close corporations to safeguard their investment.

Quicknotes

CAL. CORP. CODE, § 706 An agreement between two or more stockholders in a close corporation may prescribe voting agreements.

CLOSELY HELD CORPORATION A corporation whose shares (or at least voting shares) are held by a closely knit group of shareholders or a single person.

SPECIFIC PERFORMANCE An equitable remedy whereby the court requires the parties to perform their obligations pursuant to a contract.

Wilkes v. Springside Nursing Home, Inc.

Director (P) v. Corporation (D)

370 Mass. 842, 353 N.E.2d 657 (1976).

NATURE OF CASE: Appeal from dismissal of claim for damages resulting from shareholders' breach of fiduciary duty.

FACT SUMMARY: Wilkes (P) was terminated as director and officer of Springside Nursing Home (D) in violation of a shareholder agreement that each investor would serve as a director and receive a salary from the corporation.

🏛 RULE OF LAW
In a closely held corporation, the majority stockholders have a duty to deal with the minority in accordance with a good faith standard.

FACTS: Wilkes (P), Riche, Quinn, and Pipkin joined forces to purchase a building and operate it as a nursing home. They formed Springside (D), a corporation in which ownership of the property was vested. Each invested and received an equal share in Springside (D). They agreed that each would serve as a director and take an active role in management. As Springside (D) became profitable, each received a weekly stipend. However, as relations among the parties became strained, Wilkes (P) notified Springside (D) of his intention to sell his shares. The board ceased Wilkes's (P) salary and did not reelect him as director or officer. Wilkes (P) sued for damages based on breach of the fiduciary duty owed him by the other shareholders. The lower court dismissed the complaint. Wilkes (P) appealed.

ISSUE: May the minority shareholders in a closely held corporation charge majority shareholders with a breach of fiduciary duty in terminating his employment or ousting from his position as officer or director?

HOLDING AND DECISION: [Judge not stated in casebook excerpt.] Yes. In a closely held corporation, the majority stockholders have a duty to deal with the minority in accordance with a good faith standard. Determination of whether there was a breach of this duty is decided on a case-by-case basis. The burden of proof is on the majority to show a legitimate purpose for its decision related to the operation of the business. Then the minority may answer that the same objective could be reached through less harmful means. In reaching a determination, the court must balance the legitimacy of the intended purpose against the practicability of the less harmful alternative. In this case, there was no legitimate business purpose proffered for Wilkes's (P) termination, nor was there any evidence in the record legitimizing the majority's action. Reversed and remanded.

▶ ANALYSIS

Courts traditionally decline to intercede in the business affairs of a corporation, such as the election and removal of officers and directors, which are subject to review by the majority of shareholders. Such noninterference has led to abuse of minority shareholders under the close corporation structure. Thus, shareholders in a closely held corporation are held to a similar standard as is required between partners. This is necessary due to the unavailability of a ready market for the minority shareholder to dispose of his shares, and the greater dependency on the corporation to safeguard the shareholders' investment.

Quicknotes

CLOSELY HELD CORPORATION A corporation whose shares (or at least voting shares) are held by a closely knit group of shareholders or a single person.

FIDUCIARY DUTY A legal obligation to act for the benefit of another, including subordinating one's personal interests to that of the other person.

GOOD FAITH An honest intention to abstain from any unconscientious advantage of another.

MINORITY STOCKHOLDER A stockholder in a corporation controlling such a small portion of those shares which are outstanding that its votes have no influence in the management of the corporation.

Ingle v. Glamore Motor Sales, Inc.

Former officer (P) v. Corporation (D)

73 N.Y.2d 183, 538 N.Y.S.2d 771, 535 N.E.2d 1311 (1989).

NATURE OF CASE: Appeal from dismissal of action for wrongful termination and breach of fiduciary duty.

FACT SUMMARY: Ingle (P), a shareholder, officer, and business manager of Glamore Motor Sales (D), was terminated by Glamore's (D) board of directors, and his shares therein repurchased, consistent with a shareholders' agreement he entered into with James Glamore.

🏛 RULE OF LAW
A minority shareholder in a closely held corporation, who is also employed by the corporation, is not afforded a fiduciary duty on the part of the majority against the termination of his employment.

FACTS: Ingle (P), sales manager of Glamore Motor Sales (D), entered into a shareholders' agreement with owner James Glamore providing for the purchase by Ingle (P) of twenty-two of James Glamore's shares, with an option to purchase an additional eighteen. James Glamore agreed to nominate and vote for Ingle (P) as director and secretary of Glamore Motor Sales (D). James Glamore (D) retained the right to repurchase Ingle's (P) shares if he should terminate employment with Glamore Motor Sales (D) for any cause. Ingle (P) later exercised the option, and the parties executed a second shareholder agreement. James Glamore (D) subsequently issued an additional sixty shares, which were purchased by Glamore and his sons. The board of directors then voted to remove Ingle (P) as director and secretary, and terminated him as operating manager. James Glamore then exercised his option to repurchase Ingle's (P) shares. Ingle (P) initiated two actions claiming breach of fiduciary duty and breach of contract. The appellate division dismissed, and he appealed.

ISSUE: Is a minority shareholder of a closely held corporation, who is also employed thereby, entitled to a fiduciary duty by the majority against termination of his employment?

HOLDING AND DECISION: (Bellacosa, J.) No. A minority shareholder in a closely held corporation, who is also employed by the corporation, is not afforded a fiduciary duty on the part of the majority against the termination of his employment. A minority shareholder does not derive from that status protection against his termination in the absence of contractual provision. A court must distinguish between the fiduciary duties owed by the corporation to a minority shareholder as a shareholder, in contrast to its duties owed to him as an employee. Here Ingle (P) served as an employee at will, there being no evidence of the existence of an employment contract. The common law does not recognize an implied duty of good faith and fair dealing in such employment situations. Ingle (P) voluntarily accepted employment without the protection of a contract as to duration, without any restrictions on the Glamore Motor Sales' (D) corporation's right to terminate him, and providing for the repurchase of his shares in the event of such termination. Affirmed.

DISSENT: (Hancock, J.) The majority erroneously applied the employment-at-will rule to a minority shareholder in a closely held corporation situation. An employee's status as a minority shareholder necessitates special safeguards to protect his investment in the corporation.

▶ ANALYSIS

Courts have differed on their treatment of wrongful termination claims brought by minority shareholders in closely held corporations. Jurisdictions recognizing the fiduciary duty of good faith and fair dealing allow the claim on the demonstration that the termination was not justified by good cause, and that it frustrated the expectations of the minority shareholder. Other jurisdictions do not recognize breaches of fiduciary duty in the absence of statutory violations or the breach of express contractual provisions.

Quicknotes

CLOSELY HELD CORPORATION A corporation whose shares (or at least voting shares) are held by a closely knit group of shareholders or a single person.

EMPLOYEE AT WILL An employee who works pursuant to the agreement that either he or his employer may terminate the employment relationship at any time and for any cause.

FIDUCIARY DUTY A legal obligation to act for the benefit of another, including subordinating one's personal interests to that of the other person.

GOOD FAITH An honest intention to abstain from any unconscientious advantage of another.

MINORITY STOCKHOLDER A stockholder in a corporation controlling such a small portion of those shares which are outstanding that its votes have no influence in the management of the corporation.

Brodie v. Jordan

Minority shareholder (P) v. Majority shareholder (D)

447 Mass. 866, 857 N.E.2d 1076 (2006).

NATURE OF CASE: Appeal from affirmance of buyout of minority shareholder ordered in action for freeze-out.

FACT SUMMARY: Jordan (D) and Barbuto (D), who collectively were the majority shareholders (D) of Malden, a closely held corporation, contended that Brodie (P) was not entitled to a forced buyout of her shares, even though she had been frozen out by Jordan (D) and Barbuto (D), because this remedy would grant her a windfall and excessively penalize Jordan (D) and Barbuto (D).

🏛 RULE OF LAW
A forced buyout is an inappropriate remedy for the freeze-out of a minority shareholder in a close corporation where such a remedy effectively grants the minority a windfall or excessively penalizes the majority.

FACTS: Brodie (P), a minority shareholder in the close corporation Malden, brought suit claiming that Jordan (D) and Barbuto (D), the corporation's two other shareholders who collectively owned a majority share, had "frozen her out" from participation in the company, refused her access to company information, and denied her any economic benefit from her shares. Jordan (D) and Barbuto (D), who did receive economic benefits from their ownership, had also failed to hold an annual shareholder's meeting for the previous five years, and hindered Brodie's (P) attempts to sell her interest in the open market. The trial court found that Jordan (D) and Barbuto (D) had breached their fiduciary duties to Brodie (P) and had frustrated her reasonable expectations of benefit. Accordingly, it concluded that they were liable to Brodie (P) for freezing her out. As a remedy, the trial court ordered that Jordan (D) and Barbuto (D) purchase Brodie's (P) shares in the corporation at a price equal to her share of the corporation's net assets, as valued by an expert, even though neither the articles of organization nor any corporate bylaw obligated Malden or Jordan (D) and Barbuto (D) to purchase Brodie's (P) shares. The state's intermediate appellate court affirmed. The state's highest court granted review.

ISSUE: Is a forced buyout an appropriate remedy for the freeze-out of a minority shareholder in a close corporation where such a remedy effectively grants the minority a windfall or excessively penalizes the majority?

HOLDING AND DECISION: [Judge not stated in casebook excerpt.] No. A forced buyout is an inappropriate remedy for the freeze-out of a minority shareholder in a close corporation where such a remedy effectively grants the minority a windfall or excessively penalizes the majority. The lower courts correctly determined that Brodie (P) had been frozen-out and that Jordan (D) and Barbuto (D) had breached their fiduciary duties to her. Nonetheless, the forced buyout in this case was not an appropriate remedy. The appropriate remedy for a freeze-out should, to the extent possible, restore to the minority shareholder those benefits which she reasonably expects, but has not received because of the fiduciary breach. The remedy should neither grant the minority a windfall nor excessively penalize the majority. Here, the problem with the trial court's remedy was that it placed Brodie (P) in a significantly better position than she would have enjoyed absent the wrongdoing, and well exceeded her reasonable expectations of benefit from her shares. In ordering Jordan (D) and Barbuto (D) to purchase Brodie's (P) stock at the price of her share of the company, the trial court created an artificial market for her minority share of a close corporation—an asset that, by definition, has little or no market value. It was undisputed that neither the articles of organization nor any corporate bylaw obligated Malden or Jordan (D) and Barbuto (D) to purchase Brodie's (P) shares. Thus, there was nothing in the background law, the governing rules of Malden, or any other circumstance that could have given Brodie (P) a reasonable expectation of having her shares bought out. Thus, the trial court's remedy had the perverse effect of placing Brodie (P) in a position superior to that which she would have enjoyed had there been no wrongdoing. Accordingly, the case must be remanded for a remedy that will restore to Brodie (P) those benefits she could reasonably have expected by being a minority shareholder in a close corporation such as Malden. For quantifiable deprivations, monetary damages will be appropriate. Prospective injunctive relief may be granted to ensure that Brodie (P) is allowed to participate in company governance, and to enjoy financial or other benefits from the business, to the extent that her ownership interest justifies. If it is determined that Jordan (D) and Barbuto (D) drained off Malden's earnings from themselves, it may be appropriate to order the declaration of dividends. Reversed and remanded.

▶ ANALYSIS

This case illustrates the benefit of having a shareholder agreement—especially in a close corporation—that requires the corporation to purchase a minority shareholder's shares upon the occurrence of certain events, such as the death of a shareholder, and that otherwise spells out shareholder expectations. Here, Brodie (P) inherited her interest from her deceased husband, who had tried, but failed, to have Malden purchase his shares when his

Continued on next page.

relationship with Jordan (D) and Barbuto (D) deteriorated while he was alive. If the Malden shareholders had a shareholders agreement in place prior to the breakdown of their relationship, the costly lawsuit in this case could have been avoided and the parties could have had established expectations regarding the liquidity of their shares. In addition, this decision arguably represents a retreat from the Massachusetts Supreme Judicial Court's seminal decision in *Donahue v. Rodd Electrotype Co. of New England, Inc.,* 328 N.E.2d 505 (1975), which recognized a direct right of action between shareholders of a close corporation, and broad equitable relief, for breach of the fiduciary duty of utmost good faith and loyalty (i.e., "freeze-out" claims). The *Donahue* court remedied a freeze-out by ordering that the minority's shares be purchased on terms as favorable as those which the controlling shareholders offered to another shareholder. However, by adopting a "reasonable expectation" standard for both assessing liability and determining the scope of equitable relief available in freeze-out disputes, the court seems to have aligned itself with the current trend in other jurisdictions.

■═■

Quicknotes

FIDUCIARY DUTY A legal obligation to act for the benefit of another, including subordinating one's personal interests to that of the other person

MINORITY STOCKHOLDER A stockholder in a corporation controlling such a small portion of those shares which are outstanding that its votes have no influence in the management of the corporation.

■═■

Smith v. Atlantic Properties, Inc.

Shareholder (P) v. Corporation (D)

12 Mass. App. Ct. 201, 422 N.E.2d 798 (1981).

NATURE OF CASE: Appeal from a judgment for the plaintiff in an action for breach of a fiduciary duty owed other stockholders.

FACT SUMMARY: After disagreements arose between the parties who had formed Atlantic Properties, Inc. (D), three (P) of the four shareholders filed suit, seeking a determination of dividends to be paid and the removal of the fourth shareholder (D) as a director.

🏛 RULE OF LAW
Stockholders in a close corporation owe one another the same fiduciary duty in the operation of the enterprise that partners owe to one another.

FACTS: Smith (P), Wolfson (D), Zimble (P), and Burke (P) formed Atlantic Properties, Inc. (D) for the purpose of acquiring real estate. All four held an equal amount of shares. A clause in the articles of incorporation had the effect of giving to any one of the four original shareholders a veto in corporate decisions. Wolfson (D) wanted earnings devoted to making building repairs, while the other three wanted a declaration of dividends in order to avoid penalty taxes. Wolfson (D) refused to vote for any dividends, leading to an IRS assessment of a penalty tax. Smith (P) and the others (P) filed suit, seeking a court determination of the dividends to be paid, the removal of Wolfson (D) as a director, and an order that Atlantic (D) be reimbursed by Wolfson (D) for the penalty taxes assessed against it and for related expenses. The trial court ruled in favor of Smith (P). Wolfson (D) appealed.

ISSUE: Do stockholders in a close corporation owe one another the same fiduciary duty in the operation of the enterprise that partners owe to one another?

HOLDING AND DECISION: [Judge not stated in casebook excerpt.] Yes. Stockholders in a close corporation owe one another the same fiduciary duty in the operation of the enterprise that partners owe to one another. In this case, a clause required an affirmative vote of 80% of the capital stock issued outstanding and entitled to vote in order to effect a change. Therefore, the minority becomes an ad hoc controlling interest, thus reversing the usual roles of the majority and the minority shareholders. Wolfson (D) requested the 80% provision to protect himself from the other shareholders (P). With respect to the past damage caused to Atlantic (D), the trial judge was justified in finding that Wolfson's (D) conduct went beyond what was reasonable. In addition, the court may require information necessary to direct the adoption of a specific dividend and capital improvements policy, and reserve jurisdiction to ensure compliance. Affirmed.

▶ ANALYSIS

The possibilities of shareholder disagreement made the 80% provision seem a sensible precaution. However, to what extent may such a veto power, possessed by a minority stockholder, be exercised as its holder may wish without a violation of that shareholder's fiduciary duty? The court found this a difficult area of the law best developed on a case-by-case basis.

Quicknotes

CLOSELY HELD CORPORATION A corporation whose shares (or at least voting shares) are held by a closely knit group of shareholders or a single person.

FIDUCIARY DUTY A legal obligation to act for the benefit of another, including subordinating one's personal interests to that of the other person.

MINORITY STOCKHOLDER A stockholder in a corporation controlling such a small portion of those shares which are outstanding that its votes have no influence in the management of the corporation.

Jordan v. Duff and Phelps, Inc.

Former employee (P) v. Corporation (D)

815 F.2d 429 (7th Cir. 1987), *cert. dismissed*, 485 U.S. 901 (1988).

NATURE OF CASE: Appeal from a grant of summary judgment for the defendants in an action for fraud and breach of fiduciary duty.

FACT SUMMARY: When Jordan (P) heard of a merger announcement that would have increased the value of stock he had sold back to Duff and Phelps (D) upon leaving their employ, he filed suit, asking for damages measured by the value his stock would have had under the terms of the acquisition.

RULE OF LAW

Close corporations buying their own stock have a fiduciary duty to disclose material facts.

FACTS: Jordan (P), a securities analyst employed at will by Duff and Phelps (D), purchased stock in the company at book value. After informing Duff and Phelps (D) that he was resigning to take a new job, Jordan (P) stayed on until the end of the year in order to receive book value for his stock as of the end of that year rather than the prior year. After leaving, Jordan (P) was startled to learn of a pending merger between Duff and Phelps (D) and another company. Under the terms of the merger, Jordan's (P) stock would have been worth a great deal more. Jordan (P) refused to cash the check, demanding his stock back. Duff and Phelps (D) refused. The merger proposal was abandoned in January. Jordan (P) filed suit in March, asking for damages measured by the value his stock would have had under the terms of the acquisition. The trial court awarded summary judgment to Duff and Phelps (D). Jordan (P) appealed.

ISSUE: Do close corporations buying their own stock have a fiduciary duty to disclose material facts?

HOLDING AND DECISION: (Easterbrook, J.) Yes. Close corporations buying their own stock have a fiduciary duty to disclose material facts. Jordan (P) sold his stock in ignorance of facts that would have established a higher value. The relevance of the fact does not depend on how things turn out. So a failure to disclose an important beneficent event is a violation even if things later go sour. The news here that some firm was willing to pay $50 million for Duff and Phelps (D) in an arm's-length transaction allows investors to assess the worth of the stock. Less than a year later, Duff and Phelps (D) sold the firm to a trust for about $40 million. To recover, Jordan (P) must establish that on learning of the merger negotiations, he would have dropped plans to change jobs and stayed for another year, finally receiving payment from the leveraged buyout. A jury would be entitled to conclude that Jordan (P) would have remained. Reversed and remanded.

DISSENT: (Posner, J.) The mere existence of a fiduciary relationship between a corporation and its shareholders does not require disclosure of material information to the shareholders. The contingent nature of Jordan's (P) status as a shareholder, that is, dependent upon his continued employment, negates the existence of a right to be informed and hence a duty to disclose. By signing the stockholder agreement, Jordan (P) gave Duff and Phelps (D), in effect, an option to buy back his stock at any time at a fixed price. That option denied Jordan (P) the right to profit from any information that Duff and Phelps (D) might have about its prospects but preferred not to give him.

▶ ANALYSIS

Doubtless the news of the impending merger was the reason Jordan (P) filed this suit. If one deal for $50 million falls through, another may be possible at a similar price. Just because the first deal for $50 million fell through does not mean that the company is worth only $2.5 million, which was the book value.

■■■

Quicknotes

CLOSELY HELD CORPORATION A corporation whose shares (or at least voting shares) are held by a closely knit group of shareholders or a single person.

EMPLOYEE AT WILL An employee who works pursuant to the agreement that either he or his employer may terminate the employment relationship at any time and for any cause.

FIDUCIARY DUTY A legal obligation to act for the benefit of another, including subordinating one's personal interests to that of the other person.

MATERIALITY Importance; the degree of relevance or necessity to the particular matter.

■■■

Alaska Plastics, Inc. v. Coppock

Corporation (D) v. Minority shareholder (P)

621 P.2d 270 (Alaska 1980).

NATURE OF CASE: Appeal from a judgment for the plaintiff in an action to compel purchase of minority shares.

FACT SUMMARY: After Alaska Plastics (D) failed to notify Coppock (P) of annual shareholders meetings, she filed suit, seeking to compel Alaska Plastics (D) to purchase its stock she had received in a divorce settlement.

> ## 🏛 RULE OF LAW
> Majority shareholders in a closely held corporation owe a fiduciary duty of utmost good faith and loyalty to minority shareholders.

FACTS: As part of a property settlement related to her divorce from one of Alaska Plastics' (D) directors, Coppock (P) received one-sixth of the shares issued by Alaska Plastics (D). Alaska Plastics (D) subsequently failed to notify Coppock (P) of annual shareholders meetings, paid her no dividends, did not allow her to participate in the business, and later offered to buy her shares for $15,000. An accountant hired by Coppock (P) appraised the shares as having a value between $23,000 and $40,000. One of the directors later offered Coppock (P) $20,000, but a purchase never took place. Coppock (P) filed suit after further negotiations failed. The trial court concluded that Alaska Plastics (D) was obligated to buy Coppock's (P) shares at fair value, plus pay her attorney fees, interest, and costs. Both sides appealed.

ISSUE: Do majority shareholders in a closely held corporation owe a fiduciary duty of utmost good faith and loyalty to minority shareholders?

HOLDING AND DECISION: [Judge not stated in casebook excerpt.] Yes. Majority shareholders in a closely held corporation owe a fiduciary duty of utmost good faith and loyalty to minority shareholders. However, there is no authority which would allow a court to order specific performance on the basis of an unaccepted offer. But, in this case, payments were made to the directors and personal expenses paid for their wives, which might be characterized as constructive dividends. Whether these payments were a distribution of dividends, whether Coppock (P) was deprived of other corporate benefits, or whether the majority shareholders violated Alaska law should be determined by the trial court. The trial court did, however, properly dismiss Coppock's (P) derivative complaint, since she failed to allege that Alaska Plastics (D) itself was harmed. Remanded.

▶ ANALYSIS

On remand, the court awarded Coppock (P) the same amount for her shares that it had awarded her initially. The Alaska Supreme Court upheld the trial court's findings on appeal. The court noted that while Alaska law allows the superior court to liquidate a corporation when the acts of those in control are oppressive or fraudulent, courts retain equitable authority to fashion a less drastic remedy to fit the parties' situation.

■=■

Quicknotes

ALASKA CORP. CODE § 10.05.540 Shareholders may bring a liquidation action upon a showing that director's actions are illegal, fraudulent, or wasteful.

CLOSELY HELD CORPORATION A corporation whose shares (or at least voting shares) are held by a closely knit group of shareholders or a single person.

FIDUCIARY DUTY A legal obligation to act for the benefit of another, including subordinating one's personal interests to that of the other person.

GOOD FAITH An honest intention to abstain from any unconscientious advantage of another.

MAJORITY STOCKHOLDER A stockholder of a corporation who holds in excess of fifty percent of the corporation's shares.

MINORITY SHAREHOLDER A stockholder in a corporation controlling such a small portion of those shares which are outstanding that its votes have no influence in the management of the corporation.

■=■

Haley v. Talcott

50% LLC owner (P) v. 50% LLC owner (D)

864 A.2d 86 (Del. Ch. 2004).

NATURE OF CASE: Action to dissolve limited liability company (LLC).

FACT SUMMARY: Haley (P) and Talcott (D), each 50% owners of a limited liability company (LLC), were at an impasse. Haley (P) argued that dissolution was necessary, whereas Talcott (D) argued that Haley (P) was limited to an exit mechanism provided in the LLC's operating agreement, even if such exit mechanism was not equitable regarding Haley's (P) interests.

> ## 🏛 RULE OF LAW
> Where co-equal members of a limited liability company are at an impasse, can no longer carry on the LLC's business, and are in disagreement about whether to discontinue the business and how to dispose of its assets, and where an exit mechanism in the LLC's operating agreement is inequitable, dissolution is necessary.

FACTS: Haley (P) and Talcott (D) each owned 50% of Matt and Greg Real Estate, LLC (the LLC). A restaurant (the Redfin Grill) owned by Talcott (D) and operated by Haley (P) leased from the LLC the land on which the restaurant operated. Contractually, Haley (P) was supposed to receive 50% of the profits from the restaurant business, which the two men operated as a joint venture. Although pursuant to an employment contract Haley (P) was technically Talcott's (D) employee at the restaurant, the other terms of the contract established a relationship more similar to a partnership. Both men personally guaranteed the mortgage for the property owned by the LLC. Eventually, a rift developed between them, and the rift turned into deadlock and an impasse where the LLC could no longer carry on its business. In addition, the LLC property appreciated substantially in value (from the purchase price of $720,000 to an appraised value of $1.8 million). Absent court intervention, Haley (P) would be stuck with the status quo unless he chose to avail himself of the operating agreement's exit mechanism. This mechanism provided that upon notice of election to quit the LLC, the remaining member could elect to purchase the departing member's interest at fair market value. If the remaining member fails to elect to purchase the departing member's interest, the company is to be liquidated. However, the exit mechanism did not provide expressly for a release from the personal guarantees that the two men had given for the mortgage of the LLC's real property. Nor did the exit provision state that any member dissatisfied with the status quo had to break an impasse by exit rather than a suit for dissolution. Haley (P) brought suit for dissolution; Talcott (D) maintained that Haley's remedy (P) was limited to the contractual exit mechanism.

ISSUE: Where co-equal members of an LLC are at an impasse, can no longer carry on the LLC's business, and are in disagreement about whether to discontinue the business and how to dispose of its assets, and where an exit mechanism in the LLC's operating agreement is inequitable, is dissolution necessary?

HOLDING AND DECISION: [Judge not stated in casebook excerpt.] Yes. Where co-equal members of a limited liability company are at an impasse, can no longer carry on the LLC's business, and are in disagreement about whether to discontinue the business and how to dispose of its assets, and where an exit mechanism in the LLC's operating agreement is inequitable, dissolution is necessary. The applicable statute provides that on application by or for a member or manager, the court may decree dissolution of a limited liability company whenever it is not reasonably practicable to carry on the business in conformity with a limited liability company agreement. The elements of this statute are met here: the members are equal owners; they are engaged in a joint venture; and they are unable to agree upon whether to discontinue the business or how to dispose of its assets. Most important in this regard, Haley (P) never agreed to be a passive investor in the LLC who would be subject to Talcott's (D) unilateral dominion. Instead, the LLC agreement provided that: "no member/managers may, without the agreement of a majority vote of the managers' interest, act on behalf of the company." Because the manifest weight of the evidence is that the parties are deadlocked, if the entity were a corporation, there would be no question that Haley's (P) request to dissolve the entity would be granted. However, here, the operating agreement's exit mechanism must also be considered. First, the state's LLC statute is grounded on principles of freedom of contract. For that reason, the presence of a reasonable exit mechanism bears on the propriety of ordering dissolution. When the agreement itself provides a fair opportunity for the dissenting member who disfavors the inertial status quo to exit and receive the fair market value of his interest, it is at least arguable that the limited liability company may still proceed to operate practicably under its contractual charter because the charter itself provides an equitable way to break the impasse. Thus, so long as Haley (P) can actually extract himself fairly, it arguably makes sense for the court to stay its hand in an LLC case and allow the contract itself to solve the problem. However, forcing Haley (P) to exercise the contractual exit mechanism would not permit the LLC to proceed in a practicable way which accords with the LLC

Continued on next page.

agreement, but would instead permit Talcott (D) to penalize Haley (P) without express contractual authorization. This is so because the exit mechanism would not relieve Haley (P) of his obligation under the personal guaranty that he signed to secure the mortgage on the LLC's property. If Haley (P) is forced to use the exit mechanism, Talcott (D) and he both believe that Haley (P) would still be left holding the bag on the guaranty. It is therefore not equitable to force Haley (P) to use the exit mechanism in this circumstance. Thus, the exit mechanism fails as an adequate remedy for Haley (P) because it does not equitably effect the separation of the parties. Rather, it would leave him with no potentiality and no protection over the considerable risk that he would have to make good on any future default by the LLC (over whose operations he would have no control) to its mortgage lender. For this reason, it is necessary for the court to intervene and order dissolution.

▶ *ANALYSIS*

It is an interesting question whether the 50% member of an LLC that operates an on-going business, and who does not favor inertial policy, must exit rather than force dissolution, particularly when the cost of the exit procedure would, as here, be borne solely by him. Arguably, it is economically more efficient—absent an explicit requirement that the party disfavoring inertia exit if he is dissatisfied—to order dissolution, and allow both parties to bid as purchasers, with the assets going to the highest bidder (inside or outside) who presumably will deploy the asset to its most valuable use. It is also concomitantly arguable that if parties wish to force the co-equal member disfavoring inertia to exit rather than seek dissolution, then they should explicitly contract upfront in the LLC agreement that exit (or the triggering of a buy-sell procedure, giving incentives for the business to be retained by the member willing to pay the highest value) is the required method of breaking any later-arising stalemate.

■■■

Quicknotes

DISSOLUTION Annulment or termination of a formal or legal bond, tie or contract.

LIMITED LIABILITY COMPANY A business entity combining the features of both a corporation and a general partnership; the LLC provides its shareholders and officers with limited liability, but it is treated as a partnership for taxation purposes.

LIQUIDATION The reduction to cash of all assets for distribution to creditors.

STATUS QUO The existing circumstances at a particular moment.

■■■

Pedro v. Pedro

Minority shareholder (P) v. Shareholders (D)

489 N.W.2d 798 (Minn. App. 1992).

NATURE OF CASE: Appeal from a judgment for the plaintiff in an action requesting dissolution of a closely held corporation.

FACT SUMMARY: After Alfred Pedro (P) was fired from his position in the company by his two brothers, Carl (D) and Eugene (D), he filed this suit seeking to dissolve the company.

🏛 RULE OF LAW
Shareholders in closely held corporations have a fiduciary duty to deal openly, honestly, and fairly with one another.

FACTS: Alfred (P), Carl (D), and Eugene (D) Pedro, brothers, each owned a one-third interest in The Pedro Companies, had worked for the company all their lives, and planned to continue doing so. When Alfred (P) discovered a large discrepancy in the company's internal accounting records, he was told that if he did not cooperate and forget about the apparent discrepancy, his brothers (D) would fire him. After a second independent accountant identified a discrepancy, Alfred (P) was placed on mandatory leave of absence and subsequently fired. He brought suit, seeking dissolution of the company. His brothers (D) moved that the action proceed as a buyout under Minnesota law. Alfred (P) was awarded damages for his one-third ownership of the company, for breach of fiduciary duty, and for wrongful termination, plus attorney costs and prejudgment interest on the awards. Carl (D) and Eugene (D) appealed.

ISSUE: Do shareholders in closely held corporations have a fiduciary duty to deal openly, honestly, and fairly with one another?

HOLDING AND DECISION: [Judge not stated in casebook excerpt.] Yes. Shareholders in closely held corporations have a fiduciary duty to deal openly, honestly, and fairly with one another. Carl (D) and Eugene (D) admitted in their motion requesting a buyout, they were acting in a manner unfairly prejudicial toward Alfred (P). This admission supports a finding of breach of fiduciary duty. Furthermore, there was evidence in the record to support the measure of damages for the buyout. Finally, the unique facts in the record support the trial court's finding of an agreement to provide lifetime employment to Alfred (P). Thus, the award of lost wages was proper. Once the court found that Carl (D) and Eugene (D) had breached their fiduciary duties, the court had discretion to award attorney fees. Affirmed.

▶ ANALYSIS

In a closely held corporation, the nature of the employment of a shareholder may create a reasonable expectation by the employee-owner that his employment is not terminable at will. Here, the three brothers had worked in the company all their lives, Carl (D) since 1940, Eugene (D) since 1939, and Alfred (P) since 1942. It was thus reasonable for the court to find that they did in fact have a contract that was not terminable at will.

■══■

Quicknotes

CLOSELY HELD CORPORATION A corporation whose shares (or at least voting shares) are held by a closely knit group of shareholders or a single person.

FIDUCIARY DUTY A legal obligation to act for the benefit of another, including subordinating one's personal interests to that of the other person.

■══■

Stuparich v. Harbor Furniture Mfg., Inc.

Shareholders (P) v. Close corporation and directors (D)

83 Cal. App. 4th 1268, 100 Cal. Rptr. 2d 313 (2000).

NATURE OF CASE: Appeal from a defense summary judgment in a suit by minority shareholders of a close corporation for a statutory dissolution.

FACT SUMMARY: After an extended progression of disputes and ill-will between family board members of Harbor Furniture Mfg., Inc. (D) (a close corporation), Ann Stuparich (P) and Candi Tuttleton (P), minority shareholders, sued for the involuntary statutory dissolution of the corporation.

🏛 RULE OF LAW
Statutory dissolution of a close corporation is not reasonably necessary for shareholder protection on the grounds of animosity among the corporate directors.

FACTS: Ann Stuparich (P) and Candi Tuttleton (P) are sisters. Harbor Furniture Mfg., Inc. (D), a close corporation, was founded by their grandfather. Stuparich (P) and Tuttleton (P) obtained shares in Harbor Furniture (D) through gifts and inheritance. They became dissatisfied with the failure of the company to observe various formalities. At Stuparich's (P) insistence, Harbor Furniture (D) began holding annual meetings. Many disputes arose among the various board members, most of whom were family members, ultimately leading to severe animosity and ill-will. As a result, Stuparich (P) and Tuttleton (P), as minority shareholders, brought a suit against Harbor Furniture (D) and its directors (D), seeking, inter alia, the involuntary statutory dissolution of the corporation. The relevant legislation permits involuntary dissolution when liquidation is reasonably necessary for the protection of the rights or interests of the complaining shareholder. The trial court granted a summary judgment for Harbor Furniture (D). Stuparich (P) and Tuttleton (P) appealed.

ISSUE: Is statutory dissolution of a close corporation reasonably necessary for shareholder protection on the grounds of animosity among the corporate directors?

HOLDING AND DECISION: [Judge not stated in casebook excerpt.] No. Statutory dissolution of a close corporation is not reasonably necessary for shareholder protection on the grounds of animosity among the corporate directors. To provide close corporation shareholders with a remedy, legislation permits any shareholder of a close corporation to initiate involuntary dissolution. Since this legislation permits a going concern to be involuntarily terminated, the application of such a "drastic remedy" should be appropriately limited. Here, notwithstanding hard feelings and ill-will among the corporate directors, there was no mismanagement or unfairness nor was there evidence of a corporate deadlock. The power of minority shareholders to obtain involuntary dissolution is not unlimited. The procedure created by the statute does not authorize dissolution at will. The only evidence provided by Stuparich (P) as to whether dissolution was reasonably necessary to protect shareholder rights was that her brother had voting control of the corporation, Stuparich (P) was not allowed meaningful participation in the corporation, the dispute with the brother gave rise to a violent confrontation among certain board members, and Stuparich (P) had an economic interest in reducing the losses the company has suffered over the last 10 years. Here, such evidence was not sufficient upon which to base an involuntary close corporation termination. The distribution of voting shares in the corporation is consistent with California law and does not, in itself, present a reasonable necessity for dissolution. Furthermore, Harbor Furniture (D) properly contends that one can always argue that more profits could be made by a corporation. Courts should not become involved "in the tweaking of corporate performance." Such is the reason for the "business judgment rule." An opportunity to participate and speak, as here, is all a minority shareholder is entitled to and may expect. Affirmed.

▶ ANALYSIS

As noted in *Stuparich*, an overly broad construction of the close corporation dissolution statute would make it too easy for an obstreperous minority to interfere with the legitimate control and management of the majority by creating a cash nuisance value.

■=■

Quicknotes

BUSINESS JUDGMENT RULE Doctrine relieving corporate directors and/or officers from liability for decisions honestly and rationally made in the corporation's best interests.

INVOLUNTARY DISSOLUTION The termination of a corporation's existence through administrative or judicial action or insolvency.

MINORITY SHAREHOLDER A stockholder in a corporation controlling such a small portion of those shares that are outstanding that its votes have no influence in the management of the corporation.

■=■

Frandsen v. Jensen-Sundquist Agency, Inc.

Minority shareholder (P) v. Corporation (D)

802 F.2d 941 (7th Cir. 1986).

NATURE OF CASE: Appeal from dismissal of action for breach of a stockholder agreement.

FACT SUMMARY: Frandsen (P), a minority shareholder in Jensen-Sundquist (D), brought suit after his attempt to exercise his right of first refusal to buy the majority bloc's shares at the offer price in a proposed acquisition failed.

RULE OF LAW
In a transfer of control of a company, the rights of first refusal to buy shares at the offer price are to be interpreted narrowly.

FACTS: Frandsen (P) was a minority shareholder of Jensen-Sundquist (D), a holding company whose principal asset was the First Bank of Grantsburg. If the Jensen (D) family majority bloc ever offered to sell its shares, Frandsen (P) had a right to buy the shares at the offer price, or, if he declined, the majority had to buy Frandsen's (P) shares at the same price at which it sold its own shares. First Wisconsin (D) negotiated to acquire Jensen-Sundquist (D) because it wanted the bank. Frandsen (P) then announced that he was exercising his right of first refusal to buy the majority shares. When the deal was restructured, Frandsen (P) brought suit, charging Jensen-Sundquist (D) with breach of the stockholder agreement, and First Wisconsin (D) with tortious interference with his contract rights. The district judge granted summary judgment for Jensen-Sundquist (D) and First Wisconsin (D). Frandsen (P) appealed.

ISSUE: In a transfer of control of a company, are the rights of first refusal to buy shares at the offer price to be interpreted narrowly?

HOLDING AND DECISION: (Posner, J.) Yes. In a transfer of control of a company, the rights of first refusal to buy shares at the offer price are to be interpreted narrowly. In this case, there never was an offer within the scope of the stockholder agreement. Thus Frandsen's (P) right of first refusal was never triggered. First Wisconsin (D) was never interested in becoming a majority shareholder of Jensen-Sundquist (D), it simply wanted to acquire the bank. Therefore, a sale of stock was never contemplated. If no contractual right of Frandsen's (P) was violated by the transaction, it is difficult to see how First Wisconsin (D) could have been guilty of a tortious interference with his contractual rights. Affirmed.

▶ ANALYSIS

The effect of a right of first refusal is to add a party to a transaction, which increases the costs of transacting exponentially. If all the costs of the more complicated transaction were borne by the parties, it would not be a matter of social concern. However, since some of the costs are borne by the taxpayers who support the court system, the courts are not hospitable to such rights.

■ ══ ■

Quicknotes

MAJORITY SHAREHOLDER A stockholder of a corporation who holds in excess of fifty percent of the corporation's shares.

MINORITY SHAREHOLDER A stockholder in a corporation controlling such a small portion of those shares which are outstanding that its votes have no influence in the management of the corporation.

RIGHT OF FIRST REFUSAL Allows one to meet the terms of a proposed contract before it is executed.

TORTIOUS INTERFERENCE WITH CONTRACT RIGHTS An intentional tort whereby a defendant intentionally elicits the breach of a valid contract resulting in damages.

■ ══ ■

Zetlin v. Hanson Holdings, Inc.

Minority shareholder (P) v. Corporation (D)

48 N.Y.2d 684, 421 N.Y.S.2d 877, 397 N.E.2d 387 (1979).

NATURE OF CASE: Appeal from an order in favor of the defendants in an action involving the sale of majority shares of a corporation.

FACT SUMMARY: When Hanson Holdings (D) and the Sylvestri family (D) sold their controlling interest in Gable Industries for a premium price, Zetlin (P), a minority shareholder, brought suit, contending that minority shareholders were entitled to an opportunity to share equally in any premium paid for a controlling interest.

🏛 RULE OF LAW
Absent looting of corporate assets, conversion of a corporate opportunity, fraud or other acts of bad faith, a controlling stockholder is free to sell, and a purchaser is free to buy, that controlling interest at a premium price.

FACTS: Zetlin (P) held a 2% interest in Gable Industries. Hanson Holdings (D) and members of the Sylvestri family (D) owned 44% of Gable's shares. After the Sylvestri family (D) and Hanson (D) sold their controlling interest at a premium price per share, Zetlin (P) brought suit, contending that minority stockholders were entitled to an opportunity to share equally in any premium paid for a controlling interest in the corporation. The appellate division disagreed. Zetlin (P) appealed.

ISSUE: Absent looting of corporate assets, conversion of a corporate opportunity, fraud or other acts of bad faith, is a controlling stockholder free to sell, and is a purchaser free to buy, that controlling interest at a premium price?

HOLDING AND DECISION: [Judge not stated in casebook excerpt.] Yes. Absent looting of corporate assets, conversion of a corporate opportunity, fraud or other acts of bad faith, a controlling stockholder is free to sell, and a purchaser is free to buy, that controlling interest at a premium price. Certainly, minority shareholders are entitled to protection against abuse by controlling shareholders. They are not entitled, however, to inhibit the legitimate interests of the other stockholders. It is for this reason that control shares usually command a premium price. The premium is the added amount an investor is willing to pay for the privilege of directly influencing the corporation's affairs. Order affirmed.

▶ ANALYSIS

Zetlin's (P) contention would profoundly affect the manner in which controlling stock interests are now transferred. It would require, essentially, that a controlling interest be transferred only by means of an offer to all stockholders,

that is, a tender offer. The New York Court of Appeals declared that this would be contrary to existing law and that the legislature is best suited to make radical changes.

■■■

Quicknotes

CONTROLLING SHAREHOLDER A person who has power to vote a majority of the outstanding shares of a corporation, or who is able to direct the management of the corporation with a smaller block of stock because the remaining shares are scattered among small, disorganized holdings.

CORPORATE OPPORTUNITY An opportunity that a fiduciary to a corporation has to take advantage of information acquired by virtue of his or her position for the individual's benefit.

MINORITY SHAREHOLDER A stockholder in a corporation controlling such a small portion of those shares which are outstanding that its votes have no influence in the management of the corporation.

■■■

Perlman v. Feldmann

Minority shareholder (P) v. Former controlling shareholder (D)

219 F.2d 173 (2d Cir.), *cert. denied*, 349 U.S. 952 (1955).

NATURE OF CASE: Appeal from a judgment in an action to compel an accounting in the sale of a controlling corporate interest.

FACT SUMMARY: After Feldmann (D) sold his controlling interest in the Newport Steel Corporation, Perlman (P) and other minority stockholders (P) brought a derivative action to compel accounting for, and restitution of, allegedly illegal gains accruing to Feldmann (D) as a result of the sale.

🏛 RULE OF LAW
Directors and dominant stockholders stand in a fiduciary relationship to the corporation and to the minority stockholders as beneficiaries thereof.

FACTS: Newport Steel Corporation operated mills for the production of steel sheets for sale to manufacturers of steel products. Feldmann (D), the dominant stockholder, chairman of the board of directors, and Newport's president, negotiated a sale of the controlling interest in Newport to a syndicate organized as Wilport Company. A steel shortage existed at the time as a result of demand during the Korean War. Perlman (P) and other minority stockholders (P) brought this derivative action to compel an accounting for, and restitution of, allegedly illegal gains accruing to Feldmann (D) and the other majority stockholders as a result of the sale. The trial court found the share price to be a fair one for a control block of stock. Perlman (P) and the others (P) appealed.

ISSUE: Do directors and dominant stockholders stand in a fiduciary relationship to the corporation and to the minority stockholders as beneficiaries thereof?

HOLDING AND DECISION: (Clark, C.J.) Yes. Directors and dominant stockholders stand in a fiduciary relationship to the corporation and to the minority stockholders as beneficiaries thereof. However, a majority stockholder can dispose of his controlling block of stock to outsiders without having to account to his corporation for profits. But when the sale necessarily results in a sacrifice of an element of corporate good will and consequently unusual profit to the fiduciary which caused the sacrifice, that fiduciary should account for his gains. In a time of market shortage, where a call on a corporation's product commands an unusually large premium, a fiduciary may not himself appropriate the value of this premium. Hence, to the extent that the price received by Feldmann (D) and the others included such a bonus, he is accountable to the minority stockholders (P), who are entitled to a recovery in their own right, instead of in the right of Newport Steel. Reversed.

DISSENT: (Swan, J.) Feldmann (D) was not proved to be under any fiduciary duty as a stockholder not to sell the stock he controlled. In so doing, he acts on his own behalf, not as an agent of the corporation. If he knows or has reason to believe that the purchaser intends to exercise the power of management to the detriment of the corporation such knowledge or reasonable suspicion will terminate the dominant shareholder's privilege to sell. The lower court found that Feldmann (D) had no reason to think that Wilport would use its acquired power of management to injure Newport, and that there was no proof that it was ever so used.

▶ ANALYSIS

The court found no fraud, no misuse of confidential information, and no outright looting of a helpless corporation. On the other hand, it did not find compliance with the high standard applied as the rule of law, which other courts have come to expect and demand of corporate fiduciaries. In the words of Judge Cardozo, many forms of conduct permissible in a workaday world for those acting at arm's length are forbidden to those bound by fiduciary ties.

■━■

Quicknotes

CORPORATE OPPORTUNITY An opportunity that a fiduciary to a corporation has to take advantage of information acquired by virtue of his or her position for the individual's benefit.

FIDUCIARY DUTY A legal obligation to act for the benefit of another, including subordinating one's personal interests to that of the other person.

MINORITY SHAREHOLDER A stockholder in a corporation controlling such a small portion of those shares which are outstanding that its votes have no influence in the management of the corporation.

RESTITUTION The return or restoration of what the defendant has gained in a transaction to prevent the unjust enrichment of the defendant.

■━■

Essex Universal Corporation v. Yates

Corporation (P) v. Director (D)

305 F.2d 572 (2d Cir. 1962).

NATURE OF CASE: Appeal from summary judgment dismissing action seeking damages for breach of contract.

FACT SUMMARY: A contract calling for a sale of stock in Republic Pictures to Essex (P) included a provision calling for eight of Republic's fourteen directors to resign and be replaced by Essex (P) nominees.

🏛 RULE OF LAW
A sale of a controlling interest in a corporation may include immediate transfer of control.

FACTS: Yates (D) was a shareholder and president of Republic Pictures, Inc., which operated a film studio. He owned less than a majority of shares, but a sufficient amount to exercise de facto majority control. At one point he contracted to sell his interest to Essex Universal Corporation (P). The contract called for a transfer of Yates's (D) shares, which equaled roughly 28% of voting shares, and also called for the resignation of a majority of Republic's board, to be filled by individuals of Essex's (P) choice. At the last minute the deal fell through, due to disagreement on the value of shares. Essex (P) filed suit in New York state court, seeking damages for breach of contract. The matter was removed to federal court. Yates (D) successfully moved for summary judgment, arguing that the clause calling for immediate transfer of control was illegal and voided the contract. Essex (P) appealed.

ISSUE: May a sale of a controlling interest in a corporation include immediate transfer of control?

HOLDING AND DECISION: (Lumbard, C.J.) Yes. A sale of a controlling interest in a corporation may include immediate transfer of control. It is the law that control of a corporation may not be sold absent the sale of sufficient shares to transfer such control. This is based on the notion that control of a corporation derives from corporate voting, and is not a personal right. There can be no question but that if a block of stock is sold which is sufficient to transfer control, the buyer can, through the normal directorate voting process, install a directorate of his choosing. This being so, there is no reason why such transfer should not be assignable upon sale. Transfer of control is inevitable in such a situation, and goals of corporate efficiency will be promoted by allowing it in circumstances such as these. Because of this, the better rule is that immediate transfer of control will not void a sale of a controlling block of stock. Remanded.

CONCURRENCE: (Clark, J.) The action should be remanded for trial, but great discretion should be left to the trial court as to how to deal with the present issue.

CONCURRENCE: (Friendly, J.) In this case, a mass seriatim resignation was directed by a selling stockholder. He filled the vacancies with his henchmen at the dictation of a purchaser and without any consideration of the character of the latter's nominees. This is beyond what the stockholders contemplated or should have been expected to contemplate. And, therefore, the transaction here should be considered illegal. However, this rule should not be applied retrospectively, and would therefore not void this particular transaction.

▶ *ANALYSIS*

This particular decision produced no majority—each justice wrote his own separate opinion. It is clear that Justice Lumbard approved of immediate transfer of control, and Justice Friendly did not. Justice Clark's view is not at all clear, so the precedential value of the present opinion is dubious.

■■■

Quicknotes

CONTROLLING SHAREHOLDER A person who has power to vote a majority of the outstanding shares of a corporation, or who is able to direct the management of the corporation with a smaller block of stock because the remaining shares are scattered among small, disorganized holdings.

SERIATIM In order; successively.

■■■

Mergers, Acquisitions, and Takeovers

Quick Reference Rules of Law

Farris v. Glen Alden Corporation

Shareholder (P) v. Corporation (D

393 Pa. 427, 143 A.2d 25 (1958).

NATURE OF CASE: Action to enjoin performance of a corporate reorganization agreement.

FACT SUMMARY: Glen Alden (D) and List Corporation entered into a reorganization agreement under which Glen Alden (D) was to acquire List's assets. Farris (P), a stockholder in Glen Alden (D), sued to enjoin performance of this agreement.

🏛 RULE OF LAW
A transaction which is in the form of a sale of corporate assets but which is in effect a de facto merger of two corporations must meet the statutory merger requirements in order to protect the rights of minority shareholders.

FACTS: List, a holding company, purchased 38.5% of the outstanding stock of Glen Alden (D), a corporation engaged in mining and manufacture, and placed three of its directors on the Glen Alden (D) board. The two corporations entered into a "reorganization agreement" under which Glen Alden (D) was to purchase the assets of List and take over List's liabilities. List shareholders would receive stock in Glen Alden, and List would be dissolved. Notice of this agreement was sent to the shareholders of Glen Alden (D), who approved the agreement at their annual meeting. Farris (P), a shareholder of Glen Alden (D), filed this suit to enjoin performance of the agreement on the ground that the notice to the shareholders of the proposed agreement did not conform to the statutory requirements for a proposed merger. Glen Alden (D) defended on the basis that the form of the transaction was a sale of assets rather than a merger so the merger statute was inapplicable.

ISSUE: Do "reorganization agreements" which are de facto mergers, require conformance by the corporations to the merger statutes?

HOLDING AND DECISION: [Judge not stated in casebook excerpt.] Yes. To decide whether a transaction is in fact a merger or only a sale of assets, a court must look not to the formalities of the agreement but to its practical effect. Under Pennsylvania law, a shareholder of a corporation which is planning to merge has a right to dissent and to get paid fair value for his shares, but has no such rights if his corporation is merely purchasing the assets of another corporation. A transaction is a de facto merger, and these rights must be granted to dissenting shareholders, if the agreement will so change the corporate character that to refuse to allow the shareholder to dissent will, in effect, force him to give up his shares in one corporation and accept shares in an entirely different corporation. If this agreement is performed, Farris (P) will become a shareholder in a larger corporation which is engaged in an entirely different type of business. The new corporation will have a majority of directors appointed by List, Farris (P) will have a smaller percentage of ownership because of the shares issued to the List shareholders, and the market value of his shares will decrease. This, then, is a de facto merger and Glen Alden (D) must follow the statutory merger requirements even though the transaction is in the form of a purchase of List's assets. Also, even if this were a purchase of assets, the reality of the agreement is that List is acquiring Glen Alden, despite the form which states that Glen Alden (D) is acquiring List, and under Pennsylvania law shareholders of a purchased corporation also have a statutory right to dissent. Therefore, even if this were not a de facto merger, Farris (P) still has a right to dissent. Affirmed.

▶ ANALYSIS

Because of the statutory merger requirements, corporations will try to achieve the effect of a merger by alternative methods, such as a sale of assets or a sale of stock. The formal merger requirements are consent by the shareholders of both corporations and majority approval by the directors. *Glen Alden* illustrates the resulting rights of a dissenting shareholder to demand appraisal—requiring the corporation to purchase his shares before the merger can take place. The rationale of the appraisal right is that the shareholder purchased the shares of a specific corporation, and to force him to exchange his stock in the corporation he chose for stock in an entirely different corporation is to deprive him of his property. Compare this with the rationale in *Applestein v. United Board & Carton Corp.*

■=■

Quicknotes

DE FACTO MERGER DOCTRINE The acquisition of one company by another without compliance with the requirements of a statutory merger but treated by the courts as such.

PENNSYLVANIA BUS. CORP. LAW, § 908 Shareholders objecting to a merger are entitled to sell at market value.

■=■

Hariton v. Arco Electronics, Inc.

Shareholder (P) v. Corporation (D)

188 A.2d 123 (Del. 1963).

NATURE OF CASE: Appeal from summary judgment dismissing an action seeking to enjoin sale of stock.

FACT SUMMARY: Loral Electronics and Arco Electronics (D) agreed to an assets sale which constituted a de facto merger.

🏛 RULE OF LAW
A sale of assets involving dissolution of the selling corporation and distribution of the shares to its shareholders is legal.

FACTS: Loral Electronics and Arco Electronics (D) entered into an agreement wherein Arco (D) was to sell all of its assets to Loral. Loral was then to issue 230,000 shares of stock, to be transferred to Arco (D). Arco (D) was then to distribute the shares to its own shareholders. Hariton (P), a shareholder of Arco (D), filed an action seeking to enjoin the transaction, contending that it was a de facto merger and, as such, was subject to certain regulations that the transaction avoided by not officially being called a merger. The Chancery Court held the transaction valid, and the Delaware Supreme Court granted review.

ISSUE: Is a sale of assets that results in a de facto merger legal?

HOLDING AND DECISION: [Judge not stated in casebook excerpt.] Yes. A sale of assets involving dissolution of the selling corporation and distribution of the shares to its shareholders is legal. The statutes controlling mergers and those controlling asset sales are independent of each other, and are equal in terms of validity. If an asset sale meets the legal requirements of such a sale, the fact that it might be a de facto merger should not invalidate it any more than an otherwise legal merger should be invalidated because it is a de facto asset sale. To hold otherwise would be to create unnecessary uncertainty and litigation. Affirmed.

▶ ANALYSIS

Generally speaking, legislatures tend to place greater scrutiny on mergers than on asset sales. The perception appears to be that the chances of injuring minority shareholders are greater in a merger. For that reason, restrictions may be placed on mergers that are not placed on asset sales. Here, for instance, a right of appraisal attached to mergers, but not to asset sales.

Quicknotes

8 DEL. C., § 271 Governs mergers where purchasing corporation buys with its own shares.

DE FACTO MERGER DOCTRINE The acquisition of one company by another without compliance with the requirements of a statutory merger but treated by the courts as such.

Weinberger v. UOP, Inc.

Minority shareholder (P) v. Corporation (D)

457 A.2d 701 (Del. 1983) (en banc).

NATURE OF CASE: Appeal from judgment finding merger and price paid to shareholders fair in class action challenging cash-out merger.

FACT SUMMARY: The Signal Companies, Inc. (D) effected a freeze-out merger with subsidiary UOP, Inc. (D) without disclosing to minority shareholders the value of UOP (D) shares.

🏛 RULE OF LAW
A freeze-out merger approved without full disclosure of share value to minority shareholders is invalid.

FACTS: The Signal Companies (D) acquired, through both market purchases and a tender offer, a majority interest in UOP, Inc. (D). Signal (D) paid $21 per share. Signal (D) later decided to acquire all shares in UOP (D). A report generated by two directors of both corporations concluded that a share price of up to $24 would be a beneficial deal for Signal (D). Signal (D) announced to minority shareholders in UOP (D) that it was offering $21 per share to acquire all shares in UOP (D). At the annual shareholder meeting of UOP (D), a majority of the minority shareholders approved the sale, which resulted in a forced sale of all shares. Weinberger (P), a minority shareholder who had voted against the sale, filed an action seeking to enjoin the merger. The Chancery Court held the merger valid, and an appeal was taken.

ISSUE: Is a freeze-out merger approved without full disclosure of share value to minority shareholders valid?

HOLDING AND DECISION: [Judge not stated in casebook excerpt.] No. A freeze-out merger approved without full disclosure of share value to minority shareholders is invalid. For a freeze-out merger to be valid, the transaction must be fair. To be considered fair, two conditions must be met: shareholders must be informed of all relevant facts prior to voting and the price given must be fair. When important information is withheld from minority shareholders, their consent to the merger cannot be informed. In this particular instance, a report existed that showed that a share price of as much as $24 would be advantageous to Signal (D); had they known this, the minority shareholders might not have voted in favor of a cash-out at $21 per share. Therefore, as material information was withheld, the merger was not fair, and therefore must be voided. Reversed and remanded.

▌ *ANALYSIS*

In cases like these, burden of proof can often determine the winner. In the instance of a challenge to a freeze-out merger, the rule in this jurisdiction was that the ultimate burden to show unfairness was on Weinberger (P) and the others challenging the transaction, but the burden was on the corporations (D) to show the vote had been done with full disclosure.

═▪

Quicknotes

FAIR DEALING The duty owed by a controlling shareholder to a company's minority shareholders to deal fairly and not to act in a manner so as to exploit or oppress the minority shareholders.

FREEZE-OUT MERGER Merger whereby the majority shareholder forces minority shareholders into the sale of their securities.

TENDER OFFER An offer made by one corporation to the shareholders of a target corporation to purchase their shares subject to number, time, and price specifications.

═▪

Coggins v. New England Patriots Football Club, Inc.

Shareholder (P) v. Corporation (D)

397 Mass. 525, 492 N.E.2d 1112 (1986).

NATURE OF CASE: Appeal from judgment holding freeze-out merger illegal and assessing rescissionary damages.

FACT SUMMARY: A freeze-out merger of the New England Patriots Football Club (D) into a parent corporation was challenged as having been effected solely for the benefit of the majority shareholder.

🏛 RULE OF LAW
Controlling stockholders violate their fiduciary duties when they cause a merger to be made for the sole purpose of eliminating a minority on a cash-out basis.

FACTS: In 1959, Sullivan (D) purchased a franchise in the newly formed American Football League, later named the Boston Patriots. The team was owned by the New England Patriots Football Club, Inc. (Old Patriots) (D), in which Sullivan (D) held a controlling but nonmajority interest. To foster public interest in the team, nonvoting stock was sold to the public. In 1974 Sullivan (D) was ousted as president of the corporation. The following year he managed to acquire all voting shares. He then formed a new corporation, also called the New England Patriots Football Club, Inc. (New Patriots) (D). In a transaction effected primarily to pay off Sullivan's (D) personal debts incurred in acquiring the voting stock, New Patriots (D) acquired 100% of Old Patriots' (D) voting stock, Sullivan (D) retained 100% of the voting stock of New Patriots (D), the two corporations were merged, and the nonvoting shares of Old Patriots (D) were to be exchanged for cash at the rate of $15.00 a share. Coggins (P), who owned ten nonvoting shares of Old Patriots (D), challenged the transaction in a class action. The trial court held the merger illegal, but, rather than void the transaction, ordered rescissionary damages. An appeal was taken.

ISSUE: Do controlling stockholders violate their fiduciary duties when they cause a merger to be made for the sole purpose of eliminating a minority on a cash-out basis?

HOLDING AND DECISION: [Judge not stated in casebook excerpt.] Yes. Controlling stockholders violate their fiduciary duties when they cause a merger to be made for the sole purpose of eliminating a minority on a cash-out basis. To be valid, a freeze-out merger must be "fair." To be fair, two conditions must be met: fair dealing and fair price. Fair dealing means that the majority shareholder must act not only for his own benefit, but for the benefit of the corporation as a whole. In other words, it must serve a business purpose. If the majority shareholder acts solely for his own benefit, then fair dealing is not present. The burden to show fairness is on the majority shareholder. In

this particular instance, it appears that the sole reason for the freeze-out merger was that, under state corporation laws, the nonvoting stock had to be extinguished in order for the New Patriots (D) to assume Sullivan's (D) personal liabilities incurred in his quest to regain control of the franchise. This clearly was a purpose beneficial to Sullivan (D) personally and not to the corporation, and therefore the transaction was illegal. [The court went on to hold that, because ten years had passed since the merger had been effected, voiding the merger would be unduly harsh. The court agreed rescissionary damages were appropriate, and remanded the matter for a determination thereof.]

▶ ANALYSIS

What constitutes a business purpose can be a matter of some dispute. If, for instance, Sullivan (D) had reacquired the franchise out of a concern that the rebels that ousted him were harming the franchise, a business purpose in incurring the debts he did might have existed. There was no hint in the published opinion as to what Sullivan's (D) ulterior motives might have been, however.

Quicknotes

BUSINESS PURPOSE TEST Doctrine relieving corporate directors and/or officers from liability for decisions honestly and rationally made in the corporation's best interests.

CASH-OUT MERGER The acquisition of one company by another by exchanging cash for the shares of the target corporation, after which the acquired company ceases to exist as an independent entity.

CONTROLLING SHAREHOLDER A person who has power to vote a majority of the outstanding shares of a corporation, or who is able to direct the management of the corporation with a smaller block of stock because the remaining shares are scattered among small, disorganized holdings.

FAIR DEALING An implied warranty that the parties will deal honestly in the satisfaction of their obligations and without intent to defraud.

FIDUCIARY DUTY A legal obligation to act for the benefit of another.

FREEZE-OUT Merger whereby the majority shareholder forces minority shareholders into the sale of their securities.

RESCISSION The canceling of an agreement and the return of the parties to their positions prior to the formation of the contract.

Rabkin v. Philip A. Hunt Chemical Corporation

Shareholder (P) v. Corporation (D)

498 A.2d 1099 (Del. 1985).

NATURE OF CASE: Appeal from judgment dismissing challenge to merger.

FACT SUMMARY: Minority shareholders (P) of acquired corporation Philip A. Hunt Chemical (D) contended that their rights were violated in that the acquiring corporation delayed the merger to avoid an obligation to pay a contractual price.

🏛 RULE OF LAW
Delaying a merger to avoid paying a contractual price may give rise to liability to the minority shareholders.

FACTS: In 1983 Olin Corp. (D) agreed to purchase a majority interest in Philip A. Hunt Chemical Corp. (D). The sale contract called for any further purchases of stock within the next year to be made for $25 per share. Olin (D), over one year later, announced an intention to merge the two corporations. The merger was effected with Hunt's (D) minority shareholder being paid $20 per share; a price that Olin's (D) financial specialists had concluded was fair. Rabkin (P) and other minority shareholders (P) brought an action seeking to void the merger, calling the price unfair and alleging that Olin (D) had purposely delayed consummating the merger to avoid its obligation to pay $25 per share. The trial court dismissed the action, and subsequently, the minority shareholders appealed.

ISSUE: May delaying a merger to avoid paying a contractual price give rise to liability to the minority shareholders?

HOLDING AND DECISION: [Judge not stated in casebook excerpt.] Yes. Delaying a merger to avoid paying a contractual price may give rise to liability to the minority shareholders. The lower court apparently was of the opinion that Rabkin's (P) sole remedy in this instance was an appraisal proceeding. This was an incorrect understanding of the law in this area. While appraisal is an appropriate remedy in many instances, it is not the only remedy. In cases of fraud, self-dealing, manipulation, and the like, any remedy that will make the aggrieved shareholder whole may be considered. In the context of a cash-out merger, timing, structure, negotiation, and disclosure are all factors to be taken into account in ruling upon the fairness of the transaction. The allegation here is that Olin's (D) management knew from the beginning that it was going to acquire 100% of Hunt (D) and delayed consummating the merger for the sole purpose of avoiding a contractual obligation of paying more per share than it wanted to. This allegation is sufficient to withstand a motion to dismiss, and therefore the matter must be remanded for trial. Reversed and remanded.

▶ ANALYSIS

In the Chancery Court, the Vice Chancellor apparently relied on a passage in the case *Weinberger v. UOP, Inc.*, 457 A.2d 701 (1983), in which appraisal was cited as the appropriate remedy in a cash-out merger case. The Delaware Supreme Court used the instant case to point out that it had not meant this to be an exclusive remedy.

Quicknotes

CASH-OUT MERGER Occurs when a merging company prematurely redeems the securities of a holder as part of the merger.

FIDUCIARY DUTY A legal obligation to act for the benefit of another.

FRAUD A false representation of facts with the intent that another will rely on the misrepresentation to his detriment.

MINORITY SHAREHOLDER A stockholder in a corporation controlling such a small portion of those shares which are outstanding that its votes have no influence in the management of the corporation.

SELF-DEALING Transaction in which a fiduciary uses property of another, held by virtue of the confidential relationship, for personal gain.

Rauch v. RCA Corporation

Shareholder (P) v. Corporation (D)

861 F.2d 29 (2d Cir. 1988).

NATURE OF CASE: Appeal from judgment dismissing challenge to merger.

FACT SUMMARY: Shareholders (P) of acquired corporation RCA Corp. (D) contended that a merger that involved a forced sale of their shares triggered redemption rights contained in RCA's Articles of Incorporation.

🏛 RULE OF LAW
A cash-out merger that is otherwise legal does not trigger any right the shareholders may have with respect to share redemption.

FACTS: In 1985 General Electric Company (D), a majority shareholder in RCA Corp. (D), merged the latter into itself. A certain class of preferred stock was valued at $40 per share, and the shareholders thereof were paid this amount per share. Rauch (P), holder of 250 of these shares, challenged the merger on the grounds that the Articles of Incorporation of RCA (D) contained a provision that his class of stock, if redeemed, was to be paid at $100 per share. Rauch (P) argued that the merger had the same effect as redemption. The district court ruled in favor of the merger, and dismissed. Rauch (P) appealed.

ISSUE: Does a cash-out merger that is otherwise legal trigger any right the shareholders may have with respect to share redemption?

HOLDING AND DECISION: [Judge not stated in casebook excerpt.] No. A cash-out merger that is otherwise valid does not trigger any right the shareholders may have with respect to share redemption. It has long been the law in Delaware that when a corporate reorganization leads to a particular result, any consequence thereof is not invalidated by the mere fact that a similar result could have been reached by a different type of reorganization that would have been more advantageous to a particular plaintiff. Under Delaware law, mergers are governed by certain laws and redemptions by others, and they are considered equal in terms of validity. Having effected a cashing out of Rauch's (P) interest by a merger, the fact that he could have been cashed out in a redemption on terms more advantageous to himself does no good to Rauch (P) where, as here, there is no allegation that the merger itself was unfair or otherwise tainted. Affirmed.

▶ ANALYSIS

In this instance, the merger could have been accomplished by a sale of assets of RCA (D), along with redemption of preferred shares. This would have led to the same result, but would have triggered redemption rights. It is not clear if General Electric (D) effected the transaction as it did to avoid paying preferred shareholders their redemption amounts, but the opinion makes it clear that it makes no difference if it did.

■══■

Quicknotes

CASH-OUT MERGER The acquisition of one company by another by exchanging cash for the shares of the target corporation, after which the acquired company ceases to exist as an independent entity.

DE FACTO MERGER DOCTRINE The acquisition of one company by another without compliance with the requirements of a statutory merger but treated by the courts as such.

DEL. GEN. CORP. LAW., § 251(B) Governs merger agreements in which shares are converted to cash.

REDEMPTION The repurchase of a security by the issuing corporation according to the terms specified in the security agreement specifying the procedure for the repurchase.

■══■

VGS, Inc. v. Castiel

Newly formed company (D) v. Board member of original LLC (P)

2000 WL 1277372 (Del Ch.), *aff'd mem.*, 781 A.2d 696 (Del. Super. 2001).

NATURE OF CASE: Equity suit by an ousted manager of a limited liability company for rescission of a merger between his company and a new company.

FACT SUMMARY: When Sahagen (D) and Quinn (D), two managers of a limited liability company (LLC), took action to merge the LLC with another company, without notifying Castiel (P), who was the third manager, of the proposed action, the latter brought suit to rescind the merger, arguing that Sahagen (D) and Quinn (D) had breached their duty of loyalty and good faith.

🏛 RULE OF LAW
The managers of a limited liability company owe to one another a duty of loyalty to act in good faith.

FACTS: An LLC agreement created a three-member board of managers with sweeping authority to govern the LLC. The managers were Castiel (P), Sahagen (D), and Quinn (D). Castiel (P) was also the majority shareholder and CEO. The LLC statute, read literally, did not require notice to Castiel (P) before Sahagen (D) and Quinn (D) could act. Sahagen (D) and Quinn (D) acted to merge the original LLC with VGS, Inc. (D). They acted without notice to Castiel (P) of the proposed action, knowing that he would have blocked it. After the merger, Castiel (P) was relegated to the position of a minority shareholder and was no longer CEO. In short, the two managers acted without notice to the third under circumstances where they knew that with notice, the third could have acted to protect his majority interest. Castiel (P) brought suit in equity to have the merger declared invalid and rescinded on the grounds that it occurred based on the breach of the duty of loyalty of Sahagen (D) and Quinn (D) to have acted toward their fellow manager in good faith.

ISSUE: Do the managers of a limited liability company owe to one another a duty of loyalty to act in good faith?

HOLDING AND DECISION: [Judge not stated in casebook excerpt.] Yes. The managers of a limited liability company owe to one another a duty of loyalty to act in good faith. Although the LLC statute, read literally, did not require notice to Castiel (P) before Sahagen (D) and Quinn (D) could act by written consent, and the LLC agreement did not purport to modify the statute in this regard, such observations cannot here complete the analysis. Sahagen (D) and Quinn (D) knew what would happen if they notified Castiel (P) of their intention to act by written consent to merge the LLC into VGS, Inc. (D). Castiel (P) would have attempted to remove Quinn (D) and block the planned action. Regardless of his motivation in doing so, the removal of Quinn (D) in that circumstance would have been within Castiel's (P) rights as the LLC's controlling owner under the agreement. The purpose of permitting action by written consent without notice is to enable LLC managers to take quick, efficient action in situations where a minority of managers could not block or adversely affect the course set by the majority even if they were notified of the proposed action and objected to it. The state legislature never intended to enable two managers to deprive, "clandestinely and surreptitiously," a third manager representing the majority interest in the LLC of an opportunity to protect that interest by taking an action that the third manager's member would surely have opposed if he had knowledge of it. Equity looks to the intent rather than to the form. In this hopefully unique situation, this application of the maxim requires construction of the statute to allow action without notice only by a constant or fixed majority. It cannot apply to an illusory, will-of-the wisp majority which would implode should notice be given. Nothing in the statute suggests that a court of equity should blind its eyes to a shallow manipulative attempt to restructure an enterprise through an action taken by a "majority" that existed only so long as it could act in secrecy. Sahagen (D) and Quinn (D) owed Castiel (P) a duty to give him prior notice of the meeting even if he would have interfered with a plan that they conscientiously believed to be in the best interest of the LLC. They intentionally used a flawed process to merge the LLC into VGS, Inc. (D). Hence, they failed to discharge their duty of loyalty to him in good faith. The merger is invalid and is ordered rescinded.

▌ ANALYSIS

The court in *VGS* noted that while many hours were spent at trial focusing on contentions that Castiel (P) had proved to be an ineffective leader in whom employees and investors had lost confidence, the issue of who was best suited to run the LLC should not be resolved in a court but in board meetings where all the managers are present and all members are appropriately represented. Furthermore, observed the court, the actions of Sahagen (D) and Quinn (D) constituted a breach of their duty of loyalty; hence such actions did not entitle them to the benefit or protection of the business judgment rule.

■=■

Continued on next page.

Quicknotes

DUTY OF GOOD FAITH OF FAIR DEALINGS An implied duty in a contract that the parties will deal honestly in the satisfaction of their obligations and without intent to defraud.

DUTY OF LOYALTY A director's duty to refrain from self-dealing or to take a position that is adverse to the corporation's best interests.

LIMITED LIABILITY COMPANY A business entity combining the features of both a corporation and a general partnership; the LLC provides its shareholders and officers with limited liability, but it is treated as a partnership for taxation purposes.

Cheff v. Mathes

Corporate president (D) v. Shareholder

41 Del. Ch. 494, 199 A.2d 548 (1964).

NATURE OF CASE: Appeal from judgment in derivative action holding corporate directors liable for misuse of corporate funds.

FACT SUMMARY: Directors of Holland Furnace Co. (D) alleged that a repurchase of corporate stock at a premium was effected solely to perpetuate their control of the corporation.

RULE OF LAW
Corporate fiduciaries may not use corporate funds to perpetuate their control of the corporation.

FACTS: Holland Furnace Co. (D) was engaged in the business of making warm air furnaces and other home heating products. Most of the shares were held by several persons related by blood or marriage, as well as a holding company owned by the same individuals. At one point Maremount, who was the president of another company, began buying shares of Holland (D). At first he disclaimed any interest in gaining control of the company, but later began acquiring more and more stock therein and began voicing opinions about how Holland (D) should be run to the directors and officers. As Maremount had, in the opinion of Cheff (D), Holland's (D) president, a history of looting companies he acquired, Cheff (D) approached the other director-shareholders about fending off the acquisition. Eventually it was decided that Holland (D) would repurchase its own shares from Maremount. The agreed-upon price was significantly higher than the prevailing market price. Mathes (P), a shareholder of Holland (D), filed a derivative action, contending that the directors of Holland (D) effected the sale solely to preserve their positions. The Chancellor so held, and entered a judgment awarding damages against several of the directors (D). They appealed.

ISSUE: May corporate fiduciaries use corporate funds to perpetuate their control of the corporation?

HOLDING AND DECISION: [Judge not stated in casebook excerpt.] No. Corporate fiduciaries may not use corporate funds to perpetuate their control of the corporation. Corporate funds must be used for the good of the corporation. Activities that are undertaken for the good of the corporation that have the incidental effect of maintaining the directors' control are permissible, but acts effected for no other reason than to maintain control over the company are invalid. Consequently, the same activity might or might not be appropriate, depending on the motivations of the directors. In terms of burden of proof, it is initially presumed that a board's action is in good faith, and this presumption can be overcome only on an affirmative showing of bad faith or self-dealing. However, a repurchase is a form of self-dealing, and therefore the burden in this case should be on the directors (D) to show that there was a legitimate business purpose for the transaction. Here, the Chancellor apparently gave no weight to the argument that the Maremount takeover was perceived as a threat to Holland (D). In view of Maremount's history of corporate takeovers, the Chancellor gave insufficient weight to this concern, which in this court's opinion was a legitimate worry. The fact that a premium was paid for Maremount's stock does not change this analysis, since a premium is often paid for a large block of stock. This would appear to validate the actions of the directors of Holland (D). Reversed and remanded.

ANALYSIS

The extra price paid for Maremount's potentially controlling block of stock is what is generally known as a "control premium." A controlling or near-controlling block of stock has a value above the sum of its parts, and one selling such a block has the expectation that he will receive something over market price, which was what happened in this case.

■=■

Quicknotes

8 DEL. C., § 160 Corporations have the right to buy and sell shares of its own stock.

BUSINESS PURPOSE RULE Doctrine relieving corporate directors and/or officers from liability for decisions honestly and rationally made in the corporation's best interests.

SELF-DEALING Transaction in which a fiduciary uses property of another, held by virtue of the confidential relationship, for personal gain.

SHAREHOLDER'S DERIVATIVE ACTION Action asserted by a shareholder in order to enforce a cause of action on behalf of the corporation.

■=■

Unocal Corporation v. Mesa Petroleum Co.

Target corporation (D) v. Corporation (P)

493 A.2d 946 (Del. 1985).

NATURE OF CASE: Appeal from judgment enjoining a tender offer.

FACT SUMMARY: To ward off a hostile takeover by Mesa Petroleum (P), directors of Unocal (D) instituted a selective exchange offer.

🏛 RULE OF LAW
A selective tender offer, effected to thwart a takeover, is not in itself invalid.

FACTS: Unocal Corporation (D) was faced with a hostile tender offer by Mesa Petroleum Co. (P). The tender offer was of a "two-tier" structure such that the shareholders first tendering their stock obtained much greater value than those who tendered theirs later in the offer. The purpose of the plan was to motivate the shareholders to sell their shares lest they find themselves in the second tier of the offering. Following consultations with financial professionals, the board of directors of Unocal (D) approved a defensive tactic wherein Unocal (D) issued an exchange offer for its own stock, at an amount higher than that offered by Mesa (P). Mesa (P) was specifically excluded from the offer. Mesa (P) then filed an action seeking to enjoin Unocal's (D) selective exchange offer. The Chancery Court issued a temporary restraining order halting the proposed offer, which it extended into an injunction. Unocal (D) appealed.

ISSUE: Is a selective tender offer, effected to thwart a takeover, in itself invalid?

HOLDING AND DECISION: [Judge not stated in casebook excerpt.] No. A selective exchange offer, effected to thwart a takeover, is not in itself invalid. In the context of a battle for corporate control, the usual deference given to the decisions of the board of directors under the business judgment rule is somewhat circumscribed by the fact that directors in such a situation are in an inherent conflict of interest, as self-preservation is an issue they face. In spite of this threat to their corporate survival, directors must continue to put the interests of shareholders first. Therefore, acts of the directors to defeat a takeover must be shown to have been done because the takeover represented a danger to corporate policy and effectiveness. Further, the conclusion that such a threat existed must have been made after reasonable investigation and in good faith. Finally, the severity of the tactic must be reasonable in relation to the level of perceived threat. Here, the directors of Unocal (D) were faced with a situation where a coercive tender offer had been made by a reputed "greenmailer." The response was to effect a counteroffer that excluded the would-be acquirer to ward off the takeover. Given the facts available to the board, it appears that their response was commensurate to the threat, and therefore was valid. Reversed.

▶ ANALYSIS

This case established what has come to be known as the "*Unocal* Rule," which is a standard used in assessing a takeover defense. As the opinion states, the business judgment rule is not automatically applied to defensive tactics. Rather, a reviewing court must look at the reasonableness of the defensive tactic employed, due to the high possibility of interested acts on the part of the board.

■■■

Quicknotes

8 DEL. C., § 160 Corporations have the right to buy and sell shares of their own stock.

BUSINESS JUDGMENT RULE Doctrine relieving corporate directors and/or officers from liability for decisions honestly and rationally made in the corporation's best interests.

TENDER OFFER An offer made by one corporation to the shareholders of a target corporation to purchase their shares subject to number, time, and price specifications.

■■■

Revlon, Inc. v. MacAndrews & Forbes Holdings, Inc.

Target corporation (D) v. Corporation (P)

506 A.2d 173 (Del. 1985).

NATURE OF CASE: Appeal from judgment enjoining stock purchase.

FACT SUMMARY: Directors of target corporation Revlon, Inc. (D) instituted an antitakeover strategy that favored corporate bondholders over shareholders.

🏛 RULE OF LAW

Lockups and related defensive measures are permitted where their adoption is untainted by director interest or other breaches of fiduciary duty.

FACTS: Revlon, Inc. (D) became the object of interest of potential buyer Pantry Pride, Inc. (P). Pantry Pride (P) initially made an overture to Revlon (D) to purchase the corporation at $45 per share. Revlon's (D) board rejected the offer. As part of a defensive strategy, Revlon's (D) board adopted a plan whereby shareholders exchanged their shares for bonds. Pantry Pride (P) made a series of ever-increasing tender offers, which the board of Revlon (D) continuously opposed. The board then announced a leveraged buyout by "white knight" Forstmann (D) at $57.25 per share. Part of the deal was a lockup provision relating to a division of Revlon (D) that would have made any acquisition of Revlon (D) by another concern unprofitable. Also, Forstmann (D) agreed to support the value of the notes, which were sagging in the bond market. At this point Pantry Pride (P) filed an action seeking to enjoin the agreement between Revlon (D) and Forstmann (D). The Chancery Court so ordered and Revlon (D) appealed.

ISSUE: Are lockups and other defensive measures permitted where their adoption is untainted by director interest or other breaches of fiduciary duty?

HOLDING AND DECISION: [Judge not stated in casebook excerpt.] Yes. Lockups and related defensive measures are permitted where their adoption is untainted by director interest or other breaches of fiduciary duty. The actions taken by the Revlon directors (D) did not meet this standard, however. While a board is not required to be blind to all others having an interest in a corporation, their main responsibility is to the shareholders. This usually means maximizing share prices. When, as here, it becomes clear that a corporation is going to be taken over and the only issue remaining is the price that is to be paid, this duty of the directors becomes an obligation to maximize the sale price, not unlike an auctioneer. Here, the board of Revlon (D), to thwart an unfriendly takeover, negotiated a sale to a suitor that effectively ended the bidding for the corporation, which in turn prevented a higher share price. It had become clear that Revlon (D) was going to be sold, so it was incumbent upon the directors to maximize share price. Instead, they worked out a deal that favored the noteholders to the detriment of the shareholders, which was improper. This invalidated the entire transaction with Forstmann (D). Affirmed.

▶ ANALYSIS

Although not the central holding of this opinion, this case gave rise to what has become called the "*Revlon* Rule." This rule holds that when it is clear that a target is going to be sold, the directors become little more than auctioneers. Long-term corporate interests are no longer considered. While not binding in other states, this rule is widely followed around the nation due to the influence of the Delaware Supreme Court in matters of corporate law.

▬▬▬

Quicknotes

BUSINESS JUDGMENT RULE Doctrine relieving corporate directors and/or officers from liability for decisions honestly and rationally made in the corporation's best interests.

FIDUCIARY DUTY A legal obligation to act for the benefit of another, including subordinating one's personal interests to that of the other person.

HOSTILE TAKEOVER Refers to a situation in which an outside group attempts to seize control of a target corporation against the will of the targeted company's officers, directors or shareholders.

LOCK-UP OPTION A defensive strategy to a takeover attempt whereby a target corporation sets aside a specified portion of the company's shares for purchase by a friendly investor.

TENDER OFFER An offer made by one corporation to the shareholders of a target corporation to purchase their shares subject to number, time, and price specifications.

▬▬▬

Paramount Communications, Inc. v. Time Incorporated

Corporation (P) v. Target corporation (D)

571 A.2d 1140 (Del. 1989).

NATURE OF CASE: Appeal from judgment rejecting challenge to corporate merger.

FACT SUMMARY: Directors of Time, Inc. (D), seeing a threat by a bid for control by Paramount Communications, Inc. (P), undertook measures to defeat the takeover effort.

🏛 RULE OF LAW
Directors of a corporation involved in an ongoing business enterprise may take into account all long-term corporate objectives in responding to an offer to take over the corporation.

FACTS: Time, Inc. (D), publisher of a major newsmagazine, developed the intention of making inroads into the entertainment industry. After considering several established entertainment companies, Time's (D) board began merger discussions with the board of Warner Brothers, Inc. (D), a motion picture studio. A merger was agreed upon, consisting of a stock-for-stock swap in which Warner (D) would be merged into Time (D) with Warner (D) shareholders receiving 0.465 shares of Time (D) stock for each share of Warner (D) stock owned. Unexpectedly, Paramount Communications (P) announced an all-cash offer to purchase Time (D) for $175 per share. This led to a restructuring of the proposed Time (D)–Warner (D) merger into a cash and securities acquisition. Time's (D) board, citing concerns about Paramount's (P) acquisition posing a threat to Time's (D) corporate culture, continually rejected Paramount's (P) overtures, which eventually increased to an offer of $200 per share. The original Time (D)–Warner (D) agreement had included a "no shop" clause which prevented Time's (D) board from considering other options. Both Paramount (P) and various shareholders of Time (D) filed suit, alleging breach of fiduciary duty by Time's (D) board. The Chancery Court rejected the claims and dismissed. An appeal was taken.

ISSUE: May directors of a corporation involved in an ongoing business enterprise take into account all long-term corporate objectives in responding to an offer to take over the corporation?

HOLDING AND DECISION: [Judge not stated in casebook excerpt.] Yes. Directors of a corporation involved in an ongoing business enterprise may take into account all long-term corporate objectives in responding to an offer to take over the corporation. When a corporation is an ongoing enterprise, and is not effectively "up for sale," directors are more than mere auctioneers trying to obtain the highest price possible. A board's decision to reject a takeover offer will be upheld under the business judgment rule if the directors can show their decision was not dictated by a selfish desire to retain their jobs, but rather was in the best interests of the corporation. Share price is a component of this analysis, but is not the sole criterion. If the directors arrived at the decision to reject an offer after appropriate analysis and consideration of legitimate factors, a court will not substitute its judgment for that of the directors. Here, the directors elected to continue with a deliberately conceived corporate plan for long-term growth rather than accept an opportunity for short-term profits, which is a legitimate decision. The acts of Time's (D) board were therefore appropriate. Affirmed.

▶ ANALYSIS

The court here applied what is know as the "*Unocal*" analysis, after the case *Unocal Corp. v. Mesa Petroleum Co.,* 493 A.2d 946 (Del. 1985). In that opinion, the Delaware Supreme Court established the rule that a board's defensive tactics will not be given the deferential business judgment rule test, but will be subject to a higher level of scrutiny due to the possibility of self-interest.

Quicknotes

BUSINESS JUDGMENT RULE Doctrine relieving corporate directors and/or officers from liability for decisions honestly and rationally made in the corporation's best interests.

FIDUCIARY DUTY A legal obligation to act for the benefit of another, including subordinating one's personal interests to that of the other person.

TENDER OFFER An offer made by one corporation to the shareholders of a target corporation to purchase their shares subject to number, time, and price specifications.

Paramount Communications, Inc. v. QVC Network, Inc.

Target corporation (D) v. Corporation (P)

637 A.2d 34 (Del. 1994).

NATURE OF CASE: Appeal from judgment enjoining certain defensive measures taken in response to a takeover threat.

FACT SUMMARY: Directors of target corporation Paramount (D) instituted as deterrents to an unfriendly acquisition a no-shop clause, a "poison pill" termination fee, and a stock option agreement favoring friendly suitor Viacom (D).

🏛 RULE OF LAW
The directors of a corporation targeted by two or more suitors may not institute tactics that favor one suitor in such a manner as to allow the favored suitor to offer less than it otherwise would have.

FACTS: Paramount Communications, Inc. (D) instituted talks with Viacom, Inc. (D) for a friendly merger. An agreement was reached that included several devices to discourage other potential suitors. One was a "no-shop" agreement barring Paramount (D) directors from discussing mergers with any other suitor, absent certain specific circumstances. The second was a fee of $100,000,000 to be paid to Viacom (D) if Paramount (D) terminated the agreement. Finally, a stock option was granted to Viacom (D) which, if exercised, would be so advantageous that any party acquiring Paramount (D) would be subject to the danger of large losses. QVC (P) announced a tender offer and filed an action seeking to have the defensive measures declared invalid. The Chancery Court held the measures invalid, and Paramount (D) appealed.

ISSUE: May the directors of a corporation targeted by two or more suitors institute tactics that favor one suitor in such a manner as to allow the favored suitor to offer less than it otherwise would have?

HOLDING AND DECISION: [Judge not stated in casebook excerpt.] No. The directors of a corporation targeted by two or more suitors may not institute tactics that favor one suitor in such a manner as to allow the favored suitor to offer less than it otherwise would have. Generally speaking, the actions of a directorate are given great deference, under the business judgment rule. However, one exception to this rule is in the area of tactics employed to defeat an unfriendly takeover. This is because the board is in an inherent conflict in that there is a likelihood if an unfriendly takeover is effected they will be ousted. The specter of self-interest, rather than corporate interest, is therefore present. When control of a corporation is up for sale, the duty of the board is to seek a transaction that gives the shareholders the best value possible. Directors are not limited in this regard to cash value only, but may analyze the entire situation, both in the short and long term. Nonetheless, however, when directors by their acts do something that has the effect of lessening the value shareholders would otherwise receive, they have breached their fiduciary duty. Here, the directors of Paramount (D) were faced with the all-but-inevitable sale of control to either Viacom (D) or QVC (P); one of those two entities was going to end up with control of Paramount (D). While the Paramount (D) directors were free to conclude that Viacom (D) offered Paramount (D) the best deal in the long run, they took steps that effectively cut off the bidding process. It seems clear that Viacom (D) would have raised the ante had it needed to do so to gain control, and by cutting off the bidding, the directors of Paramount (D) made it unnecessary for it to do so. In doing this, the directors breached their duties to Paramount's (D) shareholders. Affirmed.

▶ ANALYSIS

The present case was something of an extension of a previous case, *Revlon, Inc. v. MacAndrews & Forbes Holdings*, 506 A.2d 176 (1985). In that case, the Delaware Supreme Court held that the directors of a corporation whose sale and breakup was inevitable were under a duty to maximize share value. The present action extended this rule to sales of control where breakup is not a certainty.

Quicknotes

BUSINESS JUDGMENT RULE Doctrine relieving corporate directors and/or officers from liability for decisions honestly and rationally made in the corporation's best interests.

POISON PILL A tactic employed by a company, which is the target of a takeover attempt, to make the purchase of its shares less attractive to a potential buyer by requiring the issuance of a new series of shares to be redeemed at a substantial premium over their stated value if a party purchases a specified percentage of voting shares of the corporation.

TENDER OFFER An offer made by one corporation to the shareholders of a target corporation to purchase their shares subject to number, time, and price specifications.

Omnicare, Inc. v. NCS Healthcare, Inc.

Acquiring corporation (P) v. Target corporation (D)

818 A.2d 914 (Del. 2003).

NATURE OF CASE: Appeal from decision holding that lock-up deal protection measures were reasonable.

FACT SUMMARY: Omnicare, Inc. (Omnicare) (P) sought to acquire NCS Healthcare, Inc. (NCS) (D). Genesis Health Ventures, Inc. (Genesis) had made a competing bid for NCS (D) that the NCS board had originally recommended, but the NCS board withdrew its recommendation and instead recommended that stockholders accept the Omnicare (P) offer, which was worth more than twice the Genesis offer. However, the agreement between Genesis and NCS (D) contained a provision that the agreement be placed before the NCS (D) shareholders for a vote, even if the board no longer recommended it. There was also no fiduciary out clause in the agreement. Pursuant to voting agreements, two NCS shareholders who held a majority of the voting power agreed unconditionally to vote all their shares in favor of the Genesis merger, thus assuring that the Genesis transaction would prevail. Omnicare (P) challenged the defensive measures that were part of the Genesis transaction.

🏛 **RULE OF LAW**
Lock-up deal protection devices, which when operating in concert are coercive and preclusive, are invalid and unenforceable in the absence of a fiduciary out clause.

FACTS: In late 1999, NCS Healthcare, Inc. began to experience serious liquidity problems that led to a precipitous decline in the market value of its stock. As a result, it began to explore strategic alternatives to address its situation. In the summer of 2001, Omnicare (P), an NCS (D) competitor, made a series of offers to acquire NCS's (D) assets in a bankruptcy sale—at less than face value of NCS's (D) outstanding debts, and with no recovery for NCS stockholders. NCS (D) rejected Omnicare's (P) offers. By early 2002, NCS's (D) financial condition was improving, and the NCS board began to believe it might be able to realize some value for its shareholders. An Ad Hoc Committee of NCS (D) creditors contacted Genesis Health Ventures, Inc. (Genesis), an Omnicare (P) competitor, and Genesis expressed interest in bidding on NCS (D). Genesis made it clear that it did not want to be a "stalking horse" for NCS (D) and demanded an exclusivity agreement. After Genesis steadily increased its offers, NCS (D) granted Genesis the exclusivity it sought. The NCS board consisted of Outcalt and Shaw, who together controlled more than 65% of voting power in NCS (D), and Sells and Osborne, both of whom were disinterested, outside directors. In its negotiations, Genesis sought an agreement that would require, as permitted by Delaware General Corporation Law (DGCL) § 251(c), NCS (D) to submit the merger to NCS stockholders regardless of

whether the NCS Board recommended the merger; an agreement by Outcalt and Shaw to vote their NCS stock in favor of the merger; and omission of any effective fiduciary out clause from the agreement. Meanwhile, Omnicare (P) learned that NCS (D) was negotiating with Genesis and made a proposed bid for a transaction in which all of NCS's (D) debt would be paid off and NCS stockholders would receive greater value than offered by Genesis. This offer was conditioned on satisfactory completion of due diligence. Fearing that Genesis might abandon its offer, NCS (D) refused to negotiate with Omnicare (P), but used Omnicare's (P) proposal to negotiate for improved terms with Genesis, which Genesis provided. However, in exchange, Genesis conditioned its offer on approval the next day. The NCS board gave such approval to the merger, in which NCS stockholders would receive Genesis stock and all NCS (D) debt would be paid off. The merger transaction included the provisions that Genesis had sought during negotiations, as well as the voting agreements with Outcalt and Shaw. Thus, the combined terms of the merger agreement and voting agreement guaranteed that the transaction proposed by Genesis would be approved by the NCS stockholders. Omnicare (P) filed suit to enjoin the merger and then launched a tender offer for all NCS (D) stock at a value of more than twice the then current market value of the shares to be received in the Genesis transaction. Otherwise, its offer equaled that of Genesis. Several months later, but before the NCS stockholders were to vote on the Genesis merger, as a result of Omnicare (P) irrevocably committing itself to its offer, the NCS board withdrew its recommendation of the Genesis merger and recommended, instead, that NCS shareholders vote for the Omnicare (P) merger because it was a superior proposal. The Chancery Court ruled that the voting agreements with Outcalt and Shaw, combined with the provision requiring a stockholder vote regardless of board recommendation, constituted defensive measures, but found that, under the enhanced judicial scrutiny standard of *Unocal Corp. v. Mesa Petroleum Co.*, 493 A.2d 946 (Del. 1985), these measures were reasonable. The Delaware Supreme Court granted review.

ISSUE: Are lock-up deal protection devices, which when operating in concert are coercive and preclusive, invalid and unenforceable in the absence of a fiduciary out clause?

HOLDING AND DECISION: (Holland, J.) Yes. Lock-up deal protection devices, which when operating in concert are coercive and preclusive, are invalid and

Continued on next page.

unenforceable in the absence of a fiduciary out clause. The Chancery Court concluded that because the Genesis transaction did not result in a change of control, the transaction would be reviewed under the business judgment rule standard. Under this standard, the Chancery Court concluded that the NCS board had not breached its duty of care in approving the transaction. The Chancery Court's decision to use the business judgment rule standard, rather than enhanced scrutiny, is not outcome-determinative and this court will assume that the NCS board exercised due care when it approved the Genesis transaction. However, as to the defensive measures, enhanced scrutiny is required because of the inherent potential conflict of interest between a board's interest in protecting a merger transaction it has approved and the shareholders' statutory right to make the final decision to either approve or not approve a merger. This requires a threshold determination that the board approved defensive measures comport with the directors' fiduciary duties. In applying enhanced judicial scrutiny to defensive measures designed to protect a merger agreement, a court must first determine that those measures are not preclusive or coercive before its focus shifts to a "range of reasonableness" proportionality determination. When the focus shifts to the range of reasonableness, Unocal requires that any devices must be proportionate to the perceived threat to the corporation and its stockholders if the merger transaction is not consummated. Here, the voting agreements were inextricably intertwined with the defensive aspects of the Genesis merger agreement, and under Unocal, the defensive measures require special scrutiny. Under such scrutiny, these measures were neither reasonable nor proportionate to the threat NCS (D) perceived from the potential loss of the Genesis transaction. The threat identified by NCS (D) was the possibility of losing the Genesis offer and being left with no comparable alternative transaction. The second part of the Unocal analysis requires the NCS directors to demonstrate that their defensive response was reasonable in response to the threat posed. This inquiry itself involves a two-step analysis. The NCS directors must first establish that the deal protection devices adopted in response to the threat were not "coercive" or "preclusive," and then must demonstrate that their response was within a "range of reasonable responses" to the threat perceived. Here, the defensive measures were both preclusive and coercive, and, therefore, draconian and impermissible. That is because any stockholder vote would be "robbed of its effectiveness" by the impermissible coercion that predetermined the outcome of the merger without regard to the merits of the Genesis transaction at the time the vote was scheduled to take place. They were also preclusive because they accomplished a fait accompli. Accordingly, the defensive measures are unenforceable. They are alternatively unenforceable because the merger agreement completely prevented the board from discharging its fiduciary responsibilities to the minority stockholders when Omnicare (P) presented its superior transaction. Here, the NCS board could not abdicate its fiduciary duties to the minority by leaving it to the stockholders alone to approve

or disapprove the merger because Outcalt and Shaw had combined to establish a majority of the voting power that made the outcome of the stockholder vote a foregone conclusion. Thus, the NCS board did not have authority to accede to the Genesis demand for an absolute "lock-up." Instead, it was required to negotiate a fiduciary out clause to protect the NCS shareholders if the Genesis transaction became an inferior offer. Therefore, the defensive measures—the voting agreements and the provision requiring a shareholder vote regardless of board recommendation—when combined to operate in concert in the absence of an effective fiduciary out clause are invalid and unenforceable.

DISSENT: (Veasey, C.J.) The NCS board's actions should have been evaluated based on the circumstances present at the time the Genesis merger agreement was entered into—before the emergence of a subsequent transaction offering greater value to the stockholders. The lock-ups were reached at the conclusion of a lengthy search and intense negotiation process in the context of insolvency, at a time when Genesis was the only viable bidder. Under these facts the NCS board's action before the emergence of the Omnicare (P) offer, reflected the actions of "a quintessential, disinterested, and informed board" made in good faith, and was within the bounds of its fiduciary duties and should be upheld. Moreover, situations arise where business realities demand a lock-up so that wealth enhancing transactions may go forward. Accordingly, any bright-line rule prohibiting lock-ups, such as the one put forth by the majority, could, in circumstances such as those faced by the NCS board, chill otherwise permissible conduct. Here, the deal protection measures were not preclusive or coercive in the context of what they were intended for. They were not adopted to fend off a hostile takeover, but were adopted so that Genesis—the "only game in town"—would save NCS (D), its creditors, and stockholders. Still, here there was no meaningful minority stockholder vote to coerce, given Outcalt and Shaw's majority position, so that the "preclusive" label has no application. Thus, giving Genesis an absolute lock-up under the circumstances, by agreeing to omit a fiduciary out clause, was not a per se violation of fiduciary duty. Hopefully, the rule announced by the majority will be interpreted narrowly and will be seen as sui generis.

DISSENT: (Steele, J.) When a board of directors exercises reasonable care and agrees, in good faith and without conflict, to contractually preserve a bargain in the absence of a better offer, the court should not substitute its judgment and invalidate a valid merger agreement just because a superior offer presents itself prior to closing the merger. This court lacks the business expertise to second-guess the NCS board and the majority stockholders who agreed to the voting lock-up and who had the most economically at stake. Lock-up provisions allow parties to close their deals even in the face of a subsequently emerging better offer, adding assurance to the freedom to contract and preserving the

Continued on next page.

substantial costs expended in establishing business opportunities. The principal opinion adopts a per se, bright-line, inflexible rule requiring an efficient breach of contract be applied to all merger agreements. The majority would apply this rule even where a board has exercised its fiduciary duties of care and loyalty in good faith.

▶ ANALYSIS

One of the primary troubling aspects of the majority opinion, as voiced by the dissent, is the majority's suggestion that it can make a *Unocal* determination after-the-fact with a view to the superiority of a competing proposal that may subsequently emerge. Many commentators agree with the dissent that the lock-ups in this case should not have been reviewed in a vacuum. In a separate dissent, Justice Steele argued that when a board agrees rationally, in good faith, without conflict and with reasonable care to include provisions in a contract to preserve a deal in the absence of a better one, their business judgment should not be second-guessed in order to invalidate or declare unenforceable an otherwise valid merger agreement. Given the tension between the majority's and dissenters' positions, the full impact of the court's decision will need to await further judicial development.

■▬■

Quicknotes

FIDUCIARY DUTY A legal obligation to act for the benefit of another, including subordinating one's personal interests to that of the other person.

LOCK-UP OPTION A defensive strategy to a takeover attempt whereby a target corporation sets aside a specified portion of the company's shares for purchase by a friendly investor.

SUI GENERIS Peculiar to its own type or class.

■▬■

Hilton Hotels Corp. v. ITT Corp.

Corporation (P) v. Target corporation (D)

978 F. Supp. 1342 (D. Nev. 1997).

NATURE OF CASE: Review of a request for injunctive and declarative relief preventing defensive actions by a target corporation in a takeover context.

FACT SUMMARY: When a hostile corporate takeover was attempted by Hilton Hotels (P), ITT (D), the target corporation, proposed a Comprehensive Plan as a defensive measure.

🏛 RULE OF LAW
A board has power over the management and assets of a corporation, but that power is limited by the right of shareholders to vote for the members of the board.

FACTS: Hilton (P) made a tender offer for the stock of ITT (D) and announced plans for a proxy contest at ITT's (D) annual meeting. Hilton (P) immediately filed a complaint for injunctive and declarative relief. ITT (D) formally rejected the tender offer and did not conduct its annual meeting. The court denied Hilton's (P) motion to compel ITT (D) to conduct its annual meeting, finding that Nevada law and the corporate bylaws permitted ITT (D) to hold its meeting within eighteen months, and not twelve months, of the prior meeting. ITT (D) then announced a Comprehensive Plan splitting ITT (D) into three new entities. Hilton (P) claimed that this plan contained a "poison pill" which would be triggered if Hilton (P) successfully acquired more than 50% of the largest of the new entities. Hilton (P) therefore sought to permanently enjoin ITT (D) from proceeding with its Comprehensive Plan. ITT (D) was seeking to implement the Comprehensive Plan prior to the annual meeting and without obtaining shareholder approval. ITT (D) argued that Nevada does not follow Delaware case law since Nevada law provides that a board can resist potential changes in control of a corporation based on its effect on constituencies other than the shareholders.

ISSUE: Does a board have power over the management and assets of a corporation limited by the right of shareholders to vote for the members of the board?

HOLDING AND DECISION: [Judge not stated in casebook excerpt.] Yes. A board has power over the management and assets of a corporation, but that power is limited by the right of shareholders to vote for the members of the board. To determine whether the primary purpose of ITT's (D) action to adopt a classified board structure under its Comprehensive Plan is to disenfranchise ITT's (D) shareholders, the following factors are to be considered: the timing of the action, the entrenchment of the board, whether the stated purpose of the Plan is a credible justification for it, the benefits of the proposed plan, the effect of the classified board, and whether an IRS opinion was obtained. The court will apply a heightened standard for permanent injunctive relief since a trial on the merits would not practically reverse a preliminary decision enjoining implementation of ITT's (D) Comprehensive Plan. Hilton (P) must show irreparable injury and must actually succeed on the merits of the claim in order to prevail. Since there is no Nevada statutory or case law on point for the issues raised by the anti-takeover defensive measures utilized by target companies in responding to a hostile takeover attempt, Delaware case law may be relied upon to provide persuasive case law. Since the Comprehensive Plan would violate the power relationship between ITT's (D) board and ITT's (D) shareholders by impermissibly infringing on the shareholders' right to vote on members of the board of directors, it must be enjoined. The staggered board provision is preclusive and was enacted for the primary purpose of entrenching the current board and no "compelling justification" for the action exists. Therefore, Hilton (P) has prevailed on the merits of its claim for permanent injunctive relief. Relief granted.

▶ ANALYSIS

Under the *Unocal/Blasius* analysis, any board action intended to thwart the free exercise of the shareholder franchise must satisfy the "heavy burden" of demonstrating a "compelling justification" for the action. Several amicus briefs were filed on behalf of ITT (D) shareholders in this case, requesting they be allowed to vote. Hilton (P) ultimately withdrew its tender offer after ITT's (D) board voted to accept a competing bid.

■ ▬ ■

Quicknotes

AMICUS BRIEF A brief submitted by a third party, not a party to the action, that contains information for the court's consideration in conformity with its position.

HOSTILE TAKEOVER Refers to a situation in which an outside group attempts to seize control of a target corporation against the will of the targeted company's officers, directors or shareholders.

INJUNCTIVE RELIEF A court order issued as a remedy, requiring a person to do, or prohibiting that person from doing, a specific act.

Continued on next page.

IRREPARABLE INJURY Such harm that because it is either too great, too small or of a continuing character that it cannot be properly compensated in damages, and the remedy for which, is typically injunctive relief.

POISON PILL A tactic employed by a company, which is the target of a takeover attempt, to make the purchase of its shares less attractive to a potential buyer by requiring the issuance of a new series of shares to be redeemed at a substantial premium over their stated value if a party purchases a specified percentage of voting shares of the corporation.

CTS Corporation v. Dynamics Corporation of America

Target corporation (D) v. Corporation (P)

481 U.S. 69 (1987).

NATURE OF CASE: Appeal from invalidation of state corporate anti-takeover law.

FACT SUMMARY: Indiana enacted a statutory scheme requiring shareholder approval prior to significant shifts in corporate control.

🏛 RULE OF LAW
A law permitting in-state corporations to require shareholder approval prior to significant shifts in corporate control is constitutional.

FACTS: Indiana enacted a statutory scheme whereby large Indiana public corporations if they so opted could require any entity acquiring either 20%, 33.33%, or 50% interest, to be subjected to a shareholder referendum wherein voting power of those shares could be withheld. Dynamics Corp. of America (P), holder of 9.6% of CTS Corporation's (D) shares, announced a tender offer that would have brought its control to 27.5%. Dynamics (P) challenged the statute as void on statutory and commerce clause grounds. The district court found the statute to violate federal securities laws and the Commerce Clause and invalidated the statute. The court of appeals affirmed. CTS (D) appealed.

ISSUE: Is a law permitting in-state corporations to require shareholder approval prior to significant shifts in corporate control, constitutional?

HOLDING AND DECISION: (Powell, J.) Yes. A law permitting in-state corporations to require shareholder approval prior to significant shifts in corporate control is constitutional. [The Court first held that the federal securities laws were not violated.] The principal objects of dormant commerce clause scrutiny are statutes discriminating against interstate commerce. The law in question here does not so discriminate, as it applies to both Indiana and non-Indiana would-be acquiring entities. Another type of law often struck down is that which would subject interstate commerce to inconsistent regulations. Such is not the case here, as Indiana's laws would be the only regulations applicable here. The court of appeals found the Act unconstitutional because it had great potential to hinder tender offers. This may be, but it is an insufficient reason to invalidate the Act. Corporations are creatures of state law, and states are free to formulate policy regarding the internal operations of corporations, provided they do so in a non-discriminatory manner, which is the case here. Reversed.

CONCURRENCE: (Scalia, J.) As long as a state's corporation law governs only its own corporations and does not discriminate against out-of-state-interests, it should survive this Court's scrutiny under the Commerce Clause.

DISSENT: (White, J.) The law undermines the policy of the Williams Act by effectively preventing minority shareholders, in some circumstances, from acting in their own interests. The law also indirectly discriminates against interstate commerce in violation of the Dormant Commerce Clause.

▶ ANALYSIS

The Court implies an acceptance of heavy regulation of the workings of a corporation by the state of its incorporation. States have, according to the Court, a great interest in their corporations, and this justifies the regulations. This analysis is what Justice Scalia thought unnecessary to the Court's decision.

■■■

Quicknotes

COMMERCE CLAUSE Article 1, section 8, clause 3 of the United States Constitution, granting Congress the power to regulate commerce with foreign countries and between the states.

DORMANT COMMERCE CLAUSE The regulatory effect of the Commerce Clause on state activity affecting interstate commerce, where Congress itself has not acted to control the activity; a provision inferred from, but not expressly present in, the language of the Commerce Clause.

INDIANA BUS. CORP. LAW 23-1-17-1 ET SEQ. Conditions acquisition of control of a corporation in approval of a majority of the pre-existing disinterested shareholders.

TENDER OFFER An offer made by one corporation to the shareholders of a target corporation to purchase their shares subject to number, time, and price specifications.

■■■

Corporate Debt

Quick Reference Rules of Law

Sharon Steel Corporation v. Chase Manhattan Bank, N.A.

Corporation (P) v. Debenture holders (D)

691 F.2d 1039 (2d Cir. 1982), *cert. denied*, 460 U.S. 1012 (1983).

NATURE OF CASE: Appeal from dismissal of action to declare debentures not due or payable.

FACT SUMMARY: Sharon Steel (P) contended that certain debentures issued by a corporation whose assets it had purchased, were not due and payable because of a clause that exempted accelerated maturity if all or substantially all of its assets were sold.

RULE OF LAW
A clause in a debt instrument preventing accelerated maturity in the event of a sale of all or substantially all the debtor's assets is inapplicable if the assets are sold piecemeal.

FACTS: UV Industries issued certain debentures. Subsequent to this, and before the debentures were due and payable, UV began to liquidate itself. UV consisted of three divisions. After two of the divisions had been sold, Sharon Steel Corporation (P) purchased the remaining division, which accounted for 38% of UV's revenues. The debentures were part of the package acquired by Sharon Steel (P). Sharon (P) filed an action seeking a declaration that the maturity of the debentures had not been accelerated by the dissolution of UV due to a clause in the debentures that provided that maturity would not be accelerated by a sale of "all or substantially all" of UV's assets. The district court dismissed, and Sharon Steel (P) appealed.

ISSUE: Is a clause in a debt instrument preventing accelerated maturity in the event of a sale of all or substantially all the debtor's assets applicable if the assets are sold piecemeal?

HOLDING AND DECISION: [Judge not stated in casebook excerpt.] No. A clause in a debt instrument preventing accelerated maturity in the event of a sale of all or substantially all the debtor's assets is inapplicable if the assets are sold piecemeal. Such a clause is a "boilerplate" in that it is a common clause in instruments of this type. For this reason, it is to be construed in a manner uniform with the normal construction of the term. In this particular situation, the term "all or substantially all" of UV's assets means those assets existing at a time UV continues to act as an ongoing concern. Sharon Steel (P) contends that since the assets it obtained were all of UV's assets after it had divested itself of most of its operations, it had in fact received "all" of UV's assets. This interpretation is incorrect. The common understanding of the term is that it refers to a debtor's operations before divestiture begins. Here, Sharon Steel (P) only obtained 38% worth of the revenue-producing assets of UV,

which does not come close to "all or substantially all" of UV's assets. Therefore, UV's obligations under the debentures became accelerated. Affirmed.

ANALYSIS

The reason that the maturity of the notes was at issue was their interest rate. As of the time of Sharon Steel's (P) purchase of UV's assets, the market value of the notes was less than the amount payable upon maturity. Noteholders therefore wanted acceleration to receive the amount payable upon maturity. Had the interest rate been higher, the parties would each have argued for the opposite result.

Quicknotes

DEBENTURES Long-term unsecured debt securities issued by a corporation.

DISSOLUTION Annulment or termination of a formal or legal bond, tie or contract.

DIVESTMENT The premature termination of an interest.

Metropolitan Life Insurance Company v.
RJR Nabisco, Inc.

Bond holder (P) v. Bond issuer (D)

716 F. Supp. 1504 (S.D.N.Y. 1989).

NATURE OF CASE: Action seeking contract damages.

FACT SUMMARY: Metropolitan Life (P), holder of bonds issued by RJR Nabisco (D), contended that a downgrading of RJR's (D) credit rating due to a leveraged buyout, which had made the bonds less marketable, constituted breach of the implied covenant of good faith.

🏛 RULE OF LAW
The assumption of additional debt by a bond issuer in a leveraged buyout (LBO) that results in a downgrading of the bonds does not constitute a breach of the covenant of good faith and fair dealing.

FACTS: Metropolitan Life Insurance Co. (P) purchased over $340,000,000 in bonds from RJR Nabisco (D). Subsequent to this, RJR (D) was the subject of a highly publicized leveraged buyout (LBO). As part of the LBO, RJR (D) took on substantial additional debt. As a result of this debt assumption, RJR's (D) creditworthiness was downgraded. This resulted in a significant decrease of the value of its corporate bonds in the bond market. Metropolitan Life (P) filed an action in federal district court contending that this debt assumption constituted a breach of the implied covenant of good faith and fair dealing. Metropolitan Life (P) and co-plaintiff bondholder Jefferson-Pilot Life Insurance Co. (P) moved for summary judgment.

ISSUE: Does the assumption of additional debt by a bond issuer in a leveraged buyout that results in a downgrading of the bonds constitute a breach of the covenant of good faith and fair dealing?

HOLDING AND DECISION: [Judge not stated in casebook excerpt.] No. The assumption of additional debt by a bond issuer in a leveraged buyout that results in a downgrading of the bonds does not constitute a breach of the covenant of good faith and fair dealing. The law does recognize in all contracts an implied covenant of good faith and fair dealing. However, this covenant does not go so far as to give one party to a contract rights for which he did not bargain. The bonds in issue here contain specific language, common in corporate bonds, allowing the issuer to engage in merger transactions, which often results in additional debt. Beyond this, internal memoranda generated within Metropolitan (P) indicates that it was aware of the potential of downgraded bonds subsequent to LBOs, and, in fact, contemplated attempting to insert language into the bonds it purchased prohibiting the incurrence of such debt. This plan was later dropped out of a realization that bond issuers would likely balk at such language and insistence thereon

might take Metropolitan (P) out of the bond market. Thus, Metropolitan (P) would have this court insert by operation of law a clause into its contract that it was unable or unwilling to do so itself at the time the bonds were negotiated. In sum, the implied covenant of good faith and fair dealing arises out of the language of the contract at issue, which sets the rights of the parties. Metropolitan (P) wishes to extend the covenant to apply to rights it does not have under the contracts at issue, and therefore it must fail. Motion denied.

▶ ANALYSIS

The court here gave some emphasis to the fact that Metropolitan (P) and Jefferson (P) were sophisticated investors that knew the risks of the bond market. Whether the court would be as unsympathetic to an unsophisticated investor is unclear.

Quicknotes

IMPLIED COVENANT OF GOOD FAITH AND FAIR DEALING An implied warranty that the parties will deal honestly in the satisfaction of their obligations and without intent to defraud.

INDENTURE A written instrument setting forth the terms pursuant to which a bond or debenture is issued.

LEVERAGED BUYOUT A transaction whereby corporate outsiders purchase the outstanding shares of a publicly held corporation mostly with borrowed funds.

RULE 10B-5 Unlawful to defend or make untrue statements in connection with purchase or sale of securities.

Katz v. Oak Industries, Inc.

Debt holder (P) v. Debt issuer (D)

508 A.2d 873 (Del Ch. 1986).

NATURE OF CASE: Class action suit seeking a preliminary injunction.

FACT SUMMARY: Katz (P) sought to enjoin an exchange offer and consent solicitation made in connection with Oak Industries' (D) attempted reorganization and recapitalization efforts.

🏛 RULE OF LAW
An exchange offer and consent solicitation made by a corporation seeking to maximize the benefit to its stockholders, at the potential expense of its debt holders, does not constitute a breach of the directors' duty of loyalty to the corporation.

FACTS: In an attempt to reduce some of its $230 million in outstanding debentures, Oak (D) made an exchange offer to its debt holders. Oak (D) entered into a contract with Allied-Signal, Inc., for the sale of a segment of its business. The companies entered into two agreements. The first involved the sale of Oak's (D) merger segment. The second provided for the purchase by Allied-Signal of ten million shares of Oak's (D) common stock. The second agreement was predicated upon the condition that at least 85% of Oak's (D) debt holders accept the exchange offer. Oak (D) made two exchange offers providing for payment of less than the face value of the securities but above their market value. The exchange offers were also based on the conditions that a minimum amount of debt securities of each class be tendered, and the holders thereof consent to amendments to the indentures. Katz (P) sought an injunction claiming that the terms of the exchange offer and consent solicitation constituted coercion and a breach of contract.

ISSUE: Does an exchange offer and consent solicitation, maximizing the interests of corporation's shareholders at the expense of its debt holders, constitute a breach of the directors' duty of loyalty?

HOLDING AND DECISION: [Judge not stated in casebook excerpt.] No. An exchange offer and consent solicitation made by a corporation seeking to maximize the benefit to its stockholders, at the potential expense of its debt holders, does not constitute a breach of the directors' duty of loyalty to the corporation. The proper standard to be applied is one of contract law. The appropriate test is whether the corporation violated the implied covenants of good faith and fair dealing. In reaching this determination, the court must decide whether from the terms of the contract the parties involved would have proscribed the action in question as a breach of the implied covenant of good faith had they negotiated in respect thereto. If so, then the court

may conclude that the implied covenant of good faith has been breached. Nothing in the indenture provisions at issue in this case precludes Oak (D) from offering the bondholders an inducement to consent to the proposed amendments. Furthermore, there is nothing in the agreement from which the court may infer that Oak's (D) act would have been prohibited as a breach of the implied covenant of good faith had the parties negotiated on the subject. The exchange offer is not in violation of either the express provisions of the indenture agreement nor does it violate the covenants of good faith and fair dealing. Katz (P) has failed to meet his burden of demonstrating a probability of success on the merits of his claim. Dismissed.

▶ ANALYSIS

Note that holders of debt securities stand in a contractual relationship to the corporation's board of directors. The directors' primary concern in a tender offer situation is to advance the welfare of the company's shareholders and attempt to maximize the return on their investment. In the absence of statutory provisions or express contractual protections, shifting the risk of loss from the shareholders to the bondholders does not constitute a breach of the directors' fiduciary duties.

■▬■

Quicknotes

BREACH OF CONTRACT Unlawful failure by a party to perform its obligations pursuant to contract.

CLASS ACTION A suit commenced by a representative on behalf of an ascertainable group that is too large to appear in court, who shares a commonality of interests and who will benefit from a successful result.

COERCION The overcoming of a person's free will as a result of threats, promises, or undue influence.

DEBENTURES Long-term unsecured debt securities issued by a corporation.

DUTY OF LOYALTY A director's duty to refrain from self-dealing or to take a position that is adverse to the corporation's best interests.

EXCHANGE OFFER A form of takeover in which the acquiring company makes a public offer to exchange shares of its own company for those of the target corporation.

IMPLIED COVENANT OF GOOD FAITH AND FAIR DEALING An implied warranty that the parties will deal honestly in the

Continued on next page.

satisfaction of their obligations and without intent to defraud.

INDENTURE A written instrument setting forth the terms pursuant to which a bond or debenture is issued.

PRELIMINARY INJUNCTION An order issued by the court at the commencement of an action, requiring a party to refrain from conducting a specified activity that is the subject of the controversy, until the matter is determined.

■═■

Morgan Stanley & Co. v. Archer Daniels Midland Company

Debenture holder (P) v. Debenture issuer (D)

570 F. Supp. 1529 (S.D.N.Y. 1983).

NATURE OF CASE: Appeal from court's denial of plaintiff's request for a preliminary injunction.

FACT SUMMARY: Morgan Stanley (P) claimed that Archer Daniels's (D) redemption of $125 million in debentures constituted a breach of contract and violated applicable securities law.

RULE OF LAW
An early redemption of debentures is lawful where the source of funds originates directly from the proceeds of a common stock offering.

FACTS: In May 1981, Archer Daniels (D) issued $125 million in debentures. The debenture agreement provided that Archer Daniels (D) would not redeem the debentures from the proceeds, or in the anticipation, of the issuance of debt if the interest rate fell below 16.08%. Following the issuance of the debentures, Archer Daniels (D) raised capital through borrowing at interest rates less than the stated 16.08%, and through two common stock offerings. In May 1983, Morgan Stanley (P) purchased $16 million worth in debentures. On June 1, Archer Daniels (D) called for the redemption of the debentures, the source of funds originating from the common stock offerings. Morgan Stanley (P) sought a preliminary injunction barring the redemption on the basis that it violated securities law and constituted breach of contract. The parties cross moved for summary judgment.

ISSUE: Is an early redemption of debentures lawful when it is funded directly from the proceeds of a common stock offering?

HOLDING AND DECISION: [Judge not stated in casebook excerpt.] Yes. An early redemption of debentures is lawful where the source of funds originates directly from the proceeds of a common stock offering. Where the contract in dispute involves "boilerplate" language, the court must construe the agreement so as to create uniform treatment. In doing so, the court may examine surrounding facts and circumstances in order to determine the parties' intent. Furthermore, the court must consider existing law at the time the contract was entered as part of that contract. The only other court presented with this issue interpreted such standardized language to render redemption of stock lawful where the refunding was accomplished solely from the proceeds of an issuance of common stock. However, the court must still determine the actual source of the funds subsidizing the redemption. Here the redemption was lawful under the terms of the debenture agreement, the direct source of funds being the two common stock offerings. Archer Daniels's (D) motion for summary judgment is granted.

ANALYSIS

Note that in a case where a proposed redemption is indirectly funded by the issuance of debt borrowed at an interest rate prohibited by the debenture agreement, such redemption would be unlawful. Thus, if Archer Daniels (D) contemporaneously issued new debentures at a lower interest rate, and used the proceeds of that issuance to repurchase the stock issued in the two common stock offerings, the attempted redemption would fail the test, having been indirectly funded through the proceeds of anticipated debt issued at a proscribed percentage. The result would place Archer Daniels (D) in an improved position, the new debt being repaid at a lower interest rate.

Quicknotes

BREACH OF CONTRACT Unlawful failure by a party to perform its obligations pursuant to contract.

COMMON STOCK A class of stock representing the corporation's ownership, the holders of which are entitled to dividends only after the holders of preferred stock are paid.

DEBENTURES Long-term unsecured debt securities issued by a corporation.

REDEMPTION The repurchase of a security by the issuing corporation according to the terms specified in the security agreement specifying the procedure for the repurchase.

SUMMARY JUDGMENT Judgment rendered by a court in response to a motion made by one of the parties, claiming that the lack of a question of material fact in respect to an issue warrants disposition of the issue without consideration by the jury.

Glossary

Common Latin Words and Phrases Encountered in the Law

A FORTIORI: Because one fact exists or has been proven, therefore a second fact that is related to the first fact must also exist.

A PRIORI: From the cause to the effect. A term of logic used to denote that when one generally accepted truth is shown to be a cause, another particular effect must necessarily follow.

AB INITIO: From the beginning; a condition which has existed throughout, as in a marriage which was void ab initio.

ACTUS REUS: The wrongful act; in criminal law, such action sufficient to trigger criminal liability.

AD VALOREM: According to value; an ad valorem tax is imposed upon an item located within the taxing jurisdiction calculated by the value of such item.

AMICUS CURIAE: Friend of the court. Its most common usage takes the form of an amicus curiae brief, filed by a person who is not a party to an action but is nonetheless allowed to offer an argument supporting his legal interests.

ARGUENDO: In arguing. A statement, possibly hypothetical, made for the purpose of argument, is one made arguendo.

BILL QUIA TIMET: A bill to quiet title (establish ownership) to real property.

BONA FIDE: True, honest, or genuine. May refer to a person's legal position based on good faith or lacking notice of fraud (such as a bona fide purchaser for value) or to the authenticity of a particular document (such as a bona fide last will and testament).

CAUSA MORTIS: With approaching death in mind. A gift causa mortis is a gift given by a party who feels certain that death is imminent.

CAVEAT EMPTOR: Let the buyer beware. This maxim is reflected in the rule of law that a buyer purchases at his own risk because it is his responsibility to examine, judge, test, and otherwise inspect what he is buying.

CERTIORARI: A writ of review. Petitions for review of a case by the United States Supreme Court are most often done by means of a writ of certiorari.

CONTRA: On the other hand. Opposite. Contrary to.

CORAM NOBIS: Before us; writs of error directed to the court that originally rendered the judgment.

CORAM VOBIS: Before you; writs of error directed by an appellate court to a lower court to correct a factual error.

CORPUS DELICTI: The body of the crime; the requisite elements of a crime amounting to objective proof that a crime has been committed.

CUM TESTAMENTO ANNEXO, ADMINISTRATOR (ADMINISTRATOR C.T.A.): With will annexed; an administrator c.t.a. settles an estate pursuant to a will in which he is not appointed.

DE BONIS NON, ADMINISTRATOR (ADMINISTRATOR D.B.N.): Of goods not administered; an administrator d.b.n. settles a partially settled estate.

DE FACTO: In fact; in reality; actually. Existing in fact but not officially approved or engendered.

DE JURE: By right; lawful. Describes a condition that is legitimate "as a matter of law," in contrast to the term "de facto," which connotes something existing in fact but not legally sanctioned or authorized. For example, de facto segregation refers to segregation brought about by housing patterns, etc., whereas de jure segregation refers to segregation created by law.

DE MINIMIS: Of minimal importance; insignificant; a trifle; not worth bothering about.

DE NOVO: Anew; a second time; afresh. A trial de novo is a new trial held at the appellate level as if the case originated there and the trial at a lower level had not taken place.

DICTA: Generally used as an abbreviated form of obiter dicta, a term describing those portions of a judicial opinion incidental or not necessary to resolution of the specific question before the court. Such nonessential statements and remarks are not considered to be binding precedent.

DUCES TECUM: Refers to a particular type of writ or subpoena requesting a party or organization to produce certain documents in their possession.

EN BANC: Full bench. Where a court sits with all justices present rather than the usual quorum.

EX PARTE: For one side or one party only. An ex parte proceeding is one undertaken for the benefit of only one party, without notice to, or an appearance by, an adverse party.

EX POST FACTO: After the fact. An ex post facto law is a law that retroactively changes the consequences of a prior act.

EX REL.: Abbreviated form of the term ex relatione, meaning upon relation or information. When the state brings an action in which it has no interest against an individual at the instigation of one who has a private interest in the matter.

FORUM NON CONVENIENS: Inconvenient forum. Although a court may have jurisdiction over the case, the action should be tried in a more conveniently located court, one to which parties and witnesses may more easily travel, for example.

GUARDIAN AD LITEM: A guardian of an infant as to litigation, appointed to represent the infant and pursue his/her rights.

HABEAS CORPUS: You have the body. The modern writ of habeas corpus is a writ directing that a person (body) being detained (such as a prisoner) be brought before the court so that the legality of his detention can be judicially ascertained.

IN CAMERA: In private, in chambers. When a hearing is held before a judge in his chambers or when all spectators are excluded from the courtroom.

IN FORMA PAUPERIS: In the manner of a pauper. A party who proceeds in forma pauperis because of his poverty is one who is allowed to bring suit without liability for costs.

INFRA: Below, under. A word referring the reader to a later part of a book. (The opposite of supra.)

IN LOCO PARENTIS: In the place of a parent.

IN PARI DELICTO: Equally wrong; a court of equity will not grant requested relief to an applicant who is in pari delicto, or as much at fault in the transactions giving rise to the controversy as is the opponent of the applicant.

IN PARI MATERIA: On like subject matter or upon the same matter. Statutes relating to the same person or things are said to be in pari materia. It is a general rule of statutory construction that such statutes should be construed together, i.e., looked at as if they together constituted one law.

IN PERSONAM: Against the person. Jurisdiction over the person of an individual.

IN RE: In the matter of. Used to designate a proceeding involving an estate or other property.

IN REM: A term that signifies an action against the res, or thing. An action in rem is basically one that is taken directly against property, as distinguished from an action in personam, i.e., against the person.

INTER ALIA: Among other things. Used to show that the whole of a statement, pleading, list, statute, etc., has not been set forth in its entirety.

INTER PARTES: Between the parties. May refer to contracts, conveyances or other transactions having legal significance.

INTER VIVOS: Between the living. An inter vivos gift is a gift made by a living grantor, as distinguished from bequests contained in a will, which pass upon the death of the testator.

IPSO FACTO: By the mere fact itself.

JUS: Law or the entire body of law.

LEX LOCI: The law of the place; the notion that the rights of parties to a legal proceeding are governed by the law of the place where those rights arose.

MALUM IN SE: Evil or wrong in and of itself; inherently wrong. This term describes an act that is wrong by its very nature, as opposed to one which would not be wrong but for the fact that there is a specific legal prohibition against it (malum prohibitum).

MALUM PROHIBITUM: Wrong because prohibited, but not inherently evil. Used to describe something that is wrong because it is expressly forbidden by law but that is not in and of itself evil, e.g., speeding.

MANDAMUS: We command. A writ directing an official to take a certain action.

MENS REA: A guilty mind; a criminal intent. A term used to signify the mental state that accompanies a crime or other prohibited act. Some crimes require only a general mens rea (general intent to do the prohibited act), but others, like assault with intent to murder, require the existence of a specific mens rea.

MODUS OPERANDI: Method of operating; generally refers to the manner or style of a criminal in committing crimes, admissible in appropriate cases as evidence of the identity of a defendant.

NEXUS: A connection to.

NISI PRIUS: A court of first impression. A nisi prius court is one where issues of fact are tried before a judge or jury.

N.O.V. (NON OBSTANTE VEREDICTO): Notwithstanding the verdict. A judgment n.o.v. is a judgment given in favor of one party despite the fact that a verdict was returned in favor of the other party, the justification being that the verdict either had no reasonable support in fact or was contrary to law.

NUNC PRO TUNC: Now for then. This phrase refers to actions that may be taken and will then have full retroactive effect.

PENDENTE LITE: Pending the suit; pending litigation underway.

PER CAPITA: By head; beneficiaries of an estate, if they take in equal shares, take per capita.

PER CURIAM: By the court; signifies an opinion ostensibly written "by the whole court" and with no identified author.

PER SE: By itself, in itself; inherently.

PER STIRPES: By representation. Used primarily in the law of wills to describe the method of distribution where a person, generally because of death, is unable to take that which is left to him by the will of another, and therefore his heirs divide such property between them rather than take under the will individually.

PRIMA FACIE: On its face, at first sight. A prima facie case is one that is sufficient on its face, meaning that the evidence supporting it is adequate to establish the case until contradicted or overcome by other evidence.

PRO TANTO: For so much; as far as it goes. Often used in eminent domain cases when a property owner receives partial payment for his land without prejudice to his right to bring suit for the full amount he claims his land to be worth.

QUANTUM MERUIT: As much as he deserves. Refers to recovery based on the doctrine of unjust enrichment in those cases in which a party has rendered valuable services or furnished materials that were accepted and enjoyed by another under circumstances that would reasonably notify the recipient that the rendering party expected to be paid. In essence, the law implies a contract to pay the reasonable value of the services or materials furnished.

QUASI: Almost like; as if; nearly. This term is essentially used to signify that one subject or thing is almost analogous to another but that material differences between them do exist. For example, a quasi-criminal proceeding is one that is not strictly criminal but shares enough of the same characteristics to require some of the same safeguards (e.g., procedural due process must be followed in a parole hearing).

QUID PRO QUO: Something for something. In contract law, the consideration, something of value, passed between the parties to render the contract binding.

RES GESTAE: Things done; in evidence law, this principle justifies the admission of a statement that would otherwise be hearsay when it is made so closely to the event in question as to be said to be a part of it, or with such spontaneity as not to have the possibility of falsehood.

RES IPSA LOQUITUR: The thing speaks for itself. This doctrine gives rise to a rebuttable presumption of negligence when the instrumentality causing the injury was within the exclusive control of the defendant, and the injury was one that does not normally occur unless a person has been negligent.

RES JUDICATA: A matter adjudged. Doctrine which provides that once a court of competent jurisdiction has rendered a final judgment or decree on the merits, that judgment or decree is conclusive upon the parties to the case and prevents them from engaging in any other litigation on the points and issues determined therein.

RESPONDEAT SUPERIOR: Let the master reply. This doctrine holds the master liable for the wrongful acts of his servant (or the principal for his agent) in those cases in which the servant (or agent) was acting within the scope of his authority at the time of the injury.

STARE DECISIS: To stand by or adhere to that which has been decided. The common law doctrine of stare decisis attempts to give security and certainty to the law by following the policy that once a principle of law as applicable to a certain set of facts has been set forth in a decision, it forms a precedent which will subsequently be followed, even though a different decision might be made were it the first time the question had arisen. Of course, stare decisis is not an inviolable principle and is departed from in instances where there is good cause (e.g., considerations of public policy led the Supreme Court to disregard prior decisions sanctioning segregation).

SUPRA: Above. A word referring a reader to an earlier part of a book.

ULTRA VIRES: Beyond the power. This phrase is most commonly used to refer to actions taken by a corporation that are beyond the power or legal authority of the corporation.

Addendum of French Derivatives

IN PAIS: Not pursuant to legal proceedings.

CHATTEL: Tangible personal property.

CY PRES: Doctrine permitting courts to apply trust funds to purposes not expressed in the trust but necessary to carry out the settlor's intent.

PER AUTRE VIE: For another's life; during another's life. In property law, an estate may be granted that will terminate upon the death of someone other than the grantee.

PROFIT A PRENDRE: A license to remove minerals or other produce from land.

VOIR DIRE: Process of questioning jurors as to their predispositions about the case or parties to a proceeding in order to identify those jurors displaying bias or prejudice.

Casenote Legal Briefs